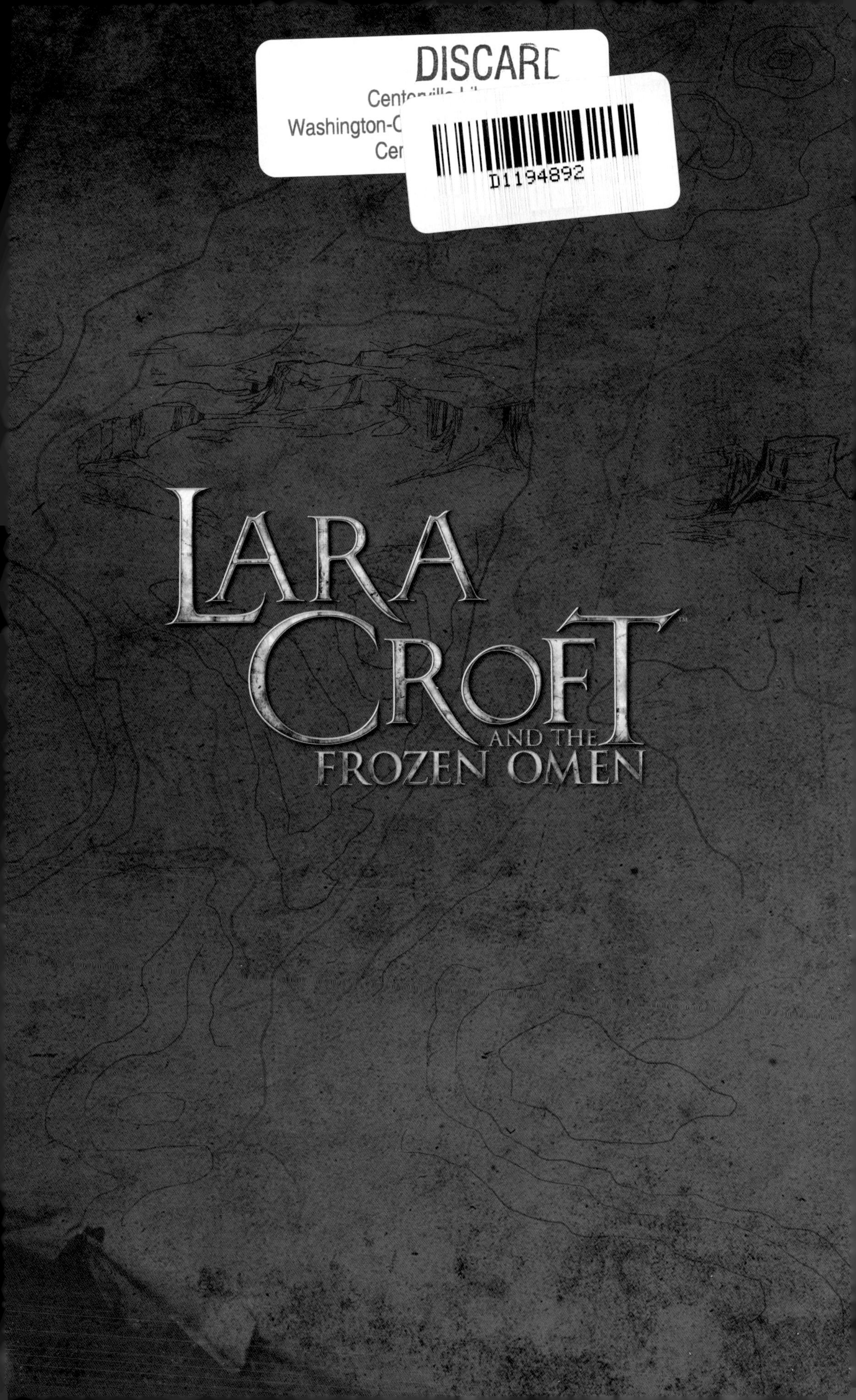

LARA CROFT AND THE FROZEN OMEN

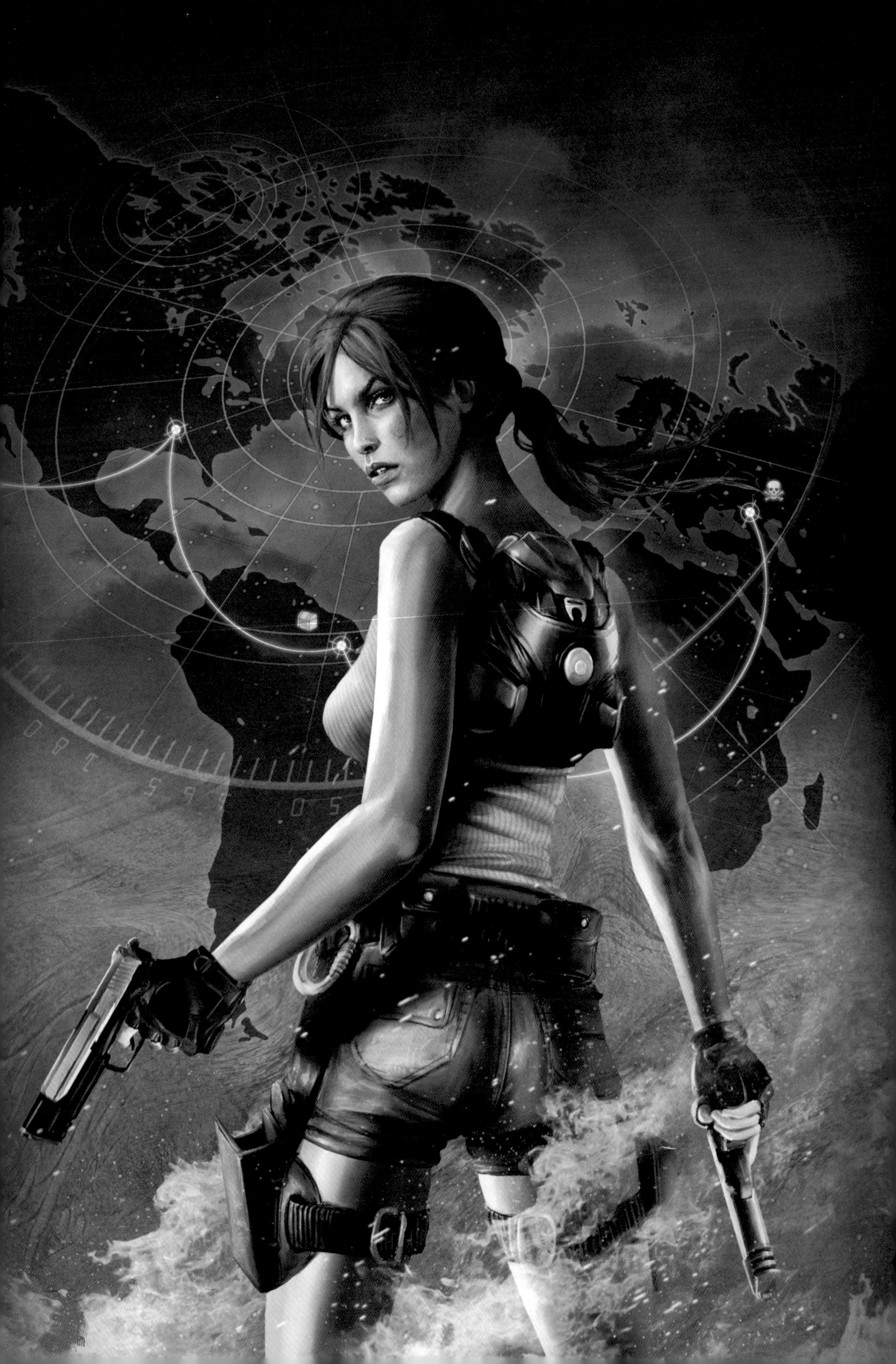

ILLUSTRATION BY
JEAN-SÉBASTIEN ROSSBACH

LARA CROFT AND THE FROZEN OMEN

SCRIPT
CORINNA BECHKO

PENCILS, PAGES 7–28, 51–72, AND 95–116
RANDY GREEN

PENCILS, PAGES 29–50
CARMEN CARNERO

PENCILS, PAGES 73–94
ROBERT ATKINS

INKS
ANDY OWENS

COLORS
MICHAEL ATIYEH

LETTERING
MICHAEL HEISLER

FRONT COVER ART
JEAN-SÉBASTIEN ROSSBACH

DARK HORSE BOOKS

PUBLISHER
MIKE RICHARDSON

EDITOR
PATRICK THORPE

ASSISTANT EDITOR
ROXY POLK

COLLECTION DESIGNER
SANDY TANAKA

DIGITAL ART TECHNICIAN
ALLYSON HALLER

SPECIAL THANKS TO CRYSTAL DYNAMICS AND SQUARE ENIX, INCLUDING:
RICH BRIGGS, BRENOCH ADAMS, AND NOAH HUGHES.

This volume collects issues #1 through #5 of the Dark Horse comic book series
Lara Croft and the Frozen Omen.

Published by
Dark Horse Books
A division of
Dark Horse Comics, Inc.
10956 SE Main Street
Milwaukie, OR 97222

DarkHorse.com
TombRaider.com

First edition: June 2016
ISBN 978-1-61655-957-1

1 3 5 7 9 10 8 6 4 2

Printed in China

Library of Congress Cataloging-in-Publication Data

Names: Bechko, Corinna, 1973- author. | Green, Randy, 1963- illustrator. | Carnero, Carmen, illustrator. | Atkins, Robert Q., illustrator. | Owens, Andy, illustrator. | Atiyeh, Michael, illustrator. | Heisler, Michael, illustrator. | Rossbach, Jean-Sébastien, illustrator.
Title: Lara Croft and the frozen omen / writer, Corinna Bechko ; penciler #1, #3, #5, Randy Green ; penciler #2, Carmen Carnero ; penciler #4, Robert Atkins ; inker, Andy Owens ; colors, Michael Atiyeh ; lettering, Michael Heisler ; cover artist, Jean-Sébastien Rossbach.
Description: First trade paperback edition. | Milwaukie, OR : Dark Horse Books, 2016. | "This volume collects issues #1 through #5 of the Dark Horse comic-book series Lara Croft and the Frozen Omen."
Identifiers: LCCN 2016001333 | ISBN 9781616559571 (pbk.)
Subjects: LCSH: Graphic novels. | Comic books, strips, etc.
Classification: LCC PN6728.L29 B43 2016 | DDC 741.5/973--dc23
LC record available at http://lccn.loc.gov/2016001333

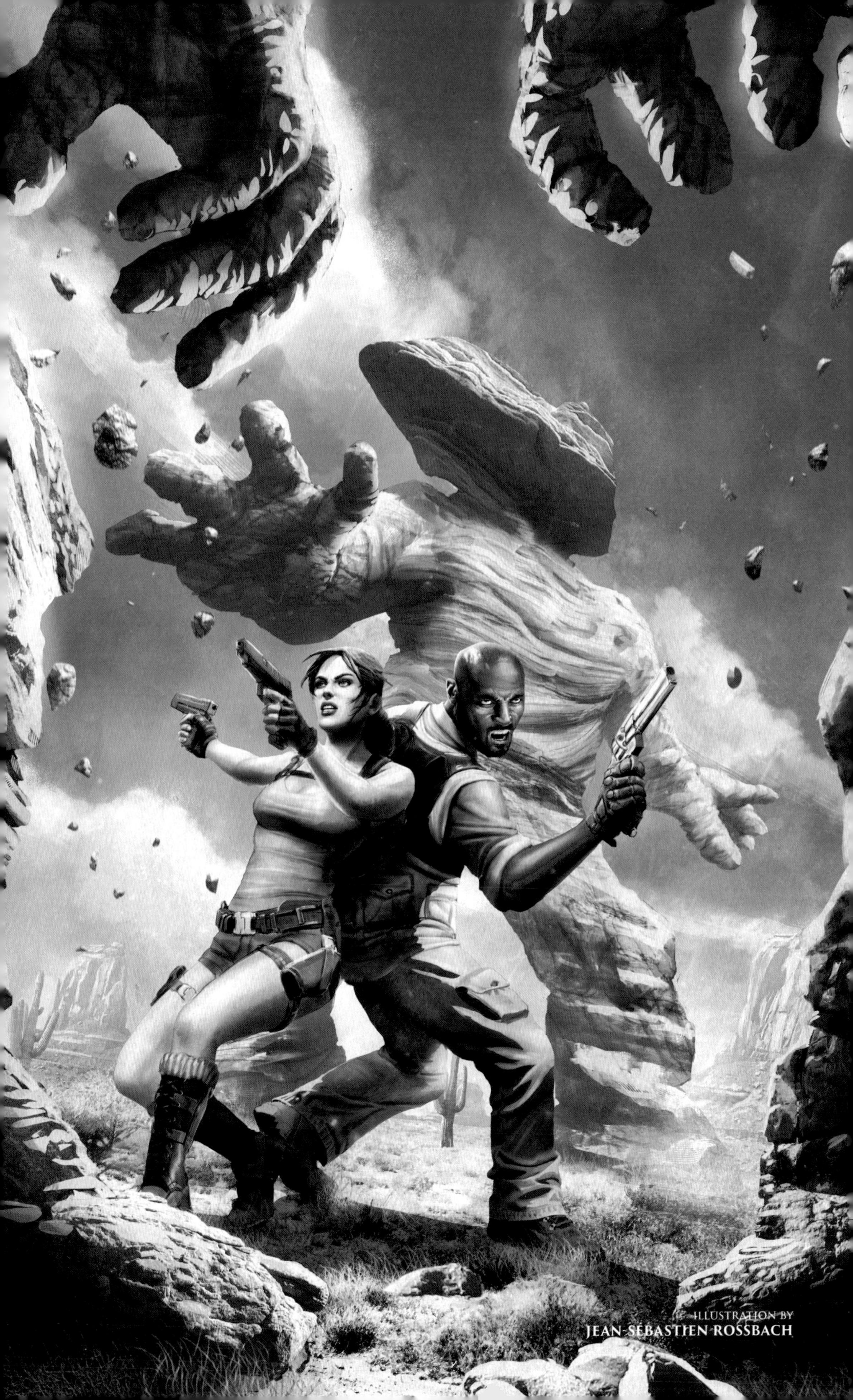
ILLUSTRATION BY
JEAN-SÉBASTIEN ROSSBACH

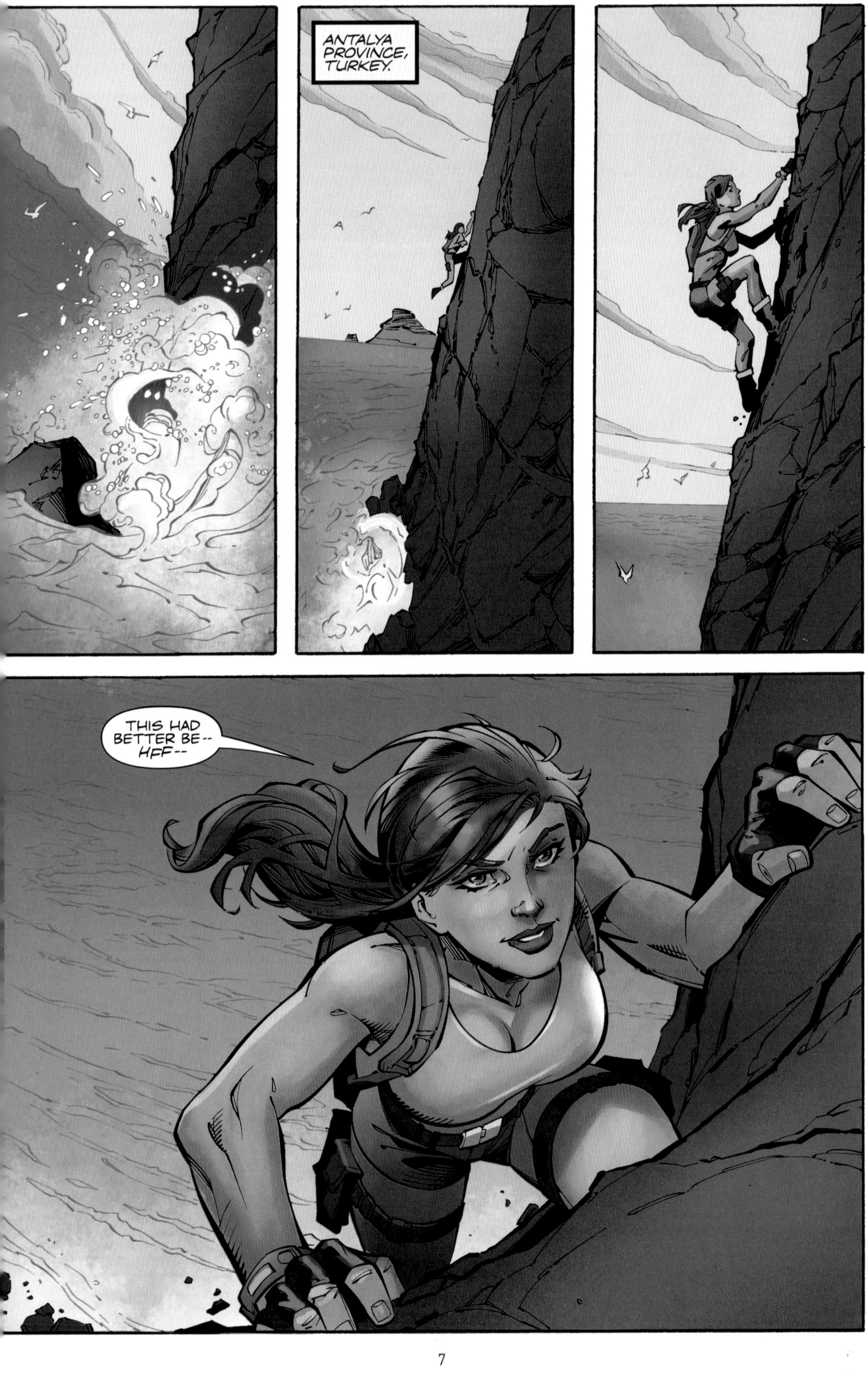
ANTALYA PROVINCE, TURKEY.
THIS HAD BETTER BE-- HFF--

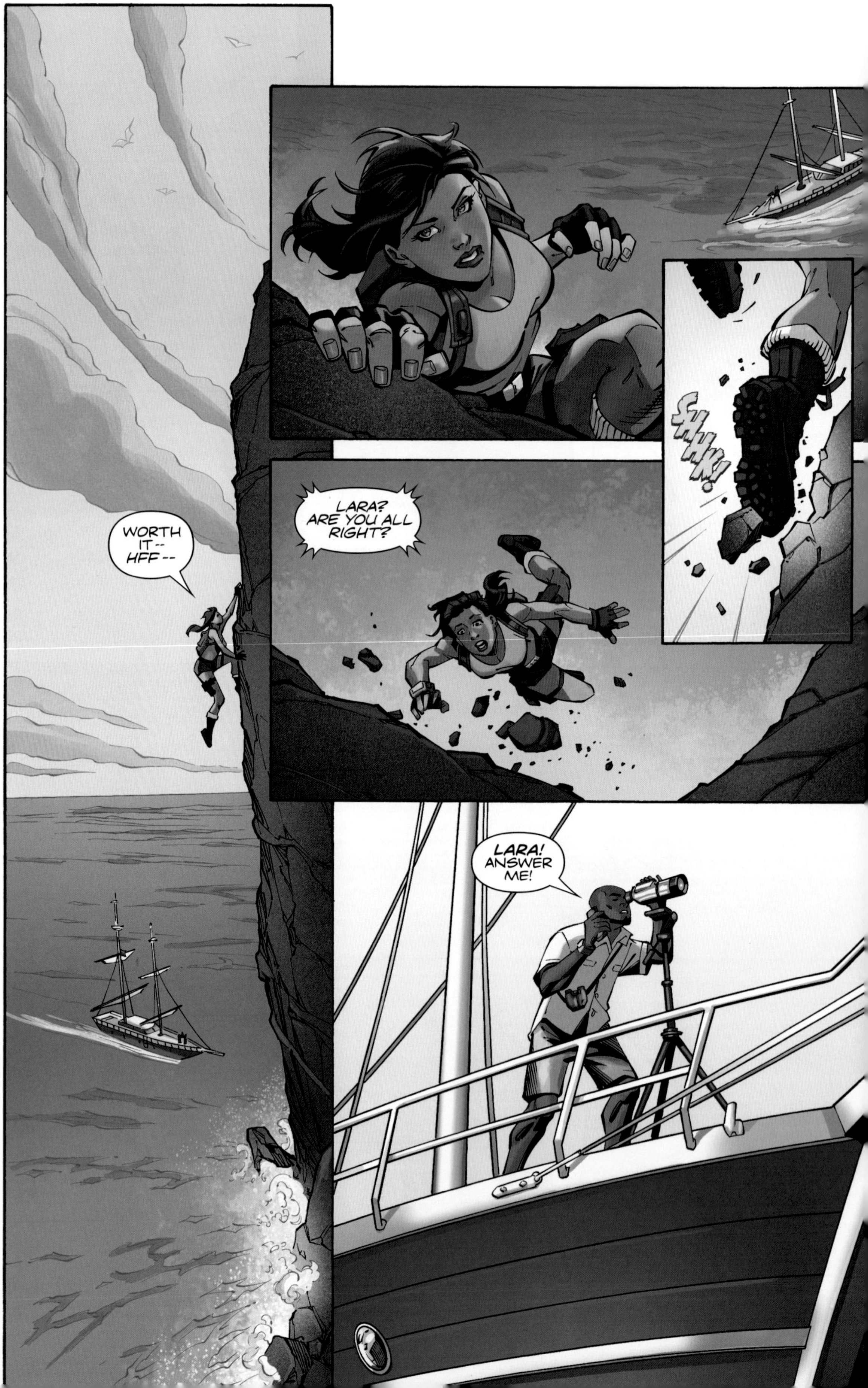
WORTH IT-- HFF--
SHHK!
LARA? ARE YOU ALL RIGHT?
LARA! ANSWER ME!

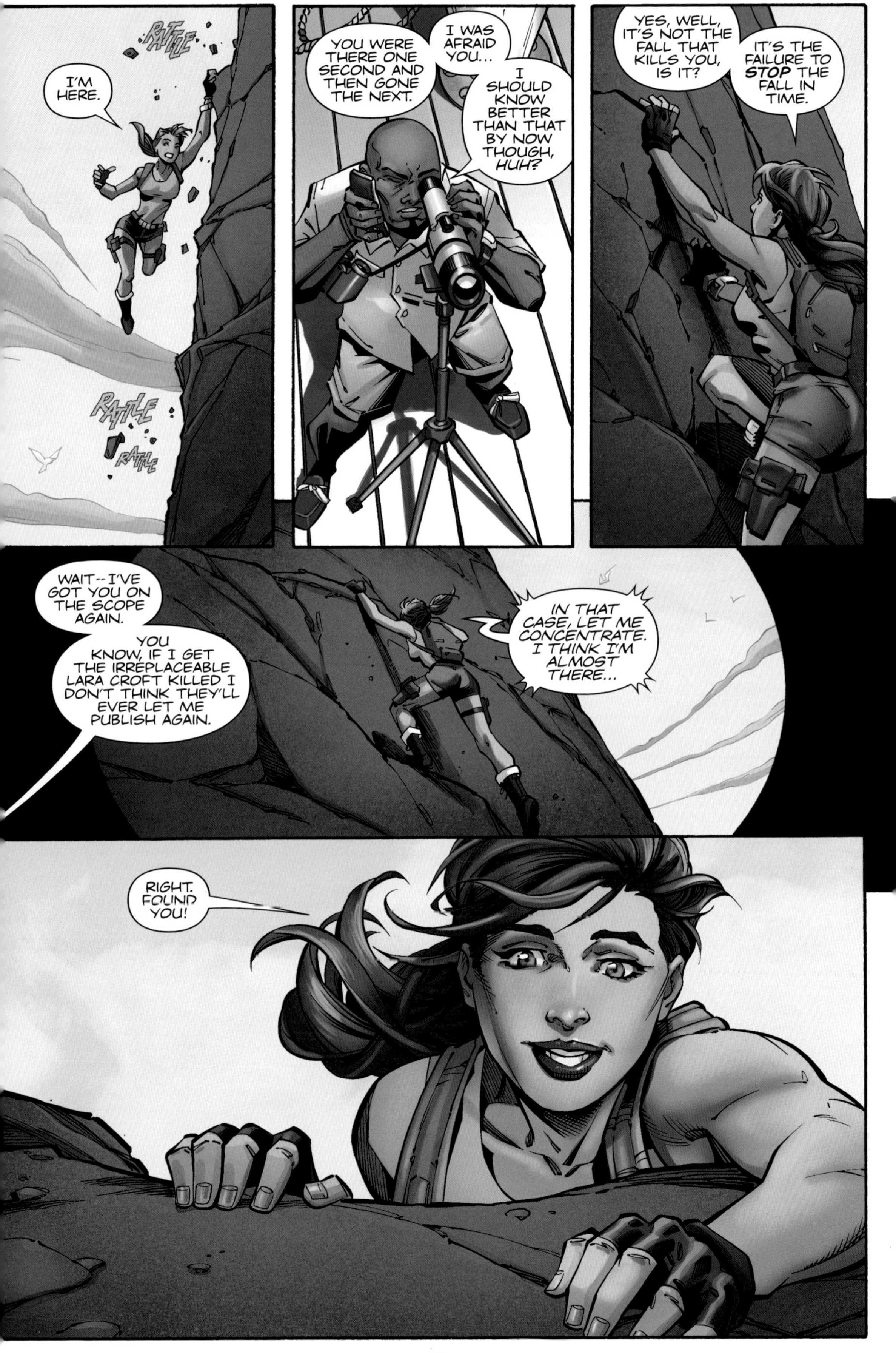
RATTLE
I'M HERE.
RATTLE
RATTLE
YOU WERE THERE ONE SECOND AND THEN GONE THE NEXT.
I WAS AFRAID YOU...
I SHOULD KNOW BETTER THAN THAT BY NOW THOUGH, HUH?
YES, WELL, IT'S NOT THE FALL THAT KILLS YOU, IS IT?
IT'S THE FAILURE TO STOP THE FALL IN TIME.
WAIT--I'VE GOT YOU ON THE SCOPE AGAIN.
YOU KNOW, IF I GET THE IRREPLACEABLE LARA CROFT KILLED I DON'T THINK THEY'LL EVER LET ME PUBLISH AGAIN.
IN THAT CASE, LET ME CONCENTRATE. I THINK I'M ALMOST THERE...
RIGHT. FOUND YOU!

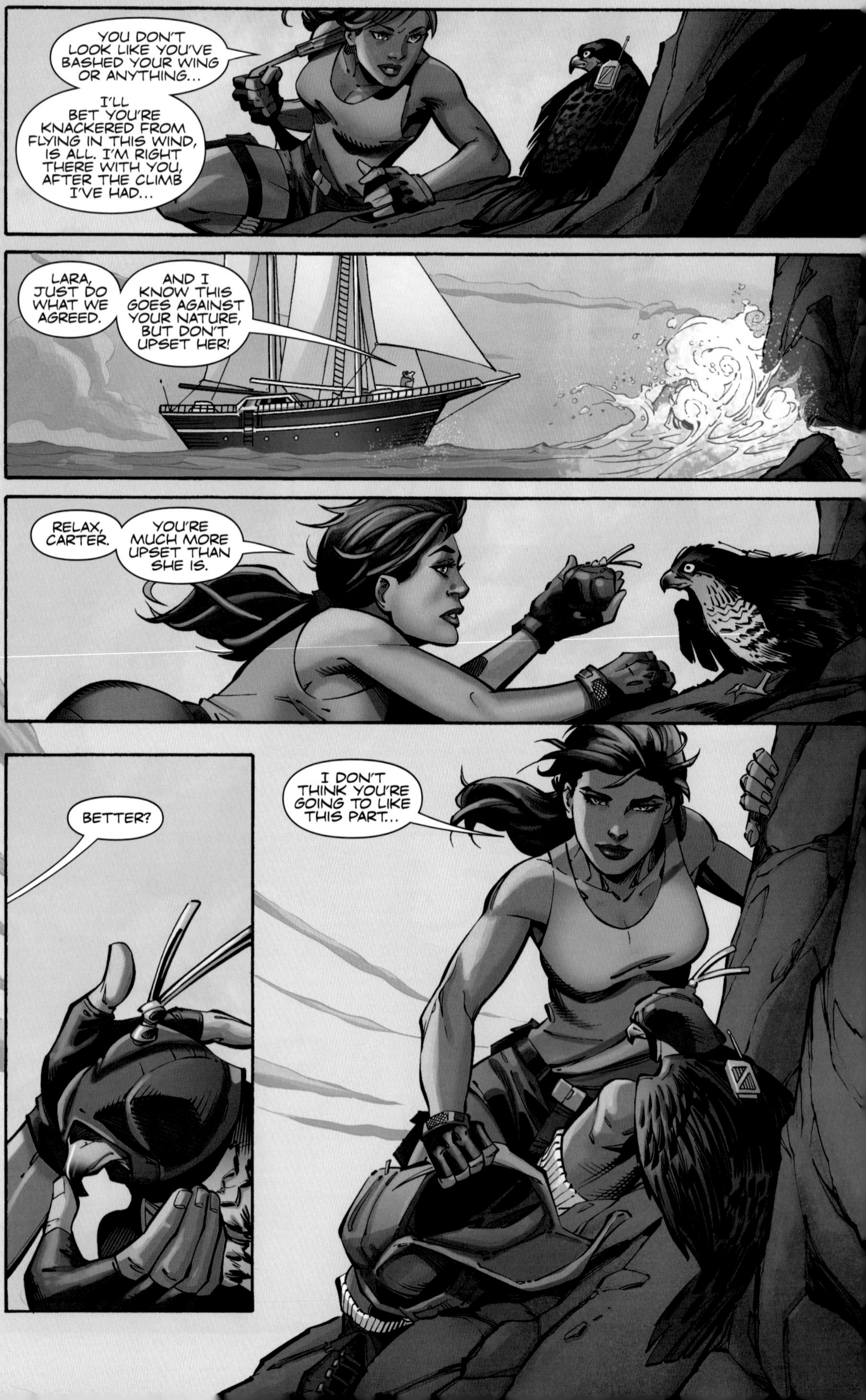
YOU DON'T LOOK LIKE YOU'VE BASHED YOUR WING OR ANYTHING...
I'LL BET YOU'RE KNACKERED FROM FLYING IN THIS WIND, IS ALL. I'M RIGHT THERE WITH YOU, AFTER THE CLIMB I'VE HAD...
LARA, JUST DO WHAT WE AGREED.
AND I KNOW THIS GOES AGAINST YOUR NATURE, BUT DON'T UPSET HER!
RELAX, CARTER.
YOU'RE MUCH MORE UPSET THAN SHE IS.
BETTER?
I DON'T THINK YOU'RE GOING TO LIKE THIS PART...

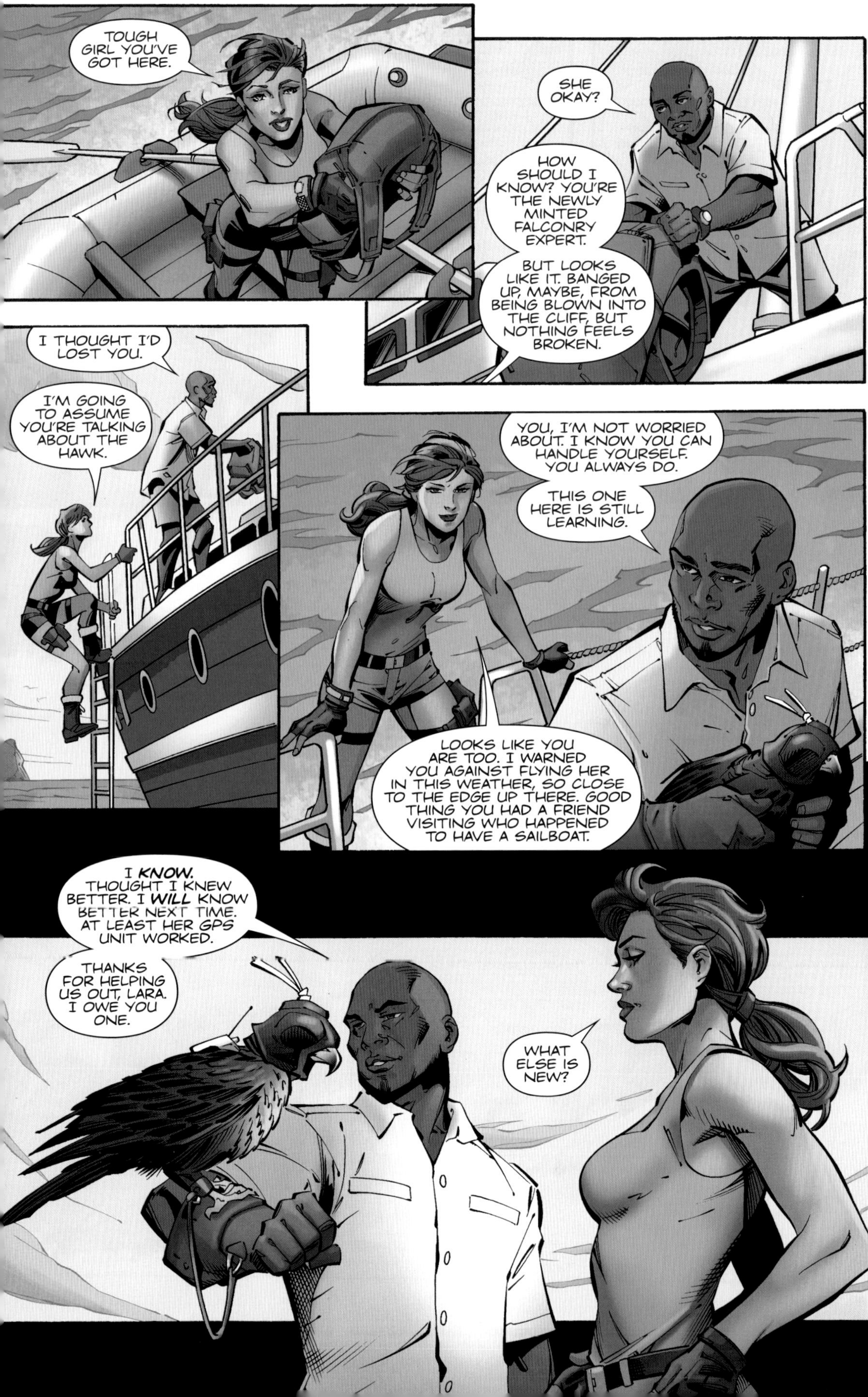
TOUGH GIRL YOU'VE GOT HERE.
SHE OKAY?
HOW SHOULD I KNOW? YOU'RE THE NEWLY MINTED FALCONRY EXPERT.
BUT LOOKS LIKE IT. BANGED UP, MAYBE, FROM BEING BLOWN INTO THE CLIFF, BUT NOTHING FEELS BROKEN.
I THOUGHT I'D LOST YOU.
I'M GOING TO ASSUME YOU'RE TALKING ABOUT THE HAWK.
YOU, I'M NOT WORRIED ABOUT. I KNOW YOU CAN HANDLE YOURSELF. YOU ALWAYS DO.
THIS ONE HERE IS STILL LEARNING.
LOOKS LIKE YOU ARE TOO. I WARNED YOU AGAINST FLYING HER IN THIS WEATHER, SO CLOSE TO THE EDGE UP THERE. GOOD THING YOU HAD A FRIEND VISITING WHO HAPPENED TO HAVE A SAILBOAT.
I **KNOW.** THOUGHT I KNEW BETTER. I **WILL** KNOW BETTER NEXT TIME. AT LEAST HER GPS UNIT WORKED.
THANKS FOR HELPING US OUT, LARA. I OWE YOU ONE.
WHAT ELSE IS NEW?

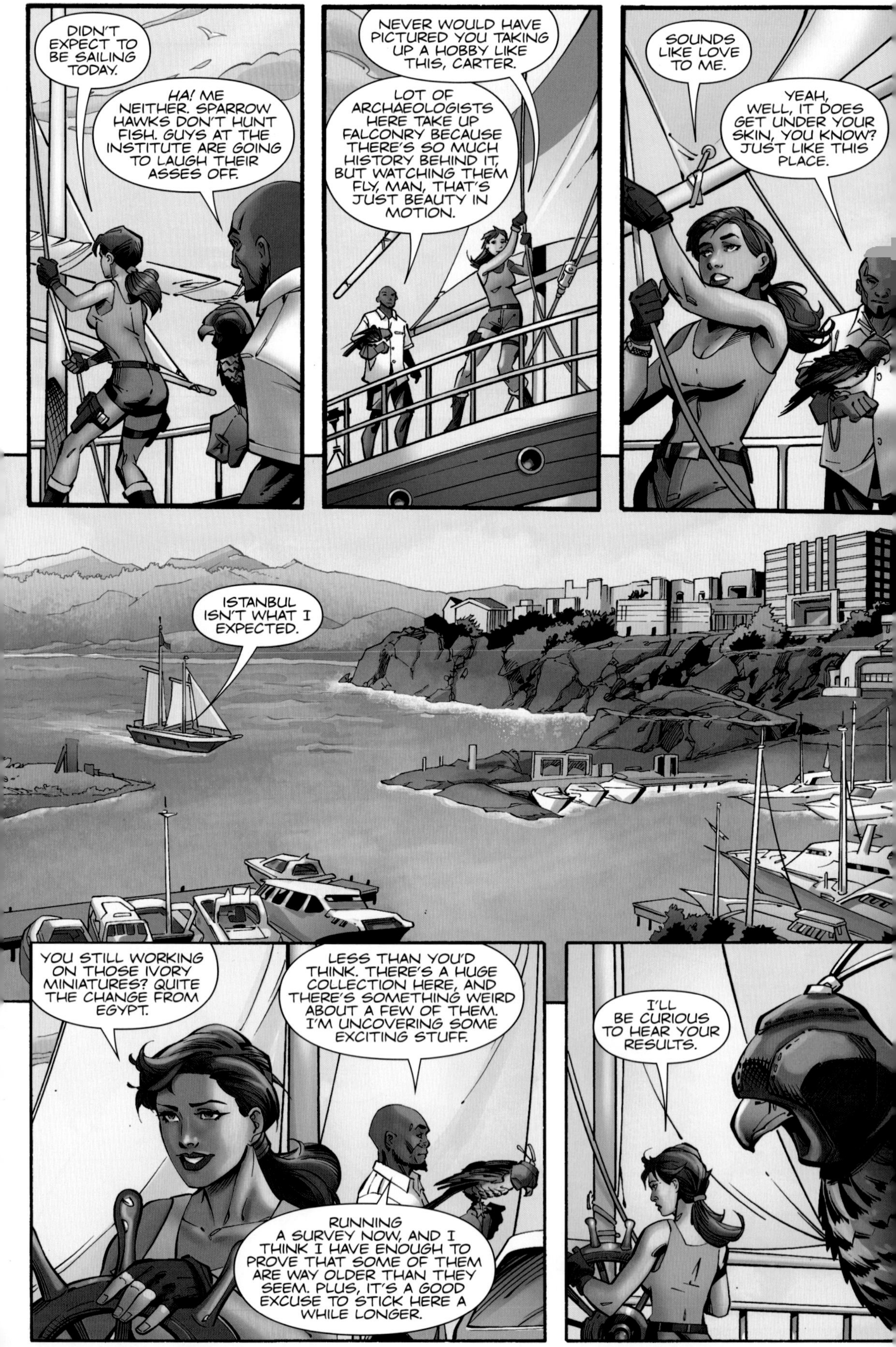
DIDN'T EXPECT TO BE SAILING TODAY.
HA! ME NEITHER. SPARROW HAWKS DON'T HUNT FISH. GUYS AT THE INSTITUTE ARE GOING TO LAUGH THEIR ASSES OFF.
NEVER WOULD HAVE PICTURED YOU TAKING UP A HOBBY LIKE THIS, CARTER.
LOT OF ARCHAEOLOGISTS HERE TAKE UP FALCONRY BECAUSE THERE'S SO MUCH HISTORY BEHIND IT, BUT WATCHING THEM FLY, MAN, THAT'S JUST BEAUTY IN MOTION.
SOUNDS LIKE LOVE TO ME.
YEAH, WELL, IT DOES GET UNDER YOUR SKIN, YOU KNOW? JUST LIKE THIS PLACE.
ISTANBUL ISN'T WHAT I EXPECTED.
YOU STILL WORKING ON THOSE IVORY MINIATURES? QUITE THE CHANGE FROM EGYPT.
LESS THAN YOU'D THINK. THERE'S A HUGE COLLECTION HERE, AND THERE'S SOMETHING WEIRD ABOUT A FEW OF THEM. I'M UNCOVERING SOME EXCITING STUFF.
RUNNING A SURVEY NOW, AND I THINK I HAVE ENOUGH TO PROVE THAT SOME OF THEM ARE WAY OLDER THAN THEY SEEM. PLUS, IT'S A GOOD EXCUSE TO STICK HERE A WHILE LONGER.
I'LL BE CURIOUS TO HEAR YOUR RESULTS.

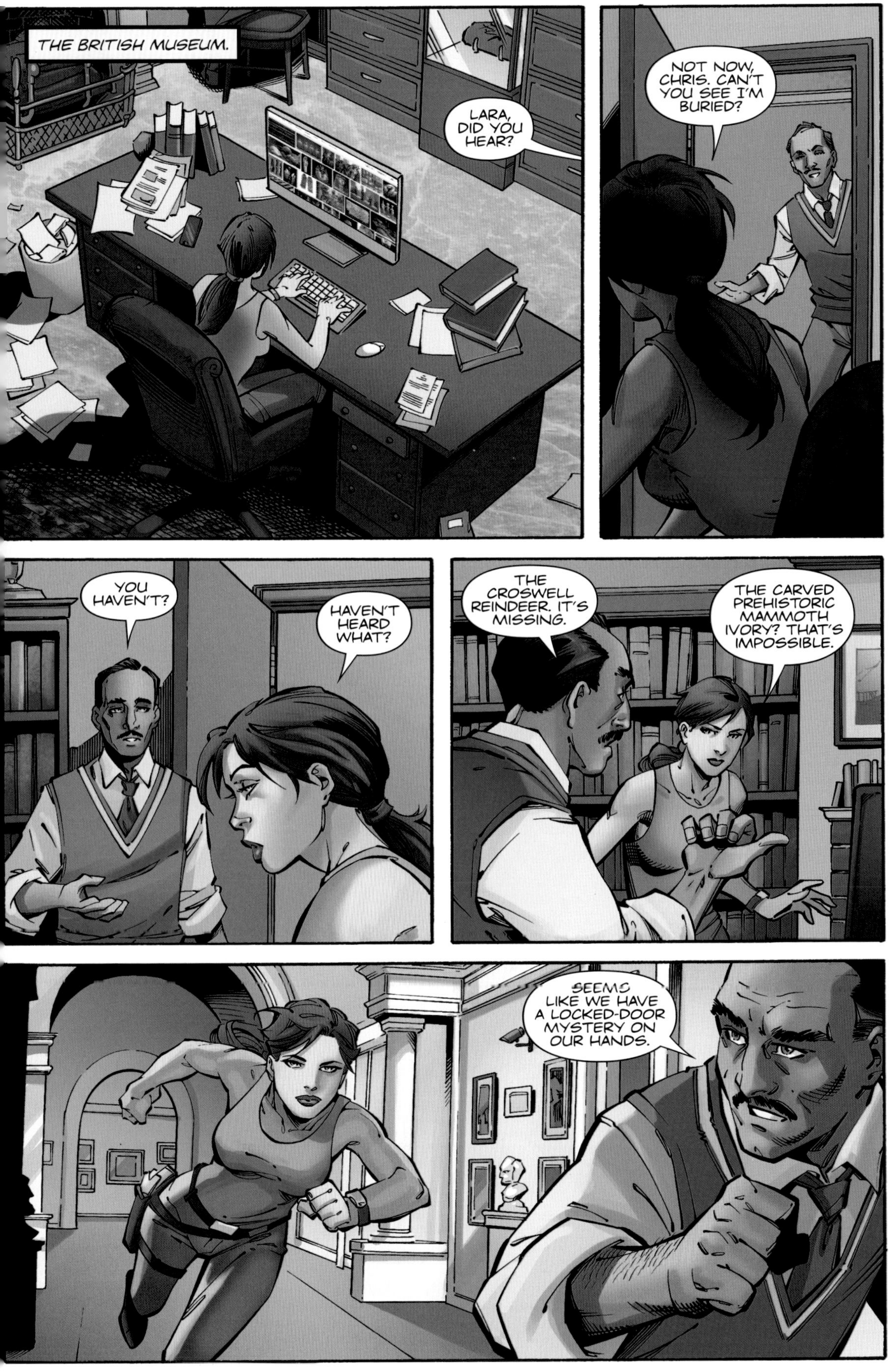
THE BRITISH MUSEUM.
LARA, DID YOU HEAR?
NOT NOW, CHRIS. CAN'T YOU SEE I'M BURIED?
YOU HAVEN'T?
HAVEN'T HEARD WHAT?
THE CROSWELL REINDEER. IT'S MISSING.
THE CARVED PREHISTORIC MAMMOTH IVORY? THAT'S IMPOSSIBLE.
SEEMS LIKE WE HAVE A LOCKED-DOOR MYSTERY ON OUR HANDS.

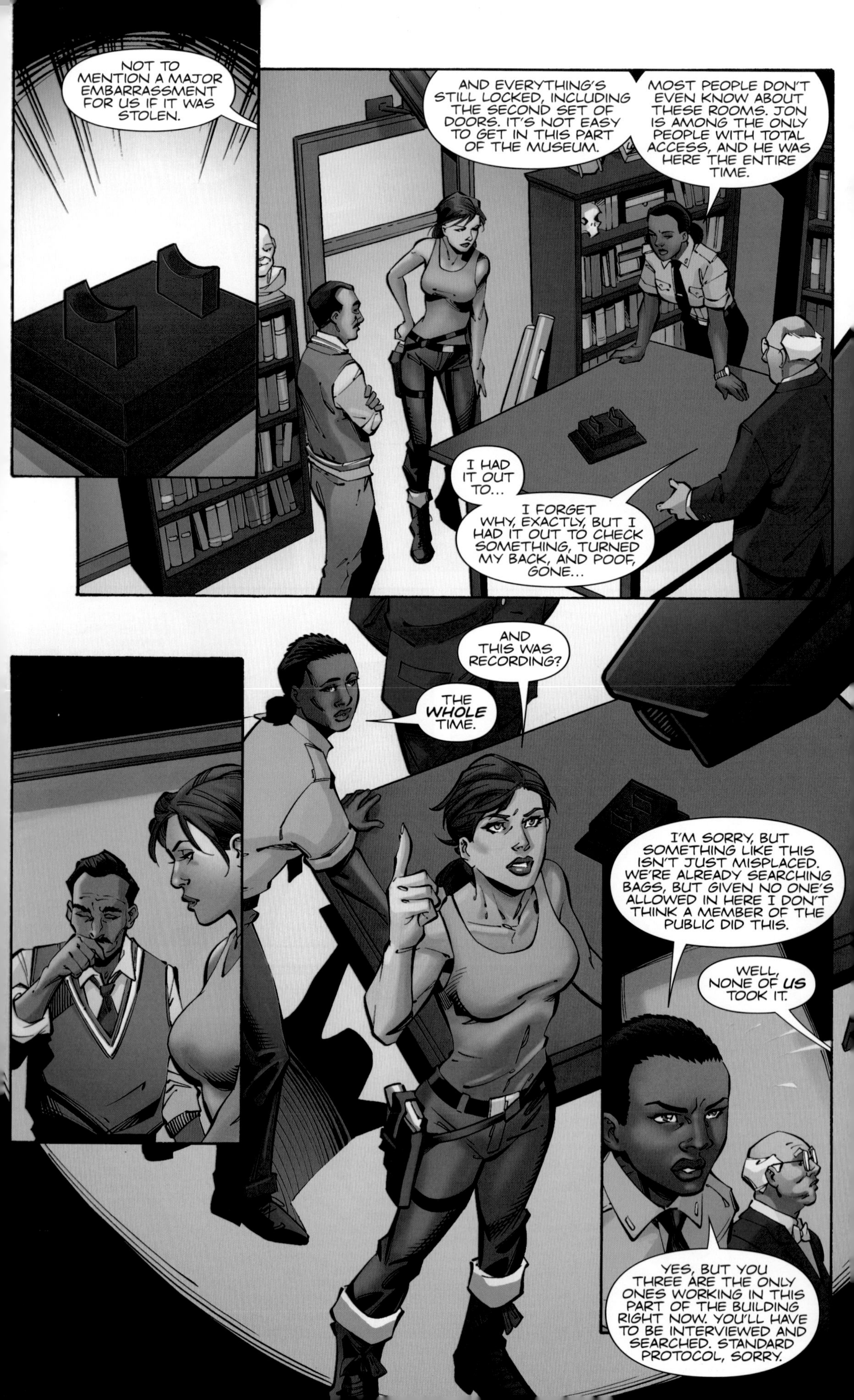
NOT TO MENTION A MAJOR EMBARRASSMENT FOR US IF IT WAS STOLEN.
AND EVERYTHING'S STILL LOCKED, INCLUDING THE SECOND SET OF DOORS. IT'S NOT EASY TO GET IN THIS PART OF THE MUSEUM.
MOST PEOPLE DON'T EVEN KNOW ABOUT THESE ROOMS. JON IS AMONG THE ONLY PEOPLE WITH TOTAL ACCESS, AND HE WAS HERE THE ENTIRE TIME.
I HAD IT OUT TO...
I FORGET WHY, EXACTLY, BUT I HAD IT OUT TO CHECK SOMETHING, TURNED MY BACK, AND POOF, GONE...
AND THIS WAS RECORDING?
THE *WHOLE* TIME.
I'M SORRY, BUT SOMETHING LIKE THIS ISN'T JUST MISPLACED. WE'RE ALREADY SEARCHING BAGS, BUT GIVEN NO ONE'S ALLOWED IN HERE I DON'T THINK A MEMBER OF THE PUBLIC DID THIS.
WELL, NONE OF *US* TOOK IT.
YES, BUT YOU THREE ARE THE ONLY ONES WORKING IN THIS PART OF THE BUILDING RIGHT NOW. YOU'LL HAVE TO BE INTERVIEWED AND SEARCHED. STANDARD PROTOCOL, SORRY.

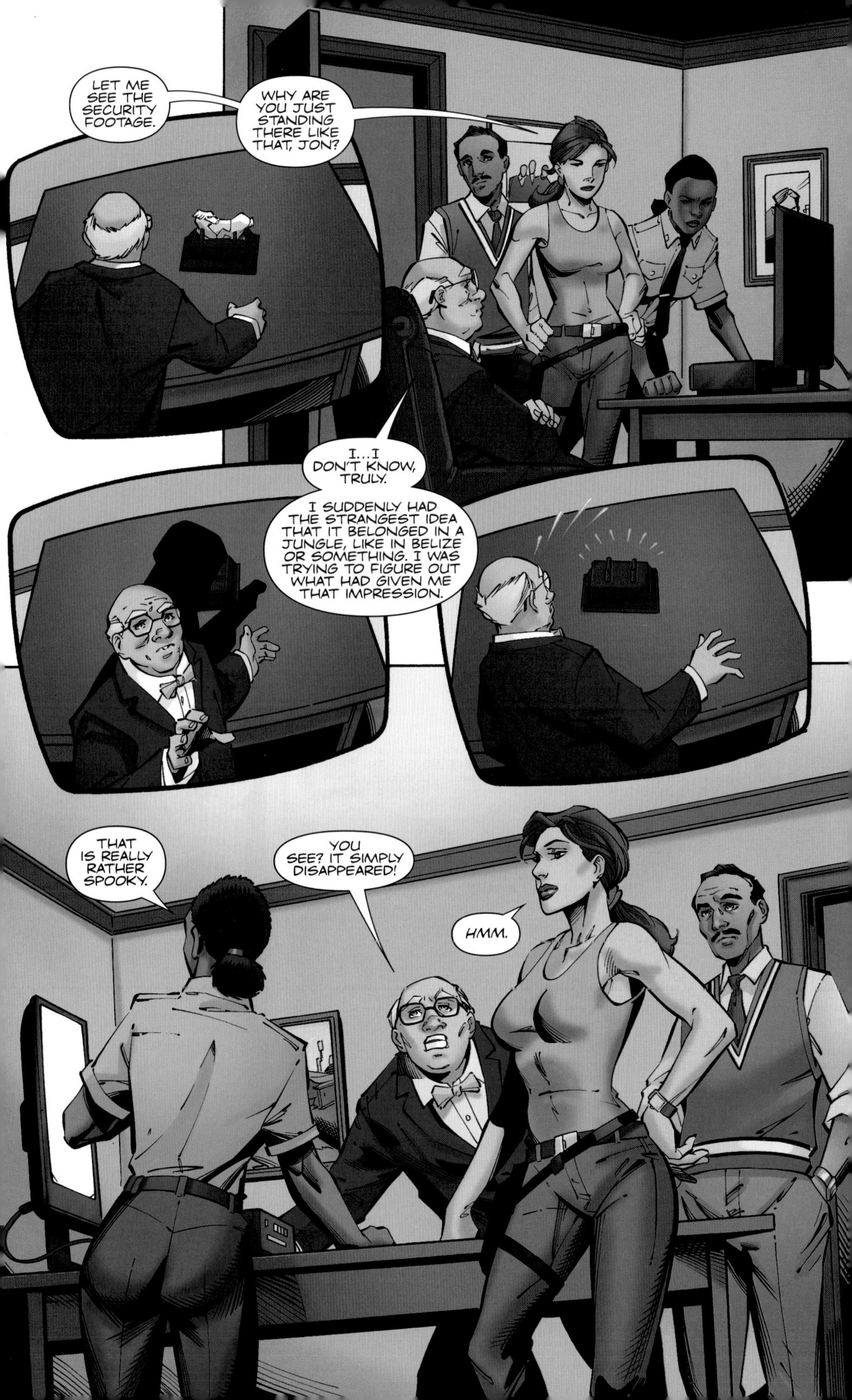
LET ME SEE THE SECURITY FOOTAGE.
WHY ARE YOU JUST STANDING THERE LIKE THAT, JON?
I...I DON'T KNOW, TRULY.
I SUDDENLY HAD THE STRANGEST IDEA THAT IT BELONGED IN A JUNGLE, LIKE IN BELIZE OR SOMETHING. I WAS TRYING TO FIGURE OUT WHAT HAD GIVEN ME THAT IMPRESSION.
THAT IS REALLY RATHER SPOOKY.
YOU SEE? IT SIMPLY DISAPPEARED!
HMM.

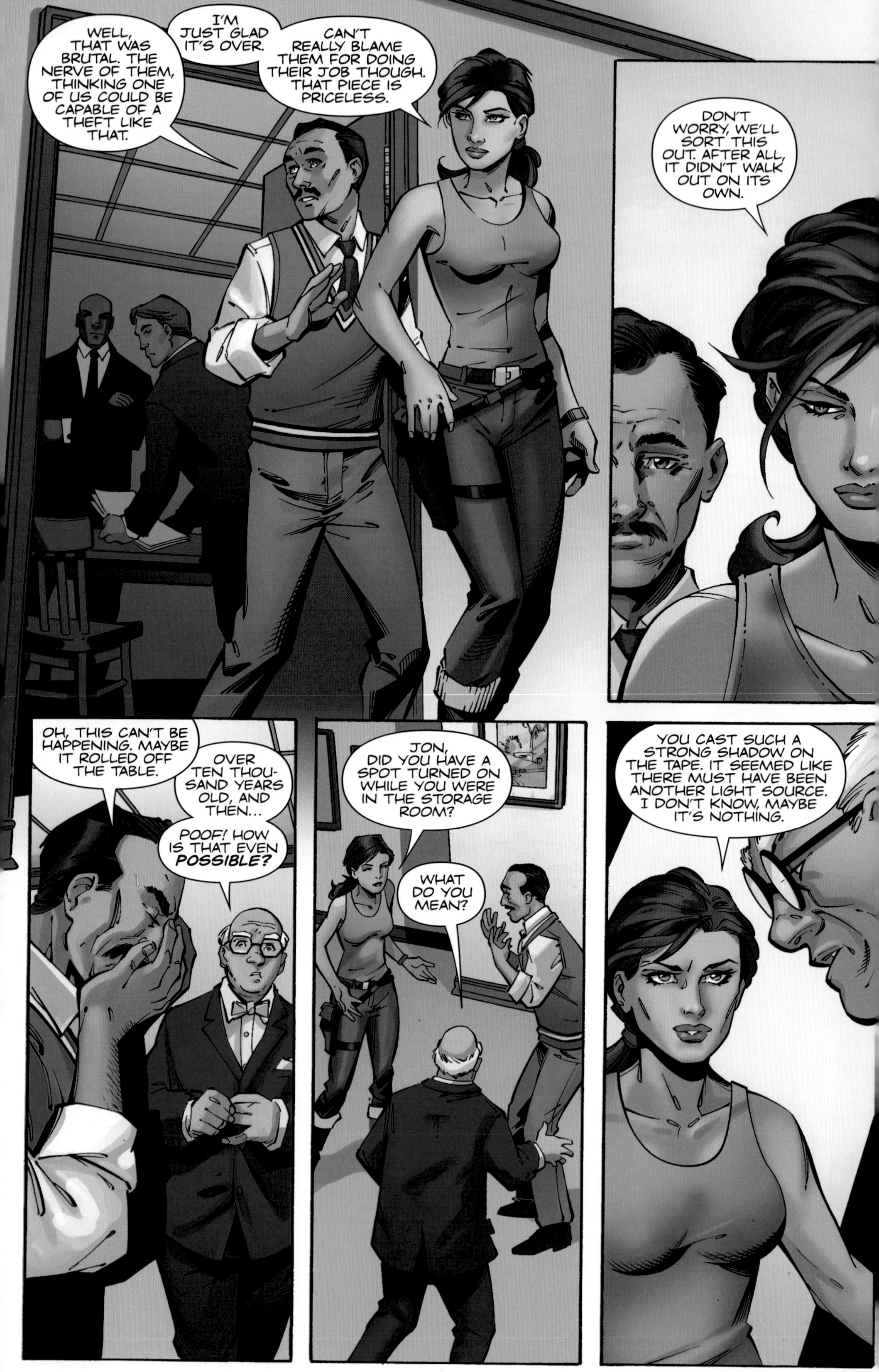
WELL, THAT WAS BRUTAL. THE NERVE OF THEM, THINKING ONE OF US COULD BE CAPABLE OF A THEFT LIKE THAT.
I'M JUST GLAD IT'S OVER.
CAN'T REALLY BLAME THEM FOR DOING THEIR JOB THOUGH. THAT PIECE IS PRICELESS.
DON'T WORRY, WE'LL SORT THIS OUT. AFTER ALL, IT DIDN'T WALK OUT ON ITS OWN.
OH, THIS CAN'T BE HAPPENING. MAYBE IT ROLLED OFF THE TABLE.
OVER TEN THOUSAND YEARS OLD, AND THEN...
POOF! HOW IS THAT EVEN **POSSIBLE?**
JON, DID YOU HAVE A SPOT TURNED ON WHILE YOU WERE IN THE STORAGE ROOM?
WHAT DO YOU MEAN?
YOU CAST SUCH A STRONG SHADOW ON THE TAPE. IT SEEMED LIKE THERE MUST HAVE BEEN ANOTHER LIGHT SOURCE. I DON'T KNOW, MAYBE IT'S NOTHING.

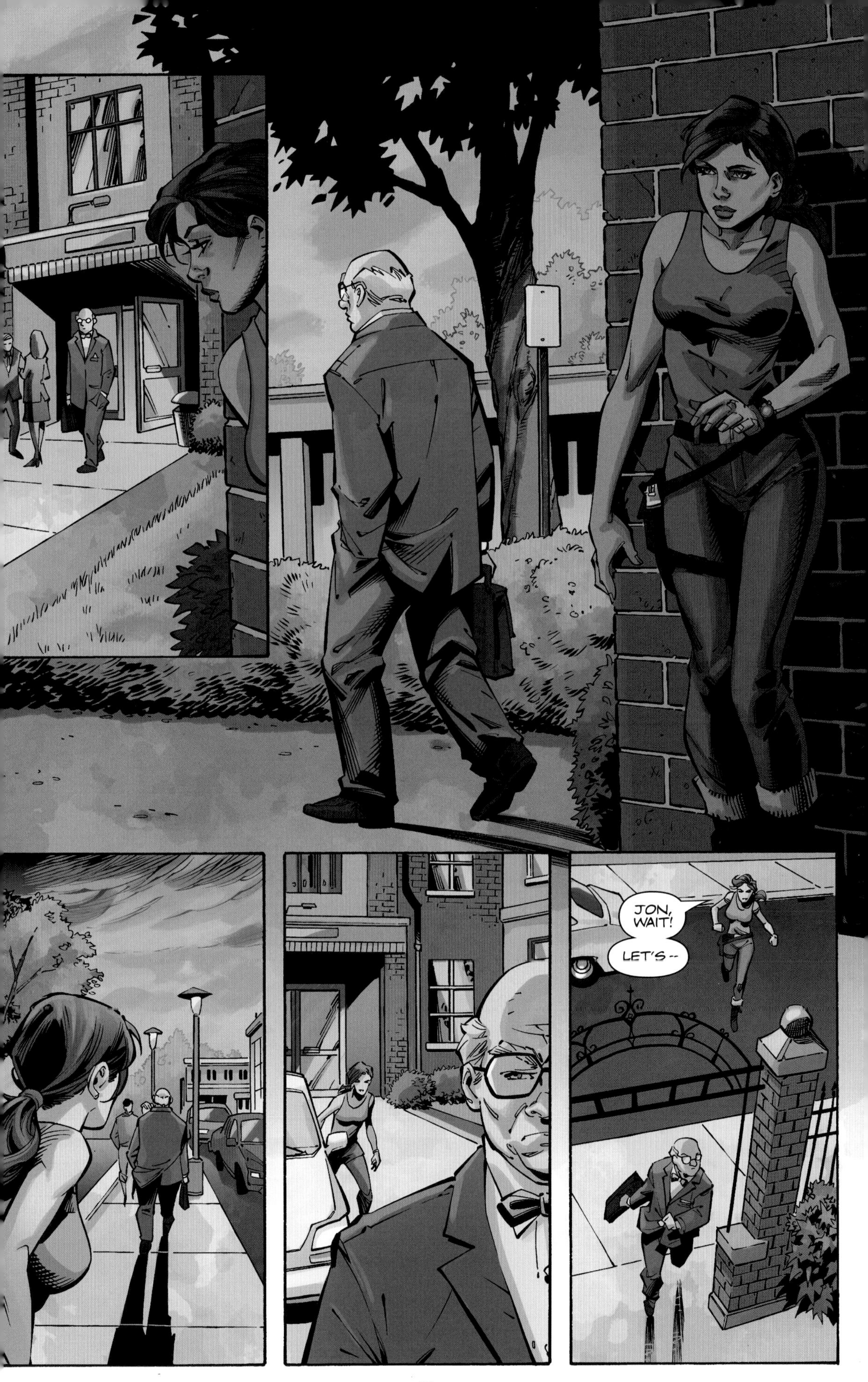
JON, WAIT!
LET'S --

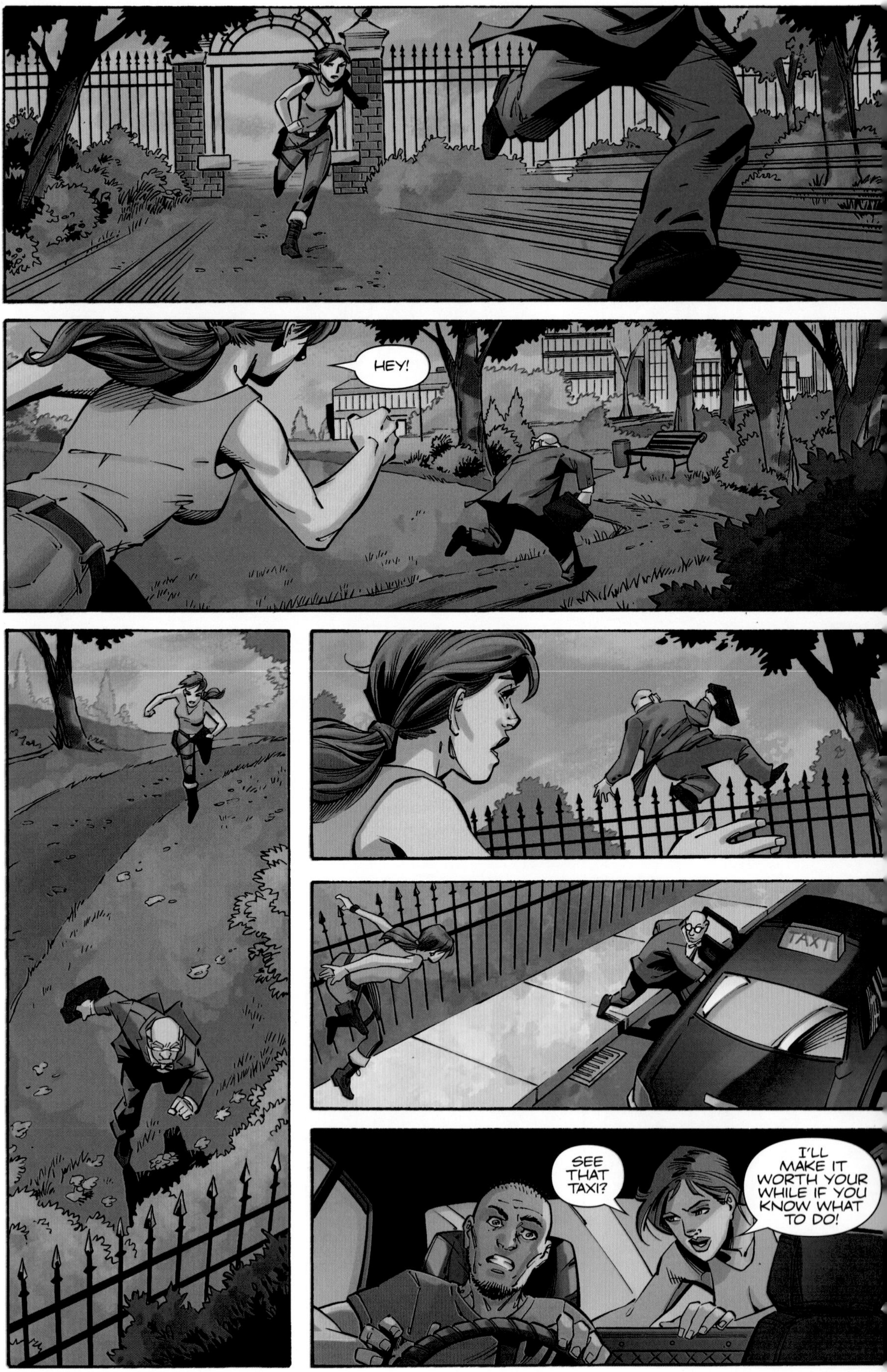
HEY!
SEE THAT TAXI?
I'LL MAKE IT WORTH YOUR WHILE IF YOU KNOW WHAT TO DO!

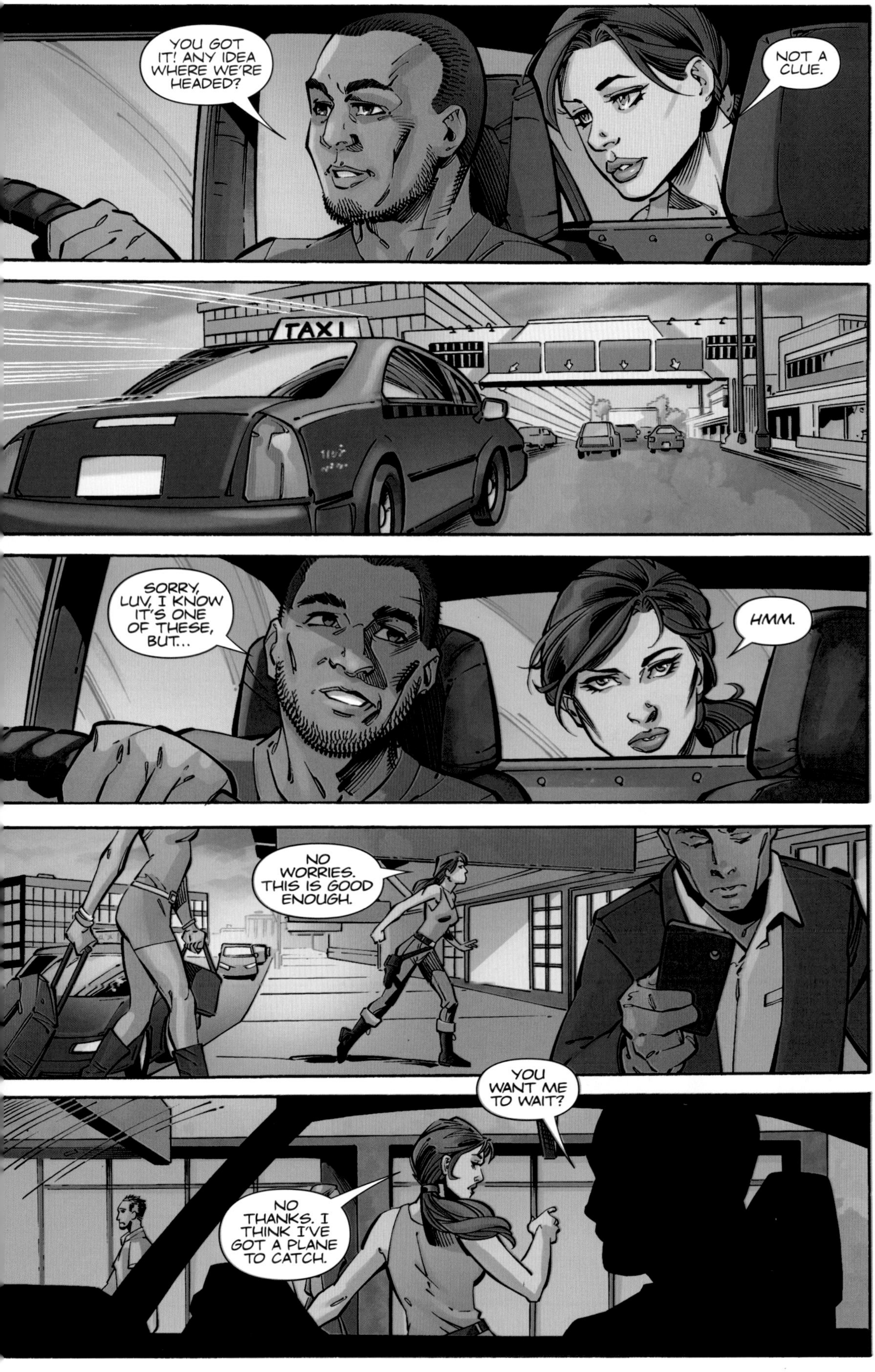
YOU GOT IT! ANY IDEA WHERE WE'RE HEADED?
NOT A CLUE.
TAXI
SORRY, LUV, I KNOW IT'S ONE OF THESE, BUT...
HMM.
NO WORRIES. THIS IS GOOD ENOUGH.
YOU WANT ME TO WAIT?
NO THANKS. I THINK I'VE GOT A PLANE TO CATCH.

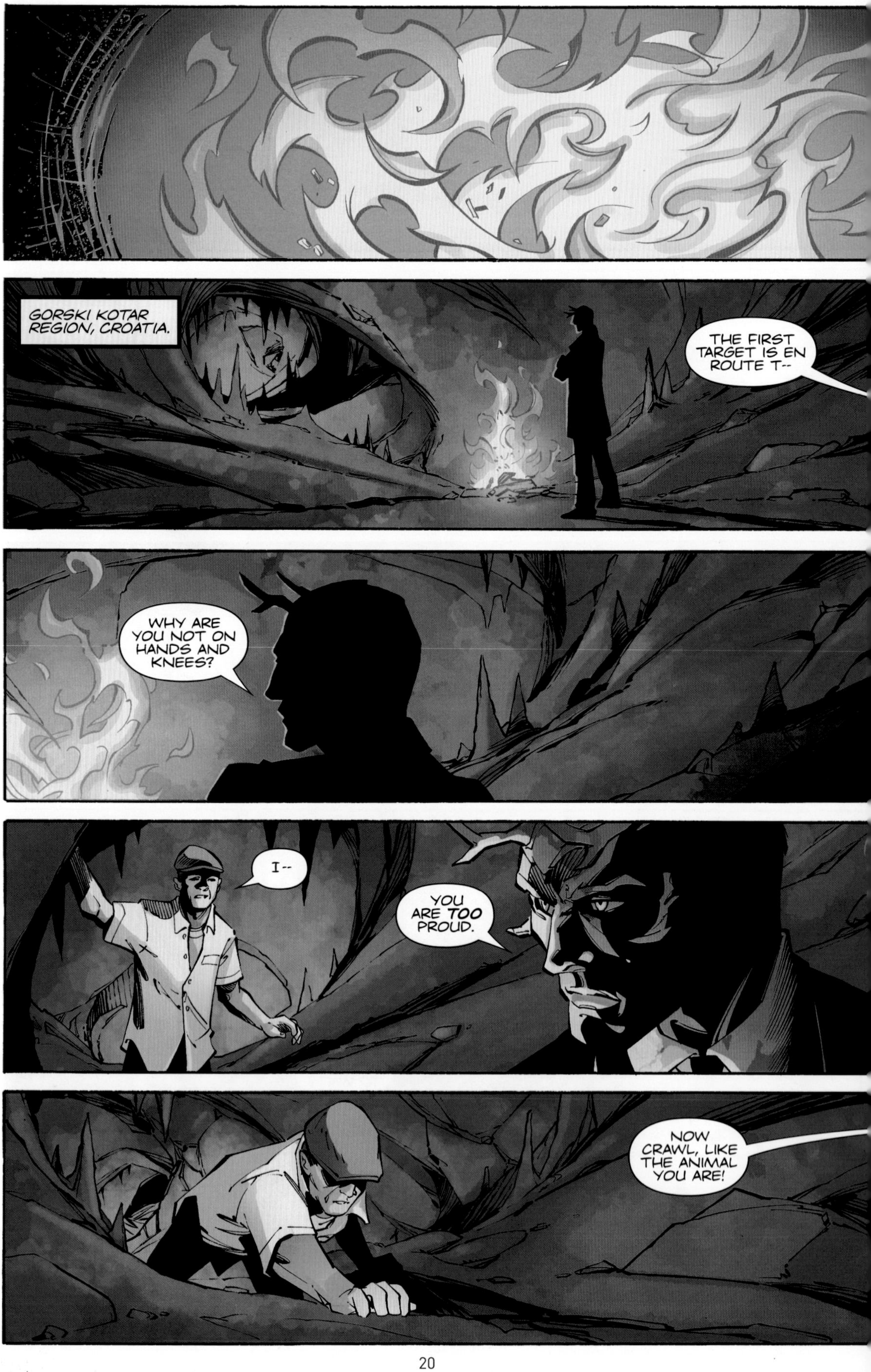
GORSKI KOTAR REGION, CROATIA.
THE FIRST TARGET IS EN ROUTE T--
WHY ARE YOU NOT ON HANDS AND KNEES?
I--
YOU ARE TOO PROUD.
NOW CRAWL, LIKE THE ANIMAL YOU ARE!

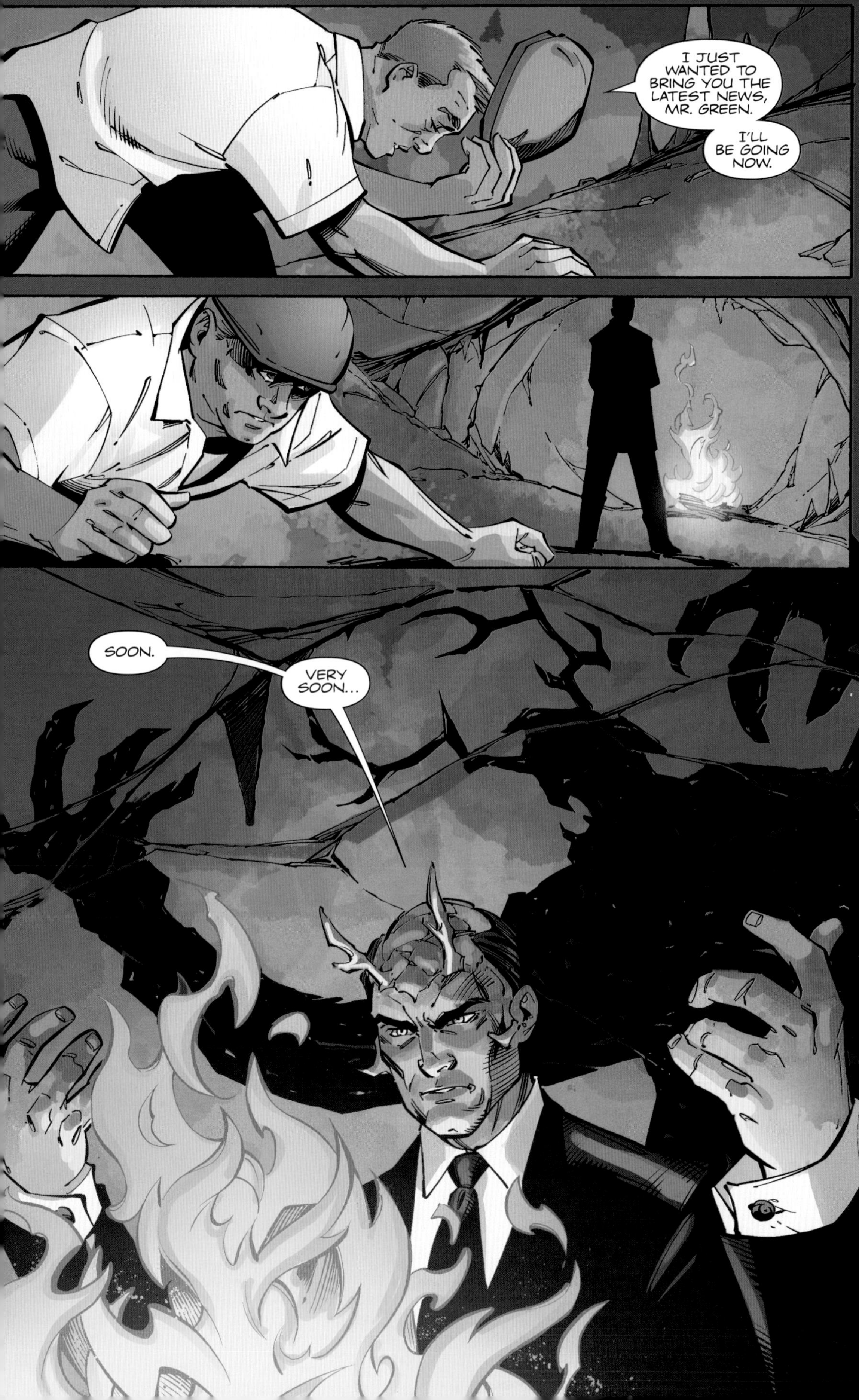
I JUST WANTED TO BRING YOU THE LATEST NEWS, MR. GREEN.
I'LL BE GOING NOW.
SOON.
VERY SOON...

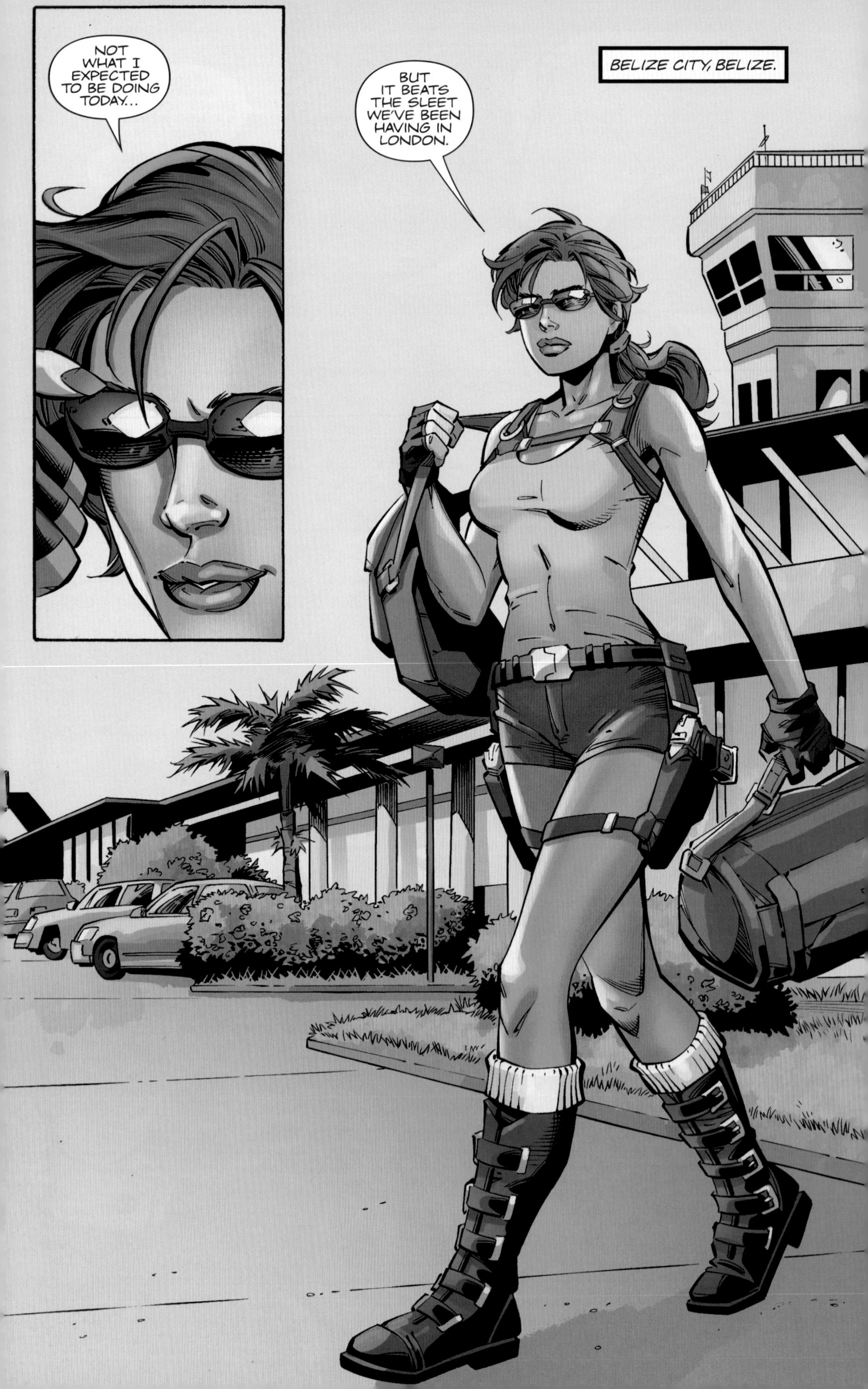
NOT WHAT I EXPECTED TO BE DOING TODAY...
BELIZE CITY, BELIZE.
BUT IT BEATS THE SLEET WE'VE BEEN HAVING IN LONDON.

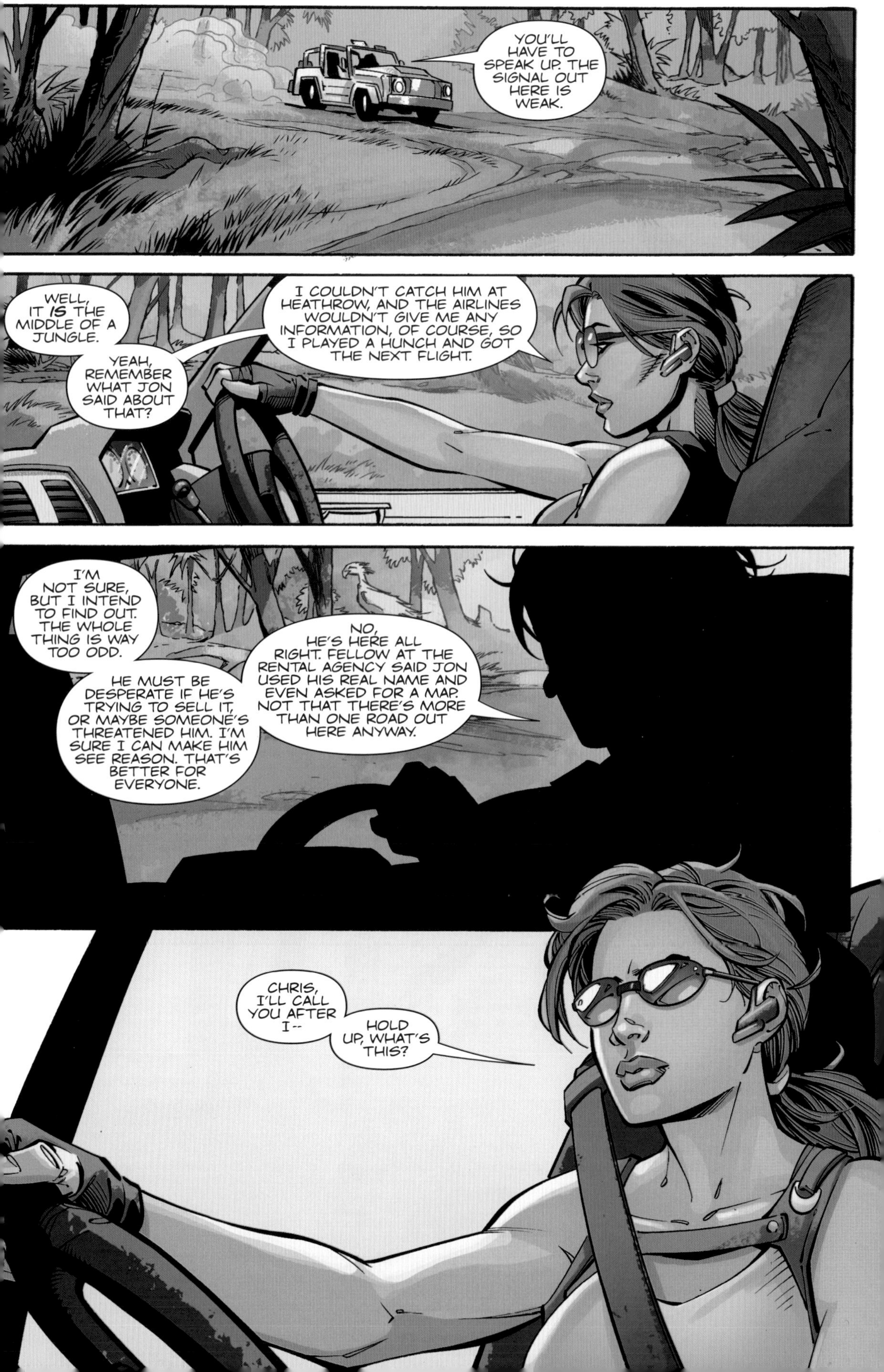
YOU'LL HAVE TO SPEAK UP. THE SIGNAL OUT HERE IS WEAK.
WELL, IT IS THE MIDDLE OF A JUNGLE.
YEAH, REMEMBER WHAT JON SAID ABOUT THAT?
I COULDN'T CATCH HIM AT HEATHROW, AND THE AIRLINES WOULDN'T GIVE ME ANY INFORMATION, OF COURSE, SO I PLAYED A HUNCH AND GOT THE NEXT FLIGHT.
I'M NOT SURE, BUT I INTEND TO FIND OUT. THE WHOLE THING IS WAY TOO ODD.
HE MUST BE DESPERATE IF HE'S TRYING TO SELL IT, OR MAYBE SOMEONE'S THREATENED HIM. I'M SURE I CAN MAKE HIM SEE REASON. THAT'S BETTER FOR EVERYONE.
NO, HE'S HERE ALL RIGHT. FELLOW AT THE RENTAL AGENCY SAID JON USED HIS REAL NAME AND EVEN ASKED FOR A MAP. NOT THAT THERE'S MORE THAN ONE ROAD OUT HERE ANYWAY.
CHRIS, I'LL CALL YOU AFTER I--
HOLD UP, WHAT'S THIS?

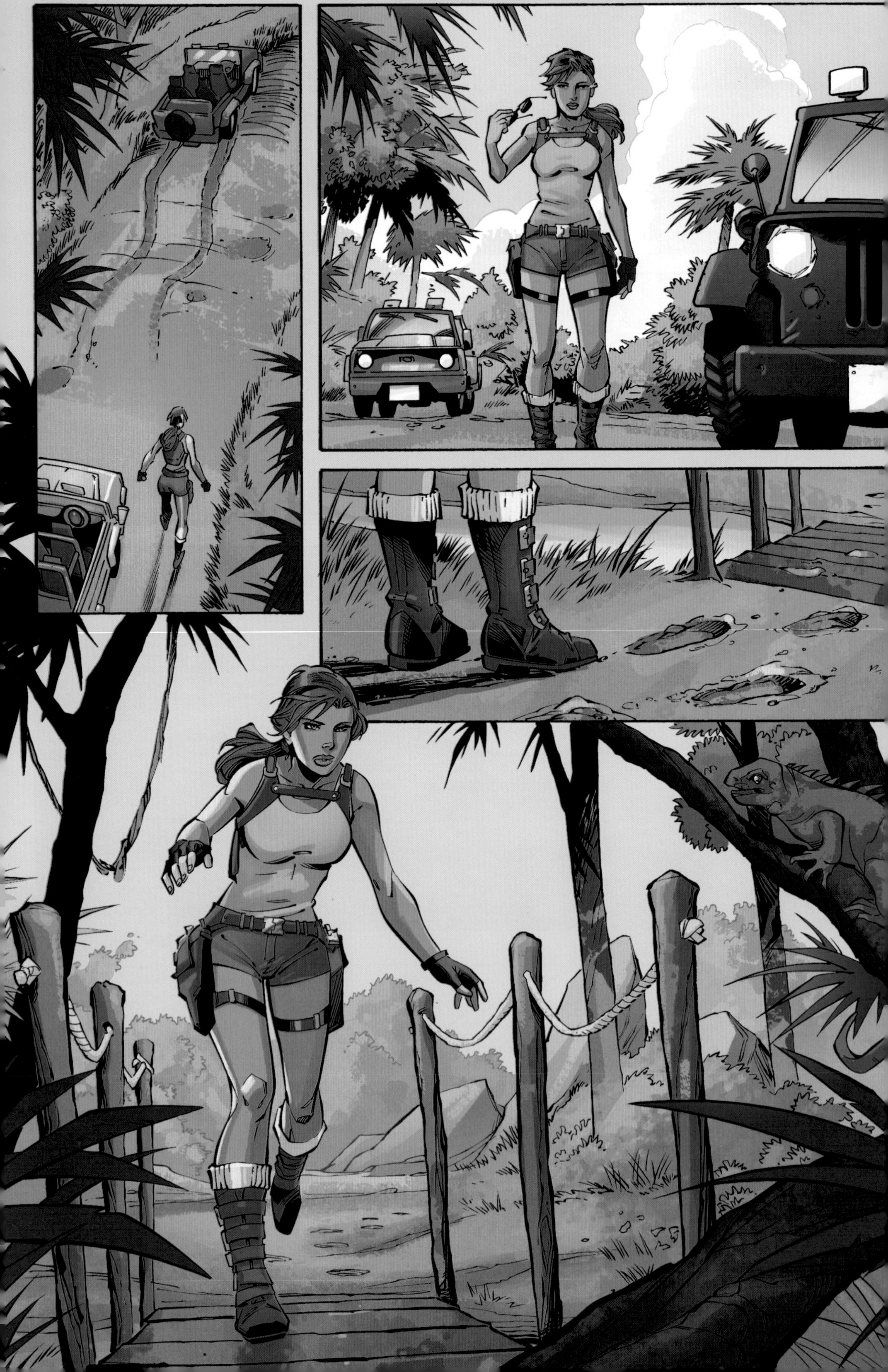

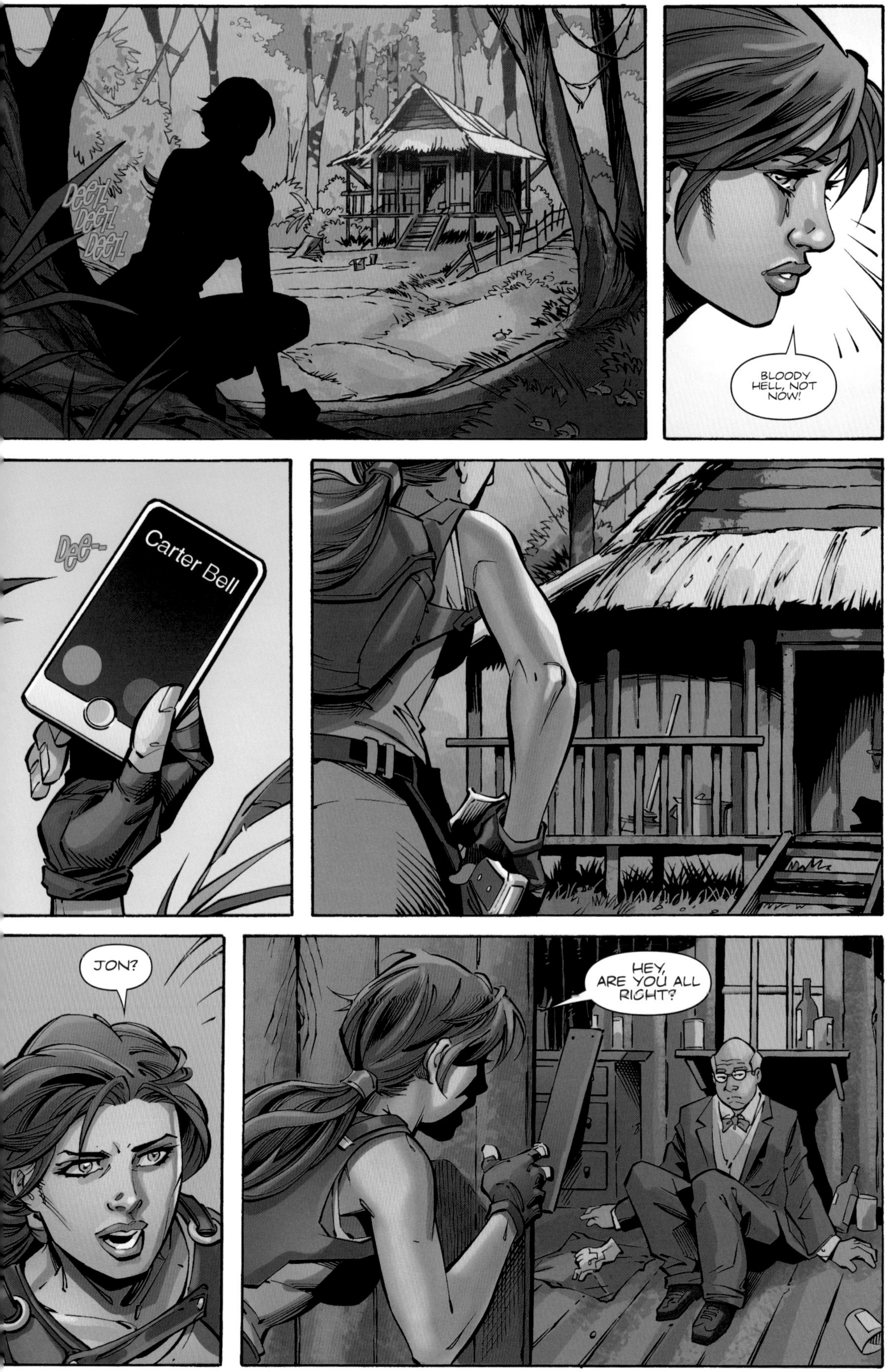
DEETL DEETL DEETL
BLOODY HELL, NOT NOW!
Dee--
Carter Bell
JON?
HEY, ARE YOU ALL RIGHT?

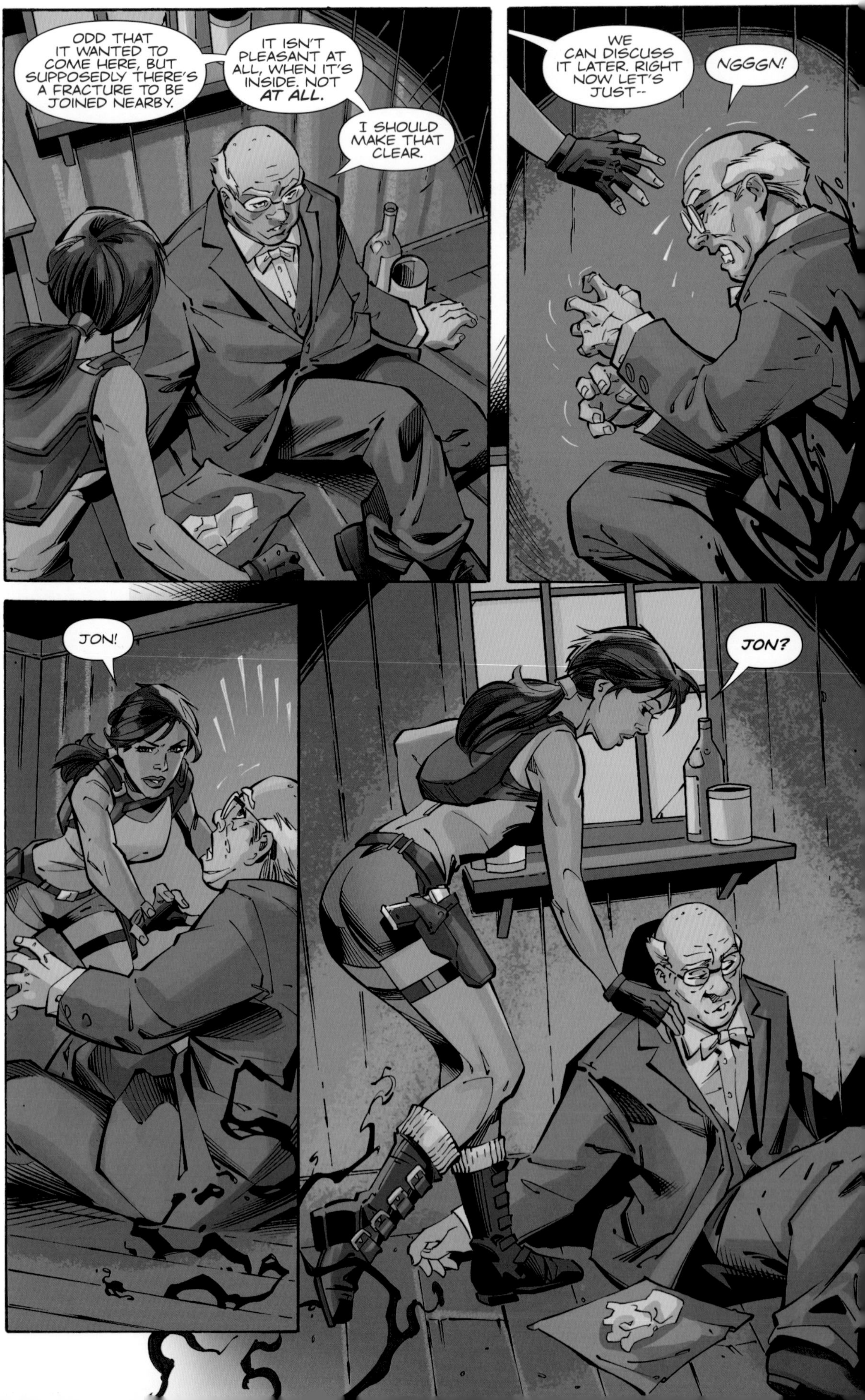
ODD THAT IT WANTED TO COME HERE, BUT SUPPOSEDLY THERE'S A FRACTURE TO BE JOINED NEARBY.
IT ISN'T PLEASANT AT ALL, WHEN IT'S INSIDE. NOT **AT ALL.**
I SHOULD MAKE THAT CLEAR.
WE CAN DISCUSS IT LATER. RIGHT NOW LET'S JUST--
NGGGN!
JON!
JON?

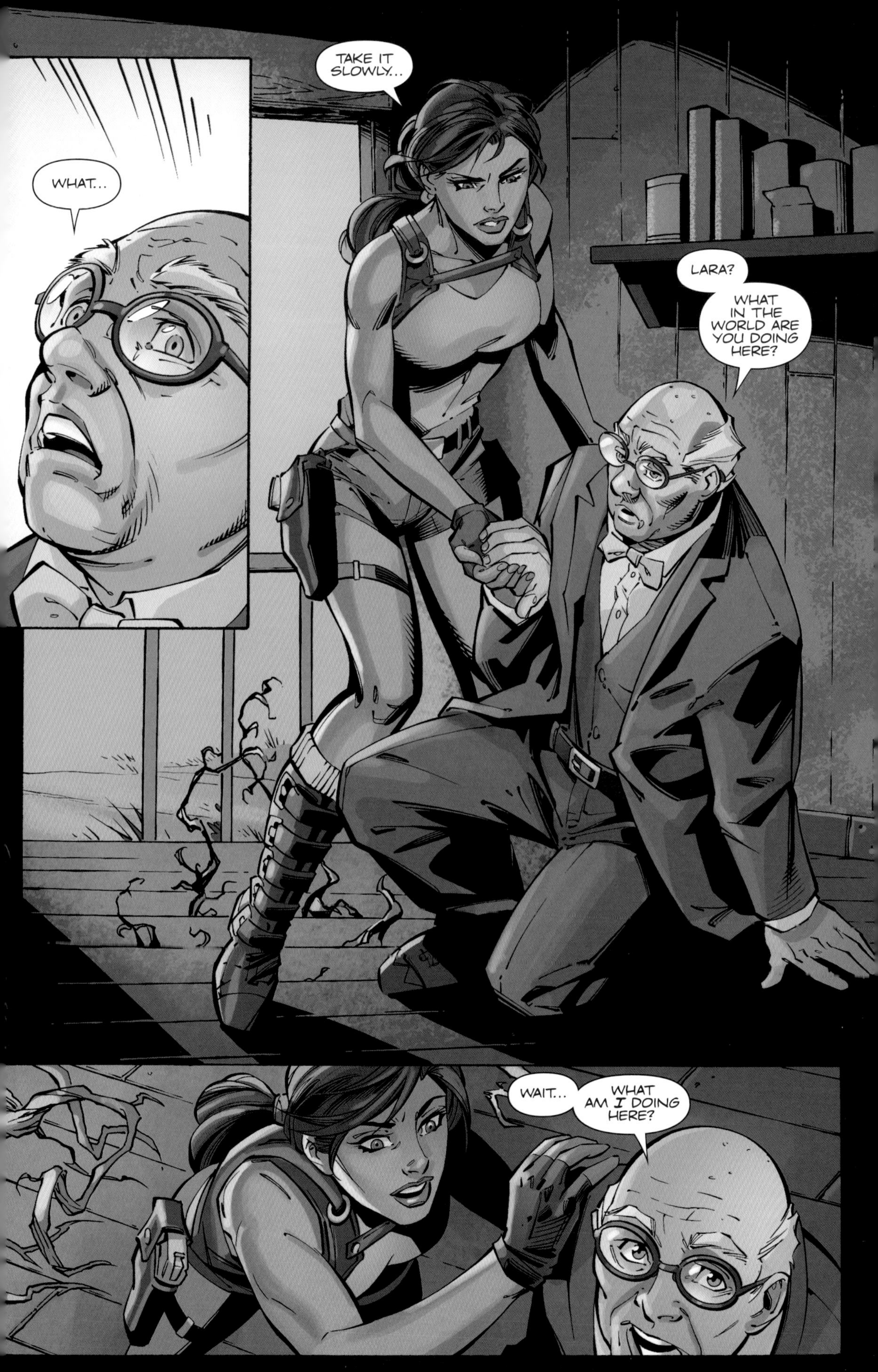
WHAT...
TAKE IT SLOWLY...
LARA?
WHAT IN THE WORLD ARE YOU DOING HERE?
WAIT...
WHAT AM I DOING HERE?

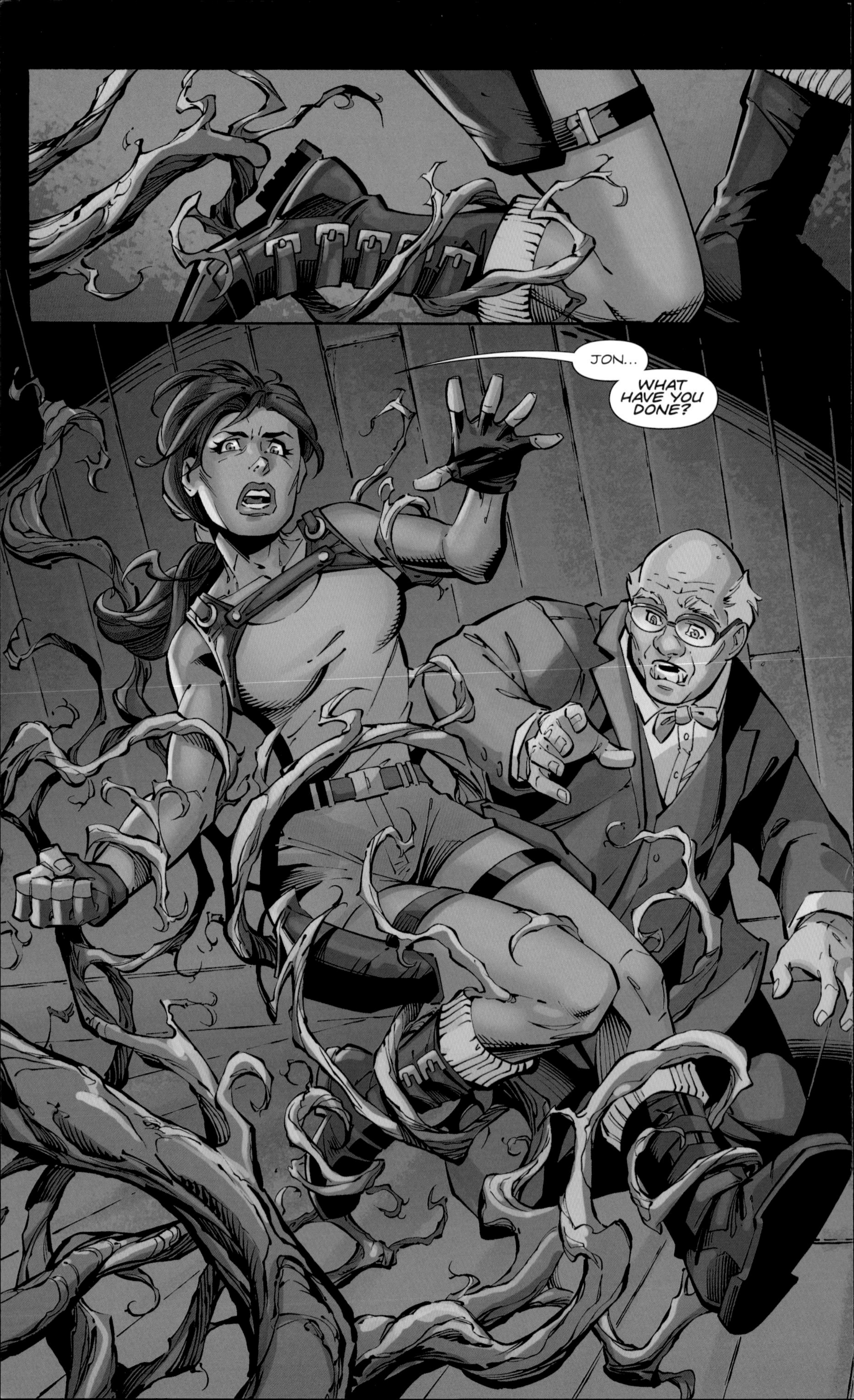
JON...
WHAT HAVE YOU DONE?

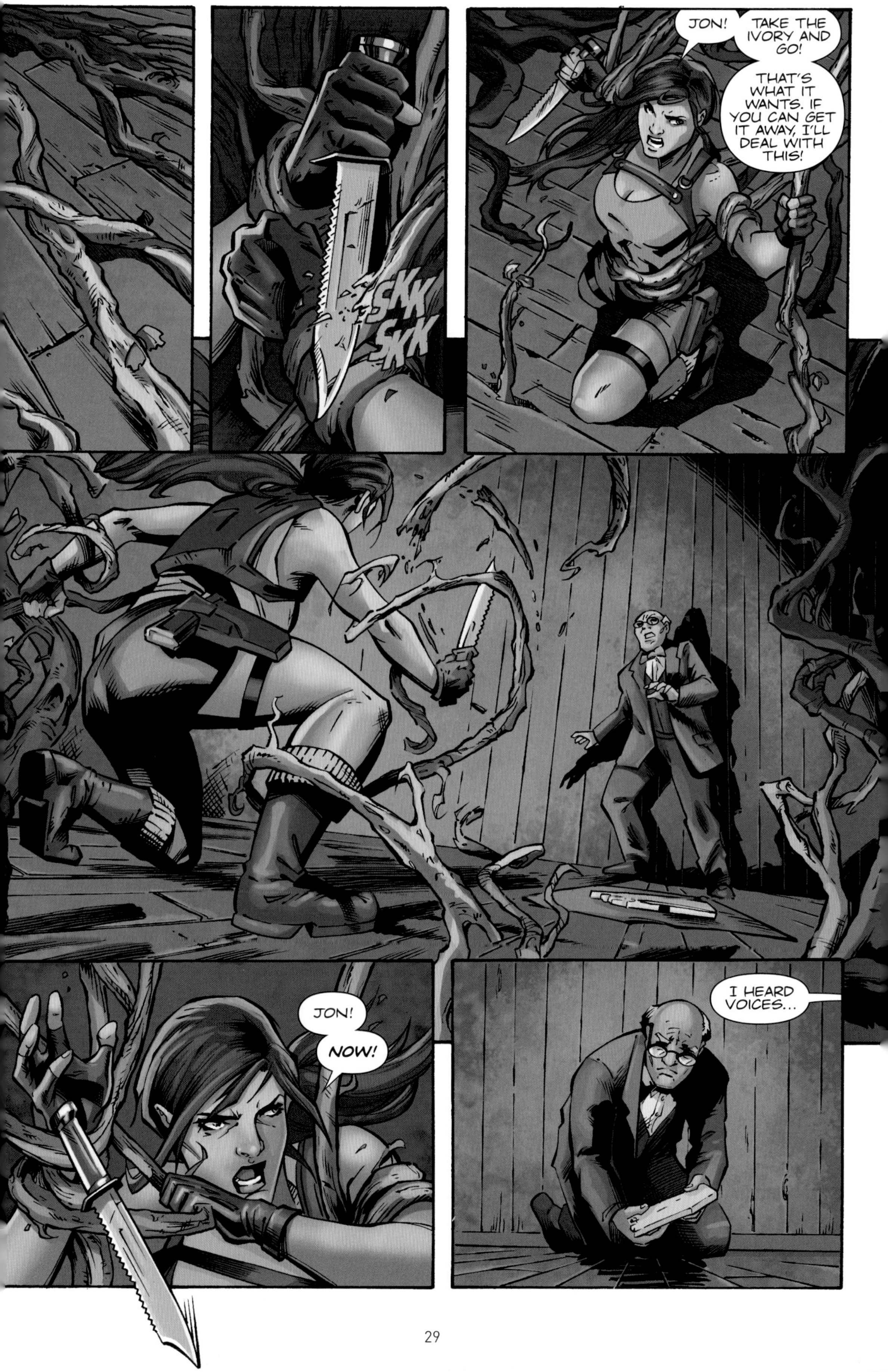
SKK
SKK
JON!
TAKE THE IVORY AND GO!
THAT'S WHAT IT WANTS. IF YOU CAN GET IT AWAY, I'LL DEAL WITH THIS!
JON!
NOW!
I HEARD VOICES...

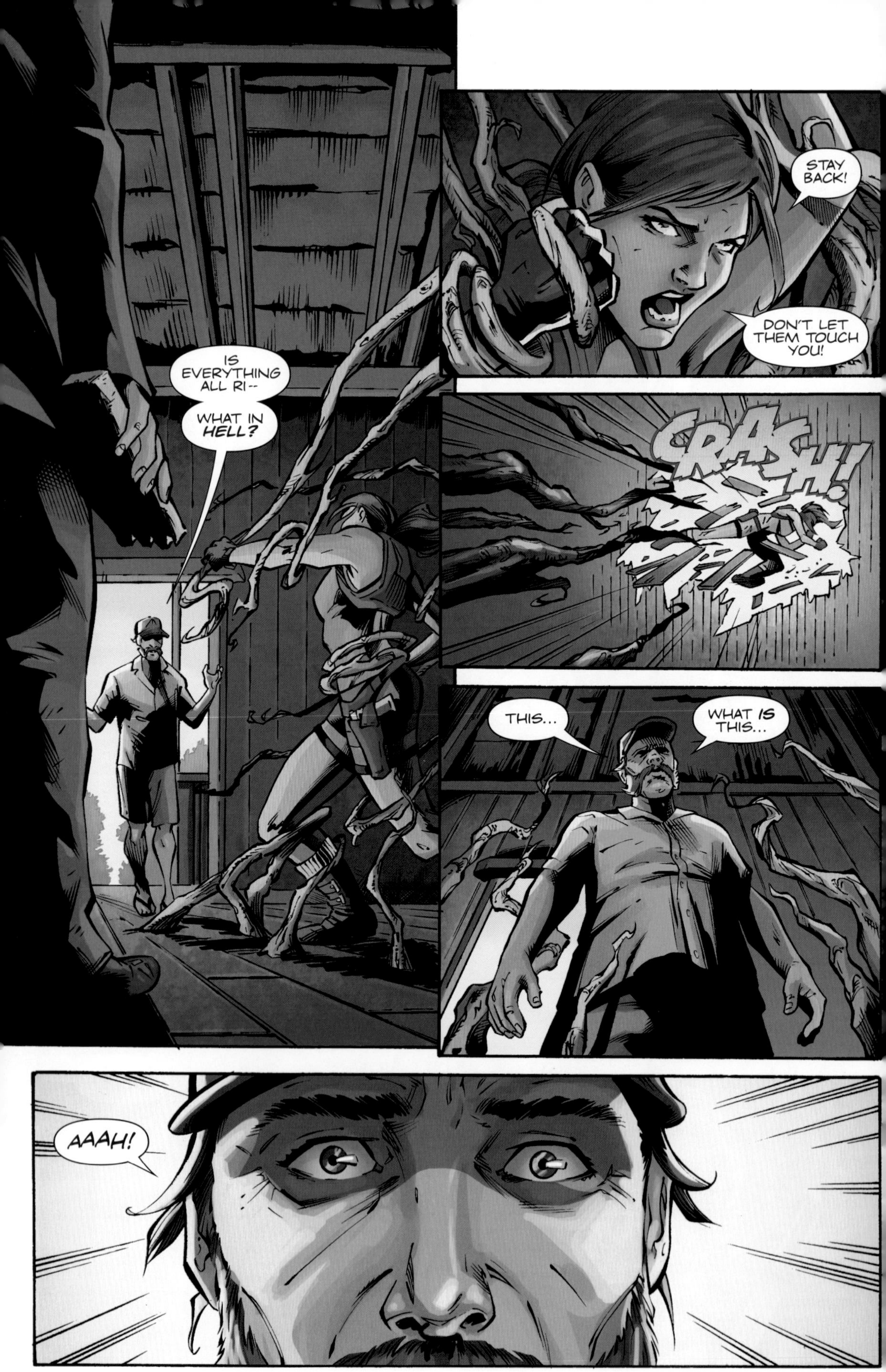
STAY BACK!
DON'T LET THEM TOUCH YOU!
IS EVERYTHING ALL RI--
WHAT IN HELL?
CRASH!
THIS...
WHAT IS THIS...
AAAH!

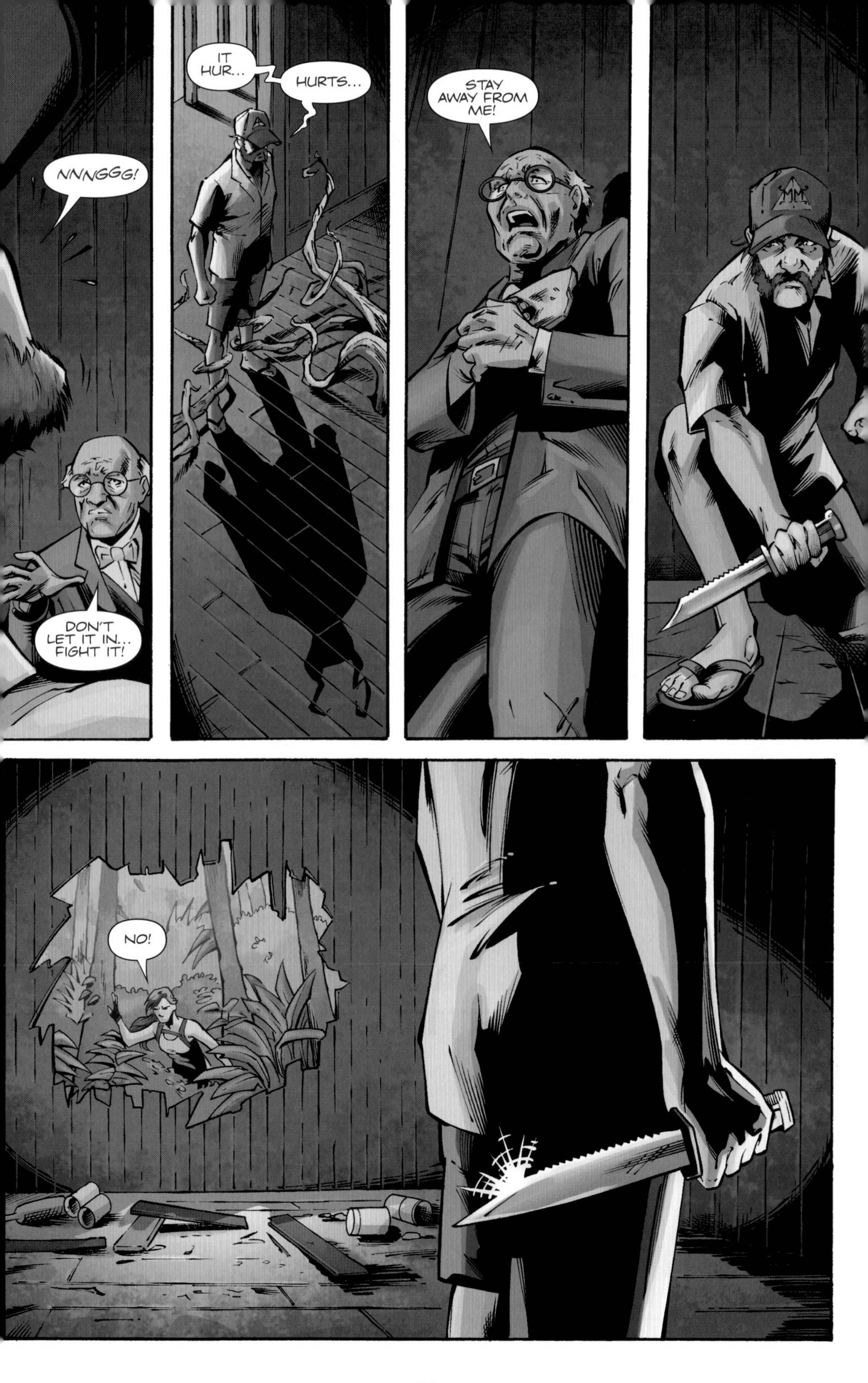
NNNGGG!
DON'T LET IT IN... FIGHT IT!
IT HUR...
HURTS...
STAY AWAY FROM ME!
NO!

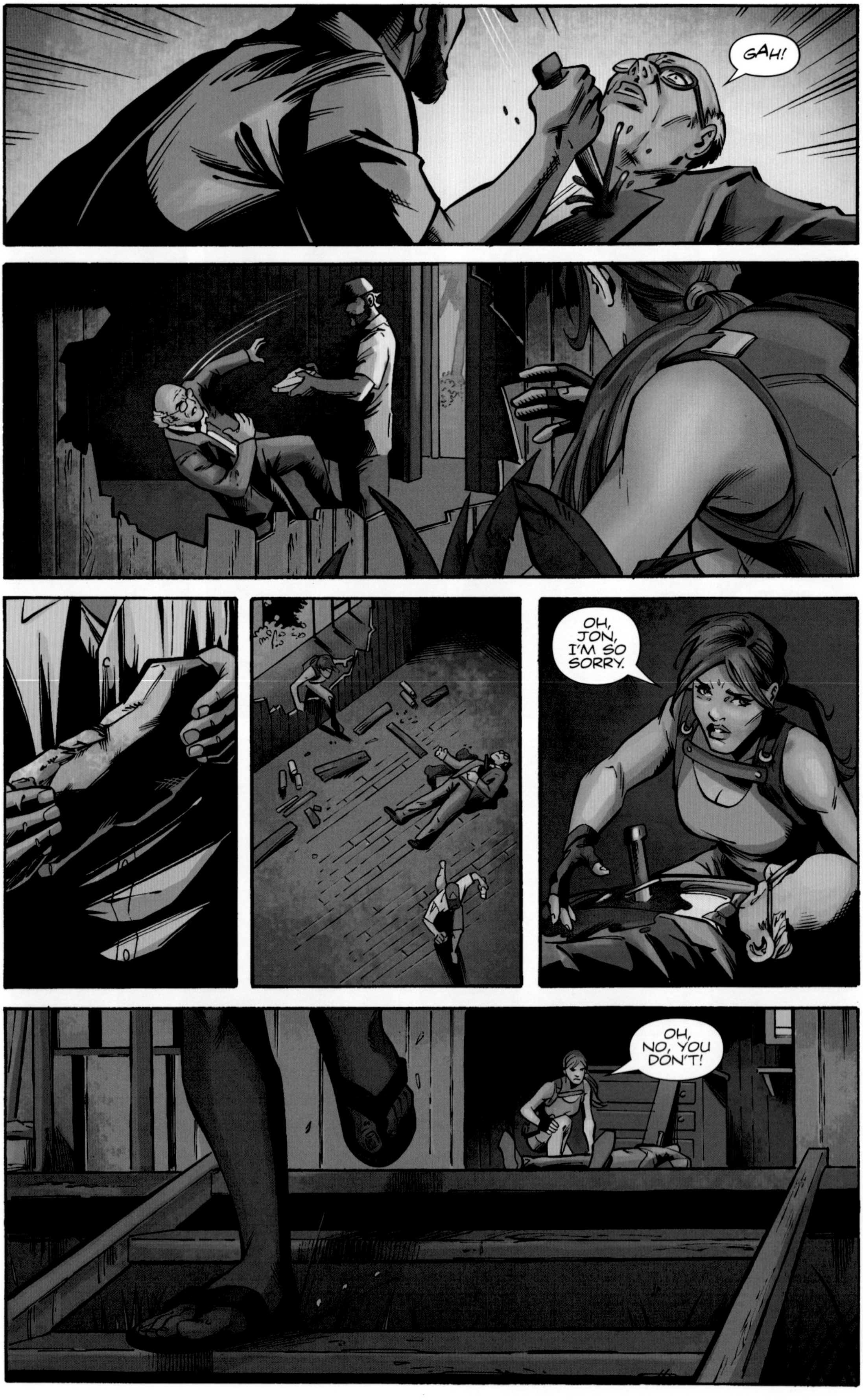
GAH!
OH, JON, I'M SO SORRY.
OH, NO, YOU DON'T!

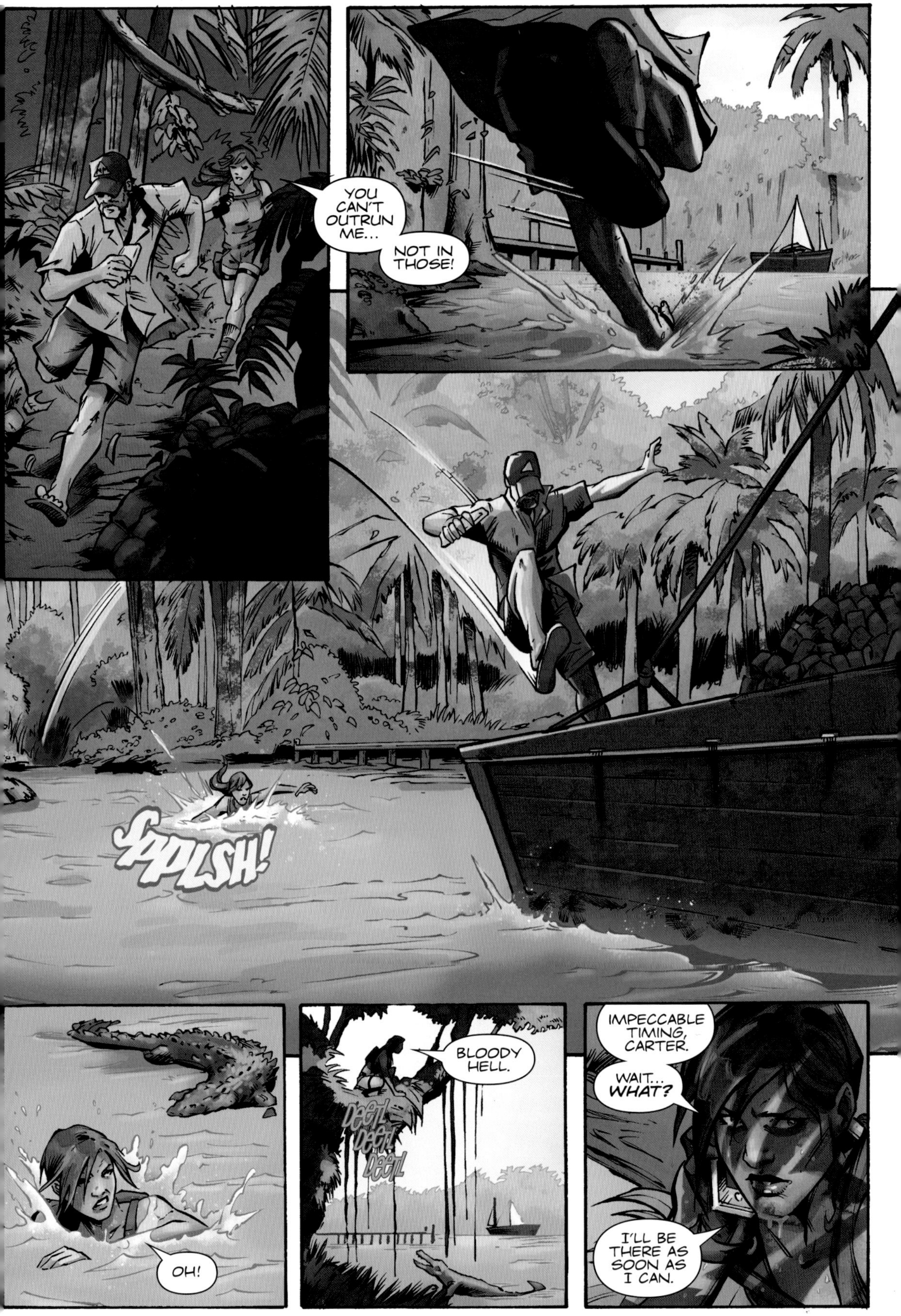
YOU CAN'T OUTRUN ME...
NOT IN THOSE!
SPPLSH!
OH!
BLOODY HELL.
DEETL DEETL DEETL
IMPECCABLE TIMING, CARTER.
WAIT... WHAT?
I'LL BE THERE AS SOON AS I CAN.

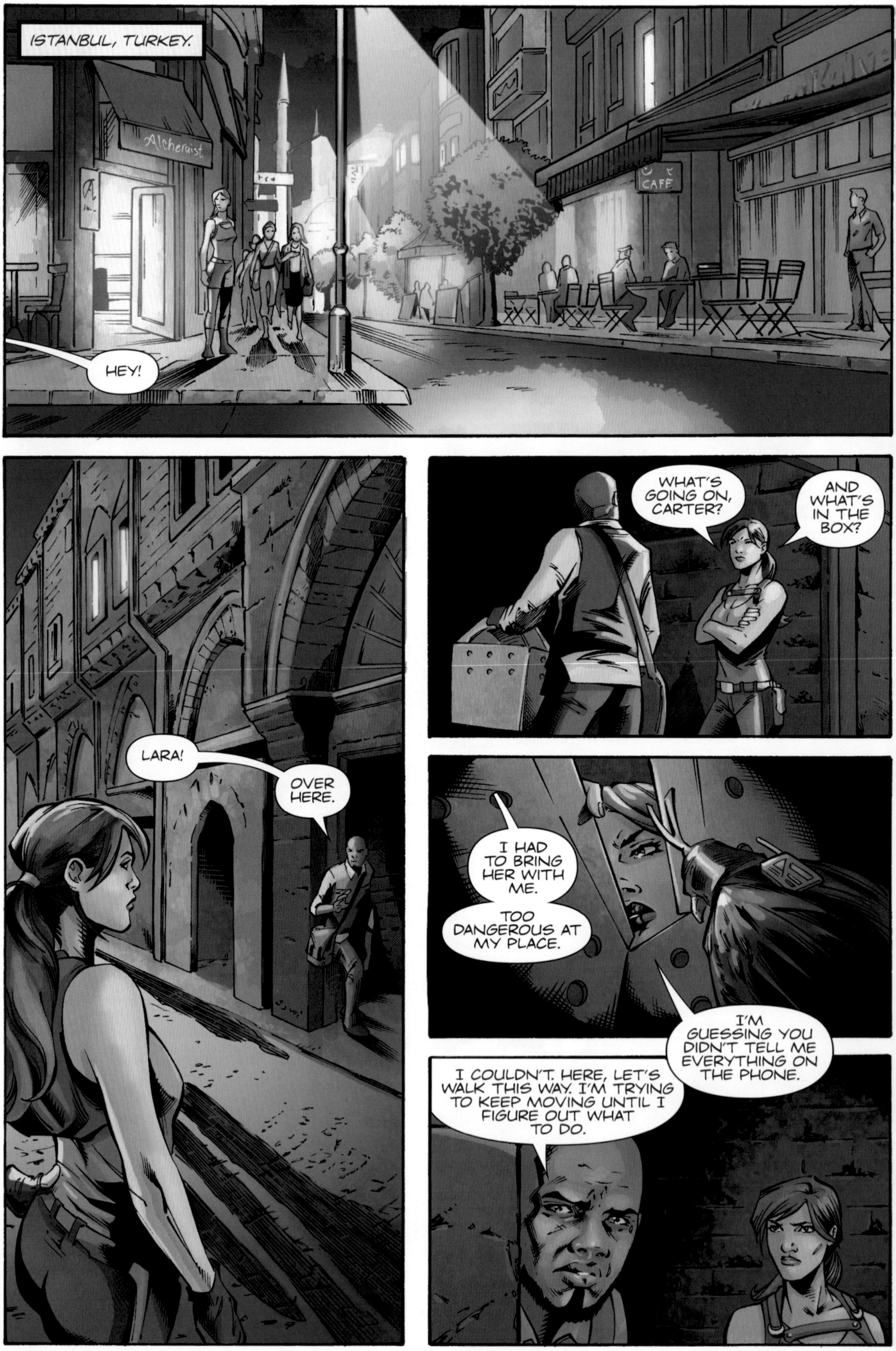
ISTANBUL, TURKEY.
HEY!
LARA!
OVER HERE.
WHAT'S GOING ON, CARTER?
AND WHAT'S IN THE BOX?
I HAD TO BRING HER WITH ME.
TOO DANGEROUS AT MY PLACE.
I'M GUESSING YOU DIDN'T TELL ME EVERYTHING ON THE PHONE.
I COULDN'T. HERE, LET'S WALK THIS WAY. I'M TRYING TO KEEP MOVING UNTIL I FIGURE OUT WHAT TO DO.

LARA, YOU'RE THE ONLY ONE I COULD CALL ABOUT THIS. NO ONE ELSE WOULD BELIEVE IT.

AND AFTER I HEARD ABOUT THE IVORY THEFT AT YOUR MUSEUM I KNEW I HAD TO TALK TO YOU.

I'VE BEEN TRACING THE ORIGIN OF INDIVIDUAL PIECES. SURPRISING HOW FAR SOME OF IT HAS TRAVELED.

ALMOST AS SURPRISING AS HOW OLD SOME OF IT IS.

OLD? WEREN'T YOU WORKING ON MEDIEVAL PIECES?

THAT'S JUST IT. SOME OF IT HAS BEEN REPURPOSED FROM MORE ANCIENT SOURCES.

THIS ONE IN PARTICULAR, THE SUBSTRATE DATES FROM THE LAST ICE AGE!

AND YOU WANT TO KNOW SOMETHING REALLY WEIRD?

I COULDN'T I.D. THE ANIMAL IT CAME FROM. IT'S NOT MAMMOTH, NOT WALRUS...

IT DOESN'T MATCH ANYTHING, LIVING OR EXTINCT. THERE'S JUST ONE MORE LIKE THAT, IN A PRIVATE COLLECTION IN ARIZONA. NOT COUNTING THE ONE JON WAS WORKING ON, OF COURSE.

HMM...

ANY IDEA WHO TOOK IT?

AS A MATTER OF FACT...

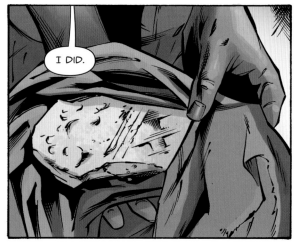

I DID.

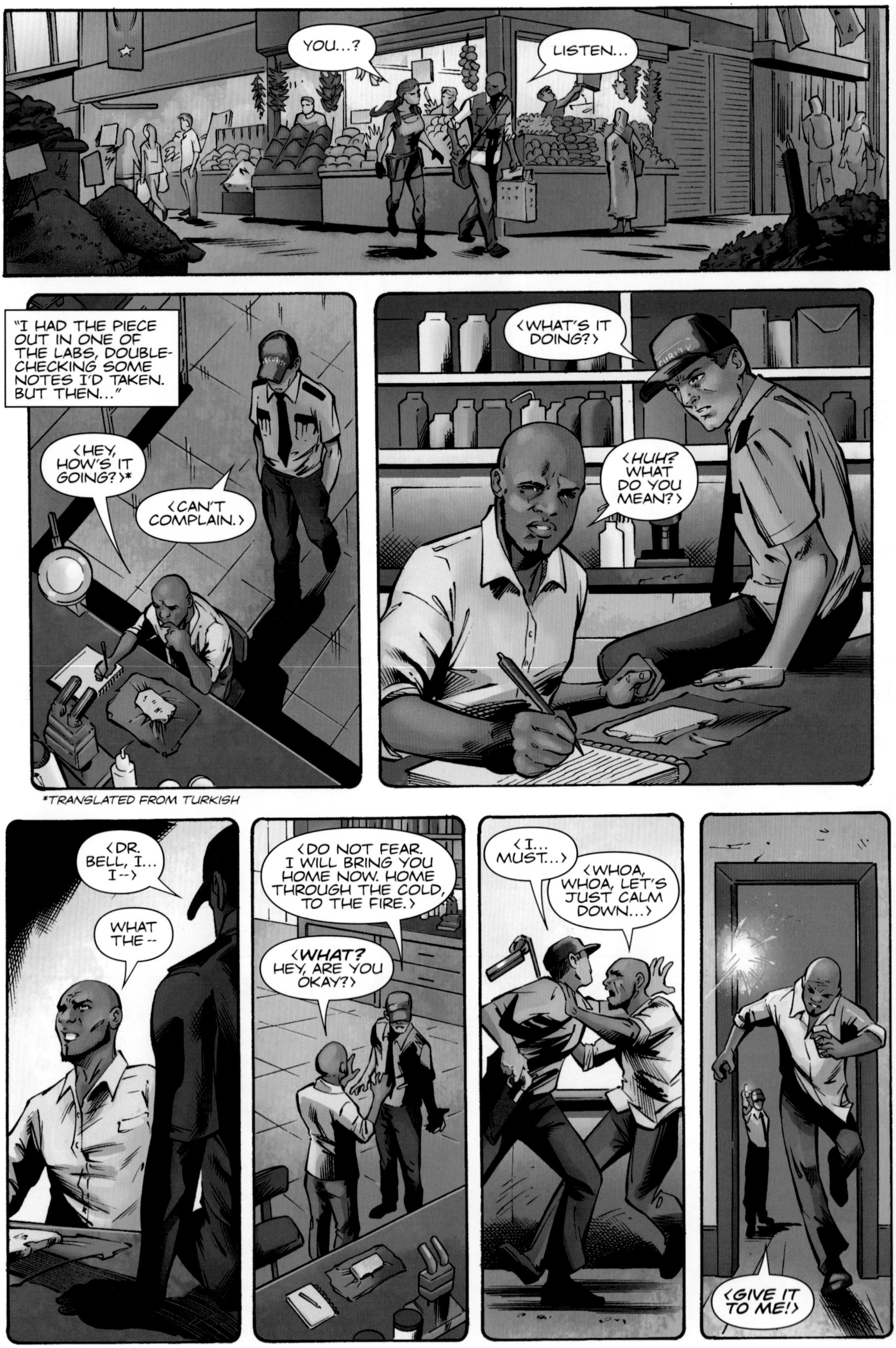
YOU...?
LISTEN...
"I HAD THE PIECE OUT IN ONE OF THE LABS, DOUBLE-CHECKING SOME NOTES I'D TAKEN. BUT THEN..."
‹HEY, HOW'S IT GOING?›*
‹CAN'T COMPLAIN.›
‹WHAT'S IT DOING?›
‹HUH? WHAT DO YOU MEAN?›
*TRANSLATED FROM TURKISH
‹DR. BELL, I... I--›
WHAT THE--
‹DO NOT FEAR. I WILL BRING YOU HOME NOW. HOME THROUGH THE COLD, TO THE FIRE.›
‹*WHAT?* HEY, ARE YOU OKAY?›
‹I... MUST...›
‹WHOA, WHOA, LET'S JUST CALM DOWN...›
‹GIVE IT TO ME!›

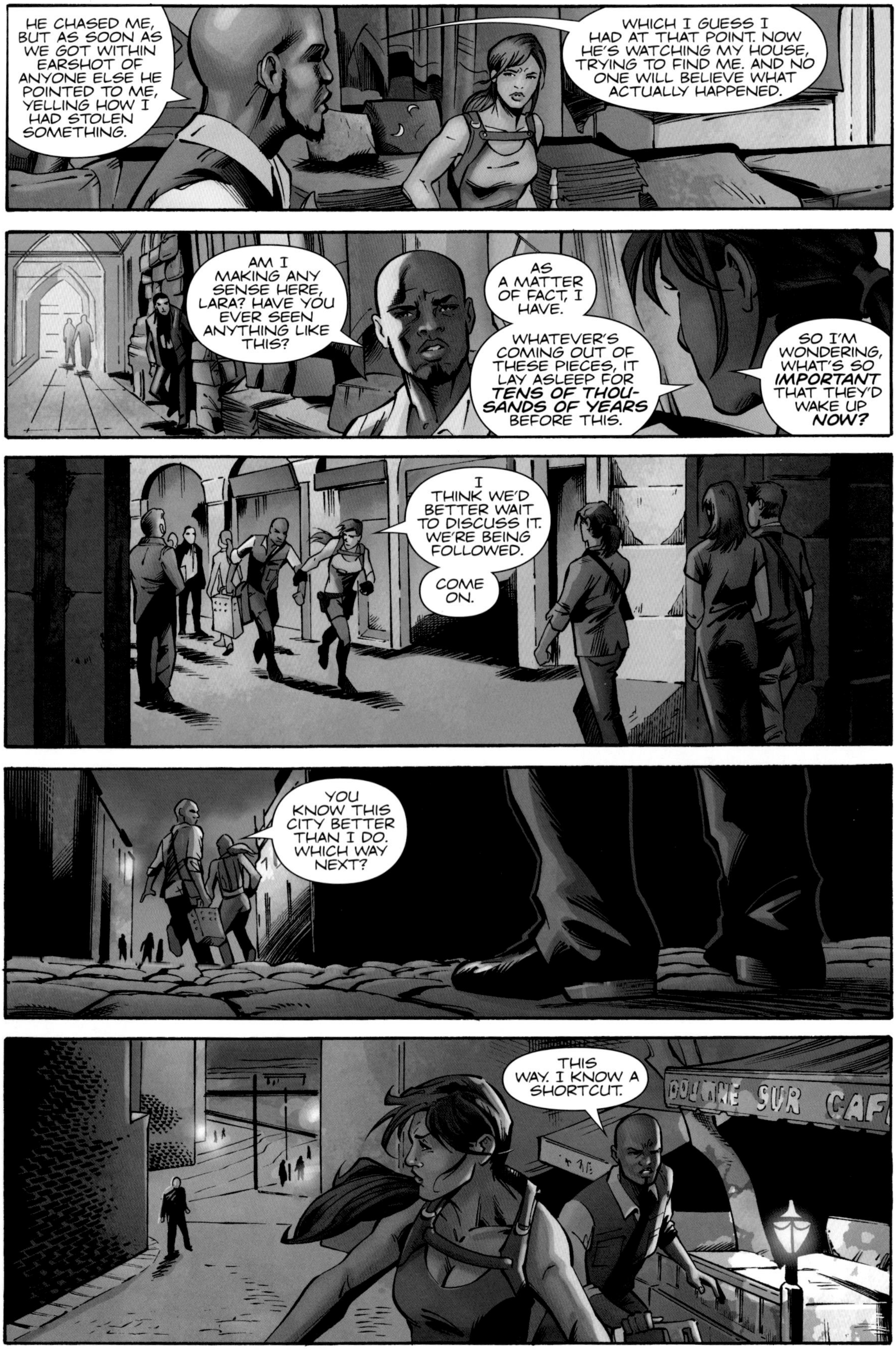
HE CHASED ME, BUT AS SOON AS WE GOT WITHIN EARSHOT OF ANYONE ELSE HE POINTED TO ME, YELLING HOW I HAD STOLEN SOMETHING.
WHICH I GUESS I HAD AT THAT POINT. NOW HE'S WATCHING MY HOUSE, TRYING TO FIND ME. AND NO ONE WILL BELIEVE WHAT ACTUALLY HAPPENED.
AM I MAKING ANY SENSE HERE, LARA? HAVE YOU EVER SEEN ANYTHING LIKE THIS?
AS A MATTER OF FACT, I HAVE.
WHATEVER'S COMING OUT OF THESE PIECES, IT LAY ASLEEP FOR TENS OF THOUSANDS OF YEARS BEFORE THIS.
SO I'M WONDERING, WHAT'S SO IMPORTANT THAT THEY'D WAKE UP NOW?
I THINK WE'D BETTER WAIT TO DISCUSS IT. WE'RE BEING FOLLOWED.
COME ON.
YOU KNOW THIS CITY BETTER THAN I DO. WHICH WAY NEXT?
THIS WAY. I KNOW A SHORTCUT.

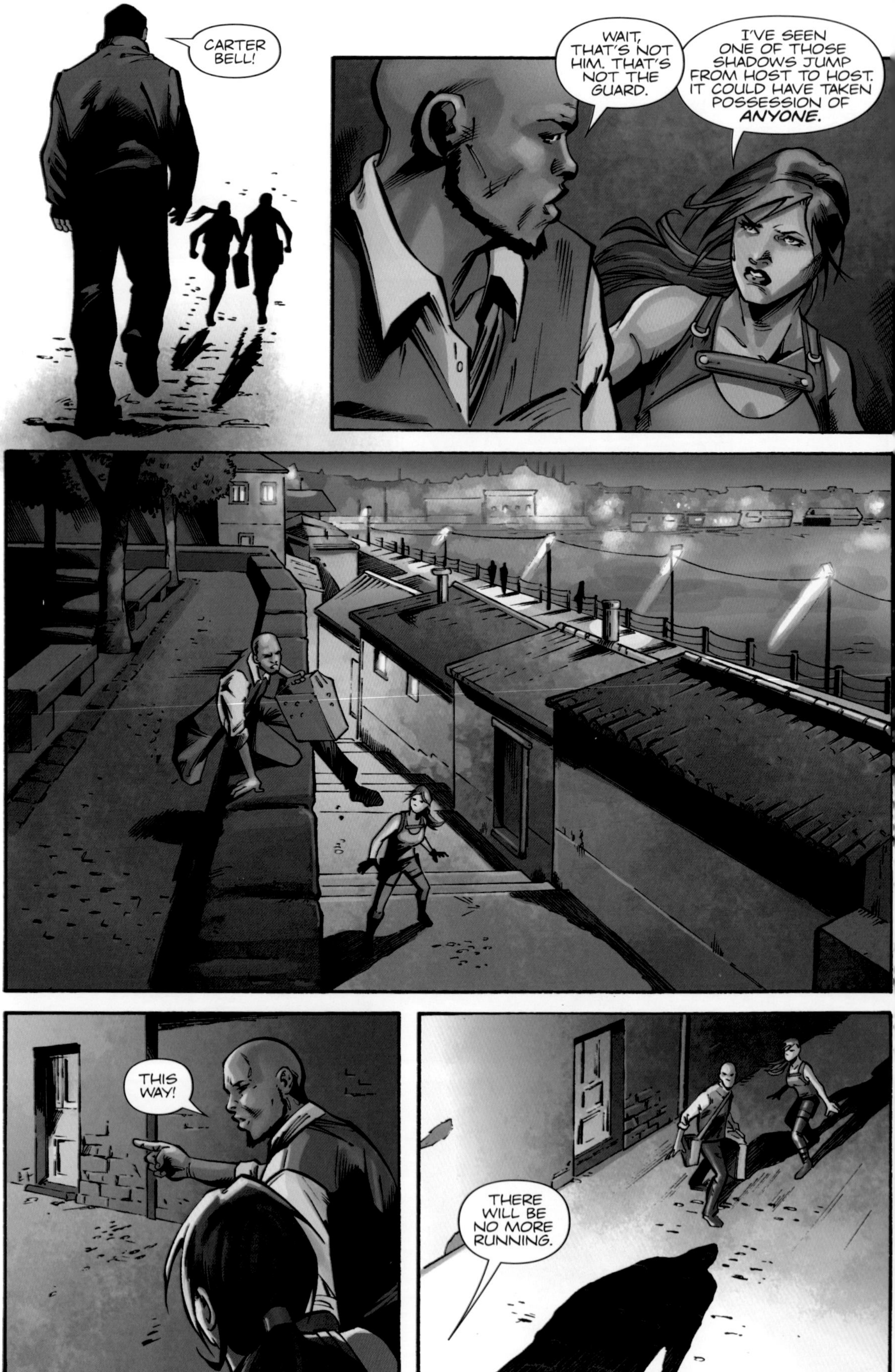
CARTER BELL!
WAIT, THAT'S NOT HIM. THAT'S NOT THE GUARD.
I'VE SEEN ONE OF THOSE SHADOWS JUMP FROM HOST TO HOST. IT COULD HAVE TAKEN POSSESSION OF ANYONE.
THIS WAY!
THERE WILL BE NO MORE RUNNING.

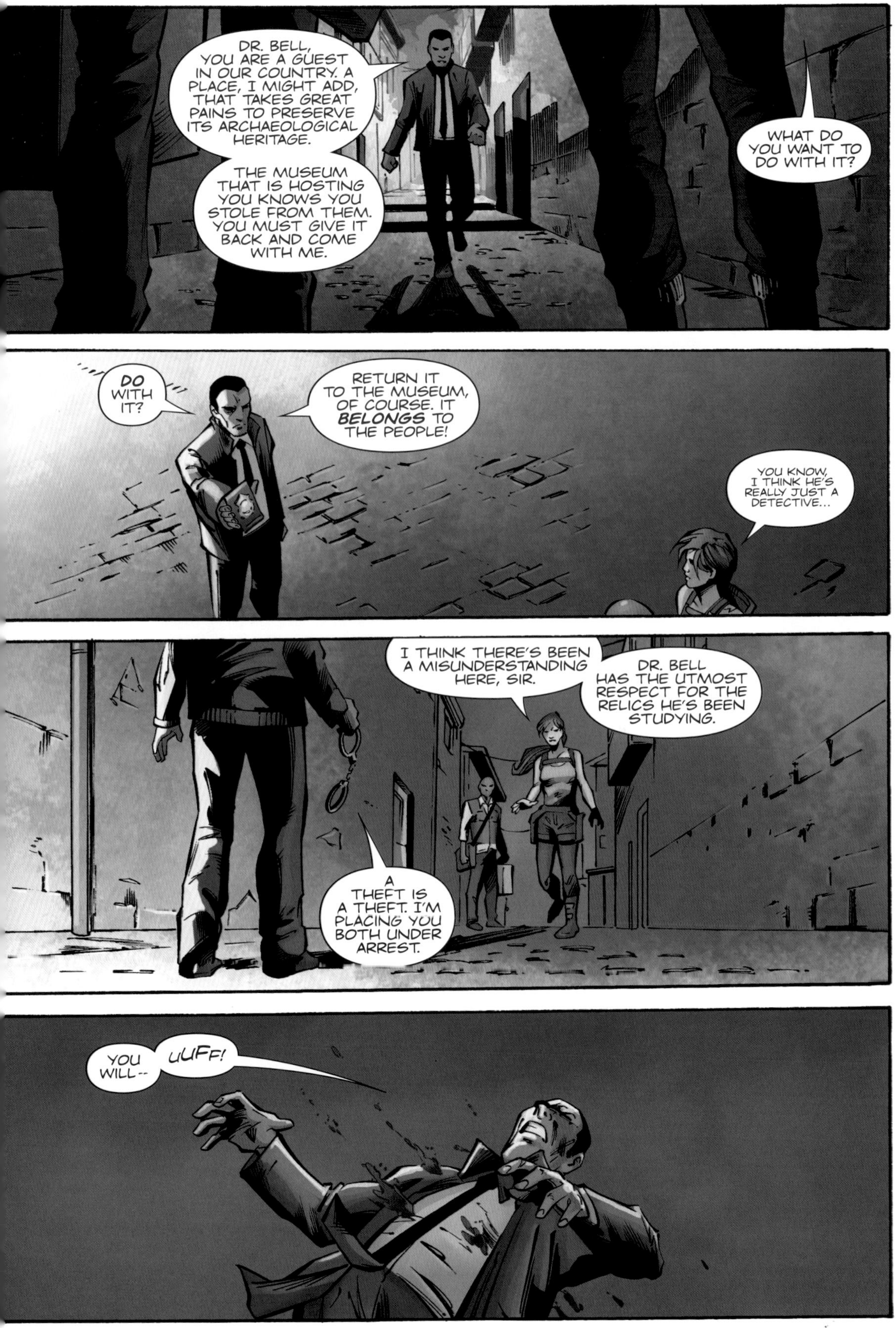

DR. BELL, YOU ARE A GUEST IN OUR COUNTRY. A PLACE, I MIGHT ADD, THAT TAKES GREAT PAINS TO PRESERVE ITS ARCHAEOLOGICAL HERITAGE.
THE MUSEUM THAT IS HOSTING YOU KNOWS YOU STOLE FROM THEM. YOU MUST GIVE IT BACK AND COME WITH ME.
WHAT DO YOU WANT TO DO WITH IT?
DO WITH IT?
RETURN IT TO THE MUSEUM, OF COURSE. IT BELONGS TO THE PEOPLE!
YOU KNOW, I THINK HE'S REALLY JUST A DETECTIVE...
I THINK THERE'S BEEN A MISUNDERSTANDING HERE, SIR.
DR. BELL HAS THE UTMOST RESPECT FOR THE RELICS HE'S BEEN STUDYING.
A THEFT IS A THEFT. I'M PLACING YOU BOTH UNDER ARREST.
YOU WILL--
UUFF!

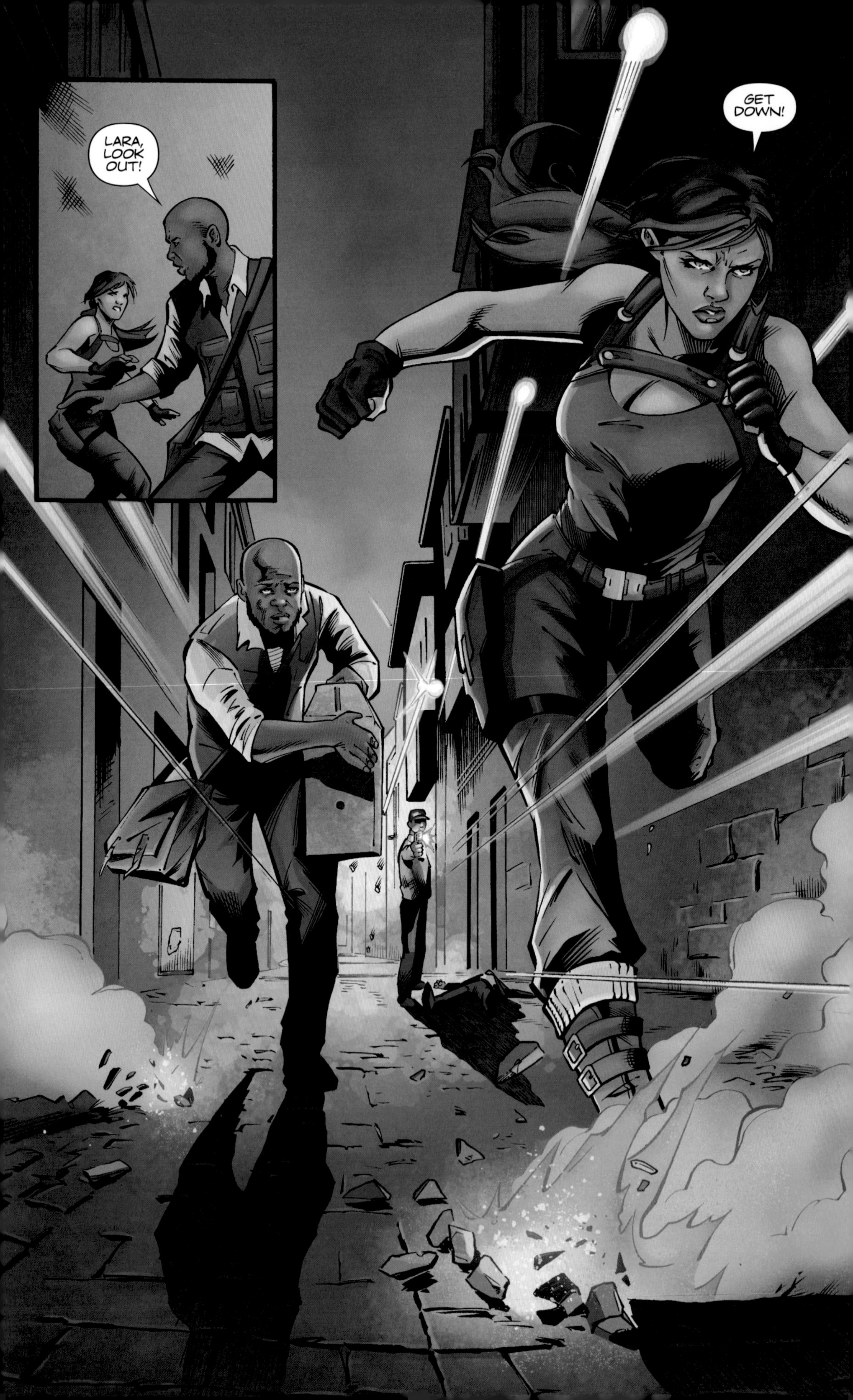
LARA, LOOK OUT!
GET DOWN!

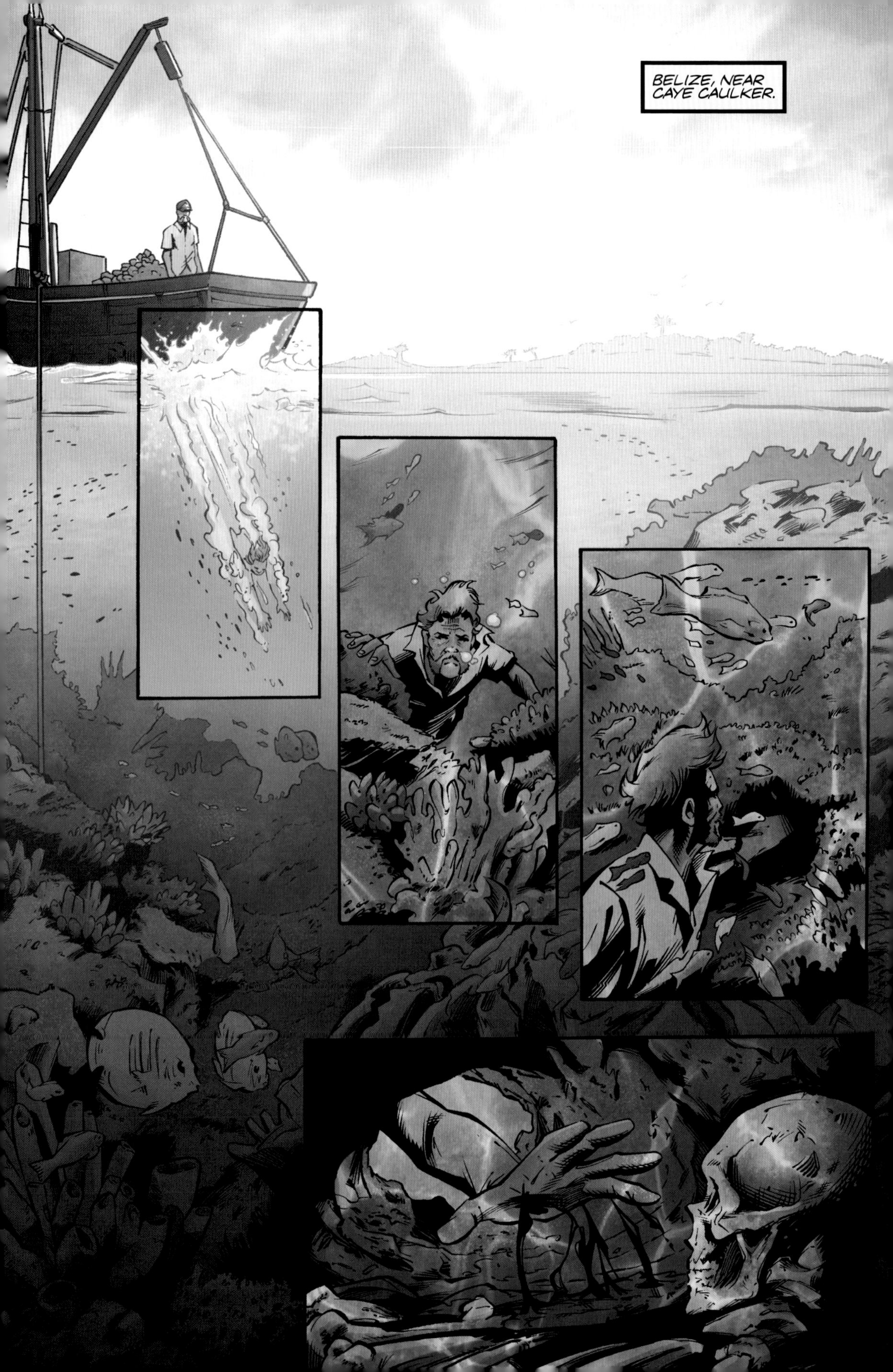
BELIZE, NEAR
CAYE CAULKER.

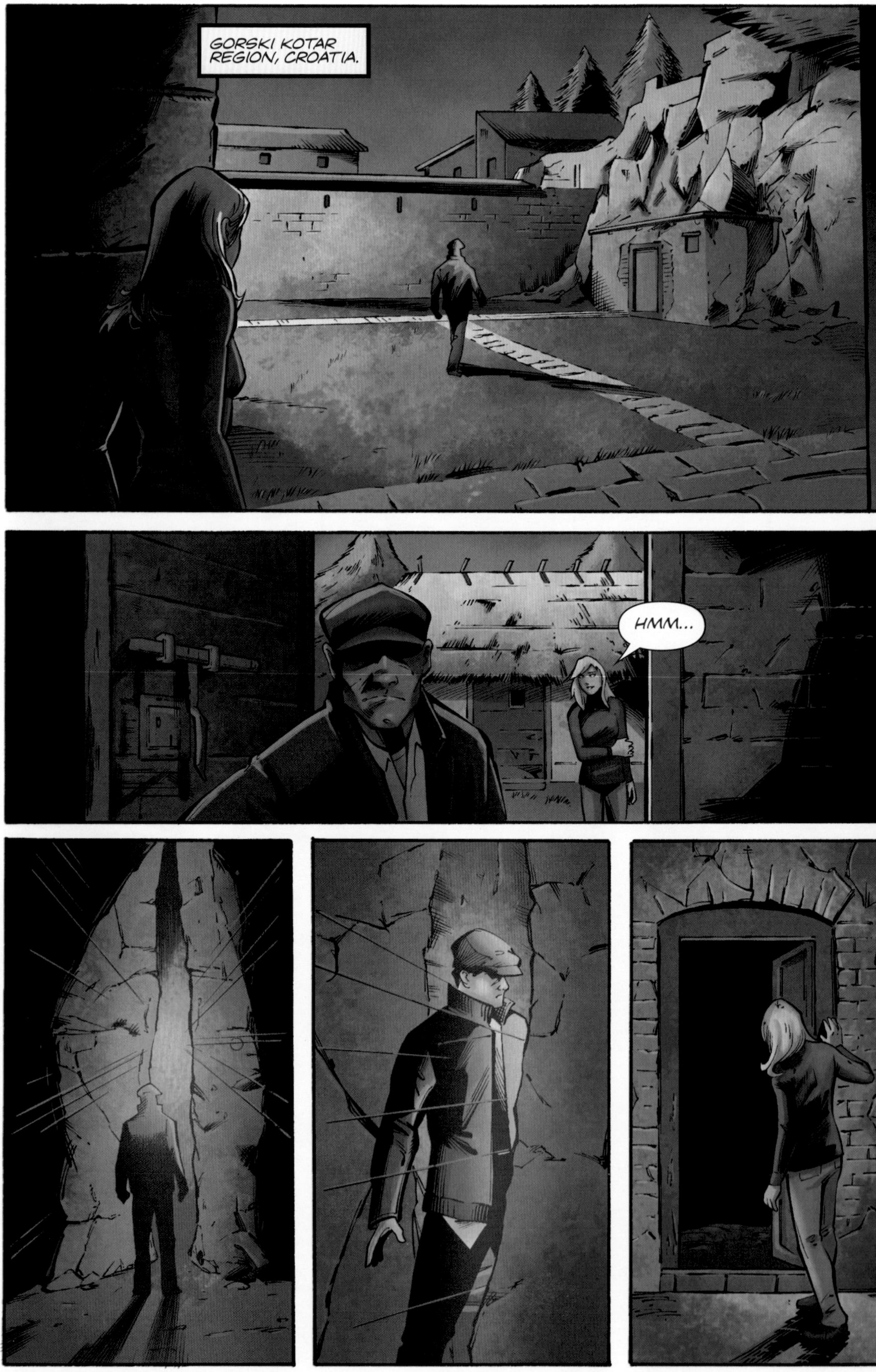
GORSKI KOTAR
REGION, CROATIA.
HMM...

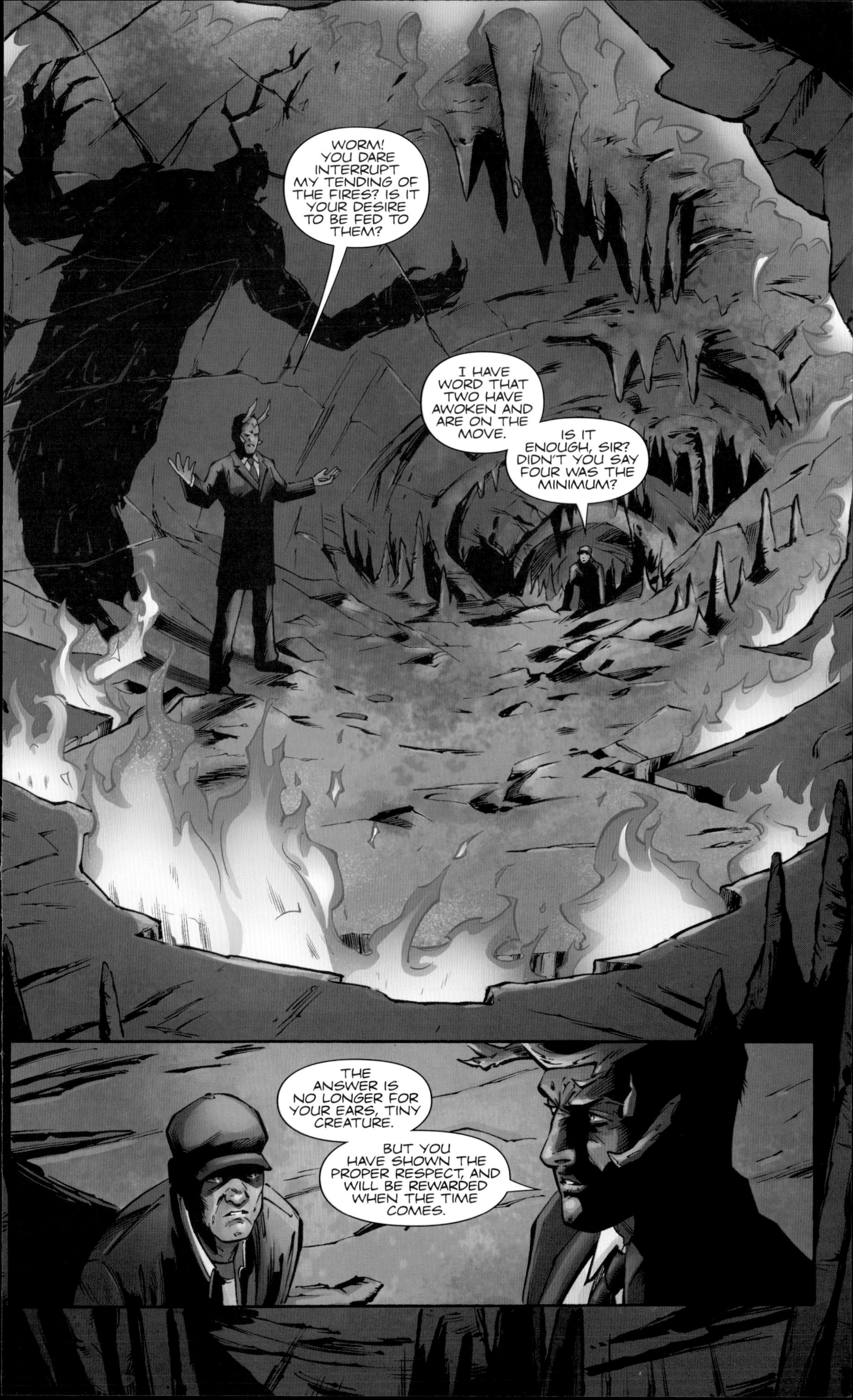
WORM! YOU DARE INTERRUPT MY TENDING OF THE FIRES? IS IT YOUR DESIRE TO BE FED TO THEM?
I HAVE WORD THAT TWO HAVE AWOKEN AND ARE ON THE MOVE.
IS IT ENOUGH, SIR? DIDN'T YOU SAY FOUR WAS THE MINIMUM?
THE ANSWER IS NO LONGER FOR YOUR EARS, TINY CREATURE.
BUT YOU HAVE SHOWN THE PROPER RESPECT, AND WILL BE REWARDED WHEN THE TIME COMES.

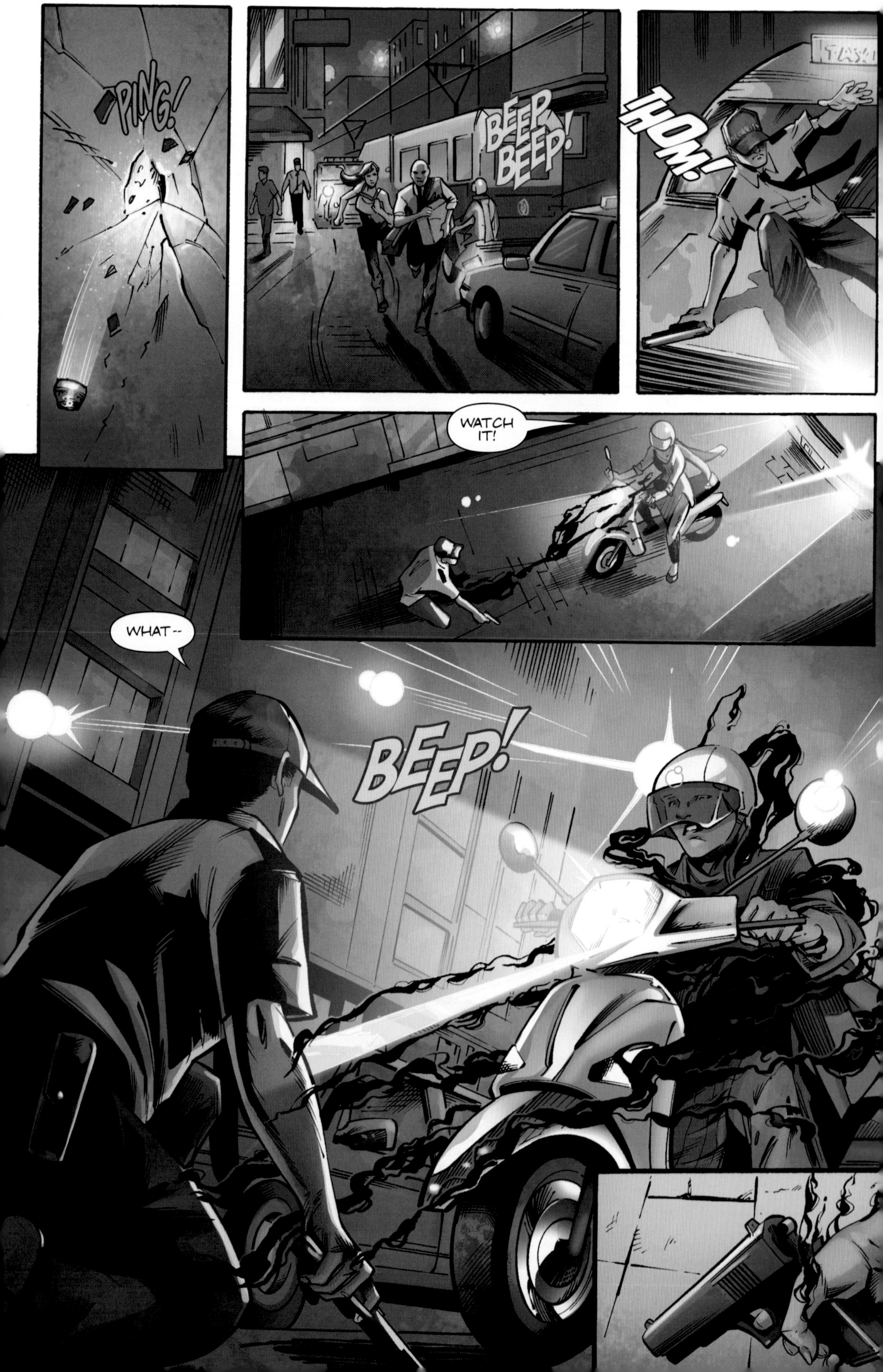
PING!
BEEP BEEP!
TAXI
THOM!
WATCH IT!
WHAT--
BEEP!

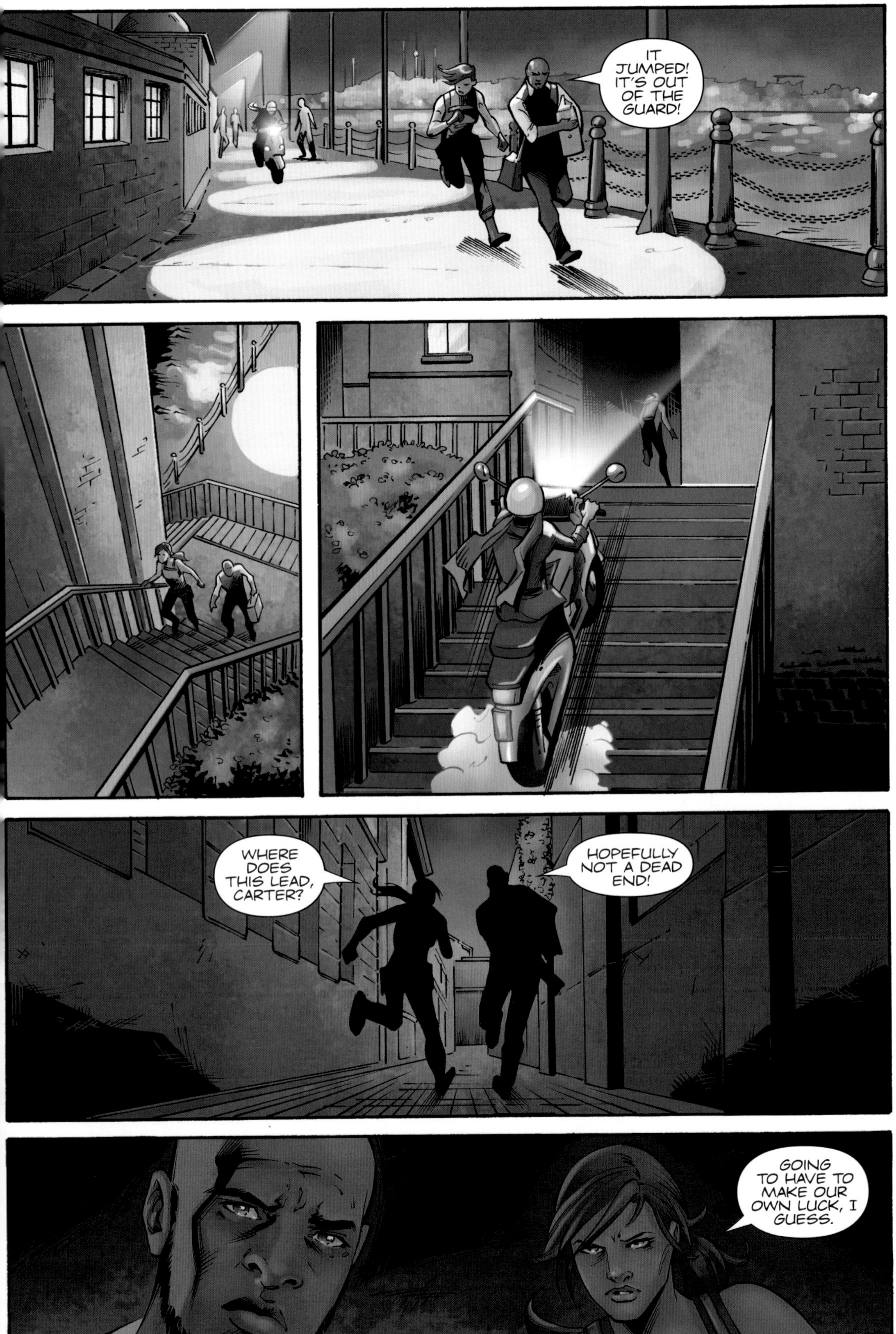
IT JUMPED! IT'S OUT OF THE GUARD!
WHERE DOES THIS LEAD, CARTER?
HOPEFULLY NOT A DEAD END!
GOING TO HAVE TO MAKE OUR OWN LUCK, I GUESS.

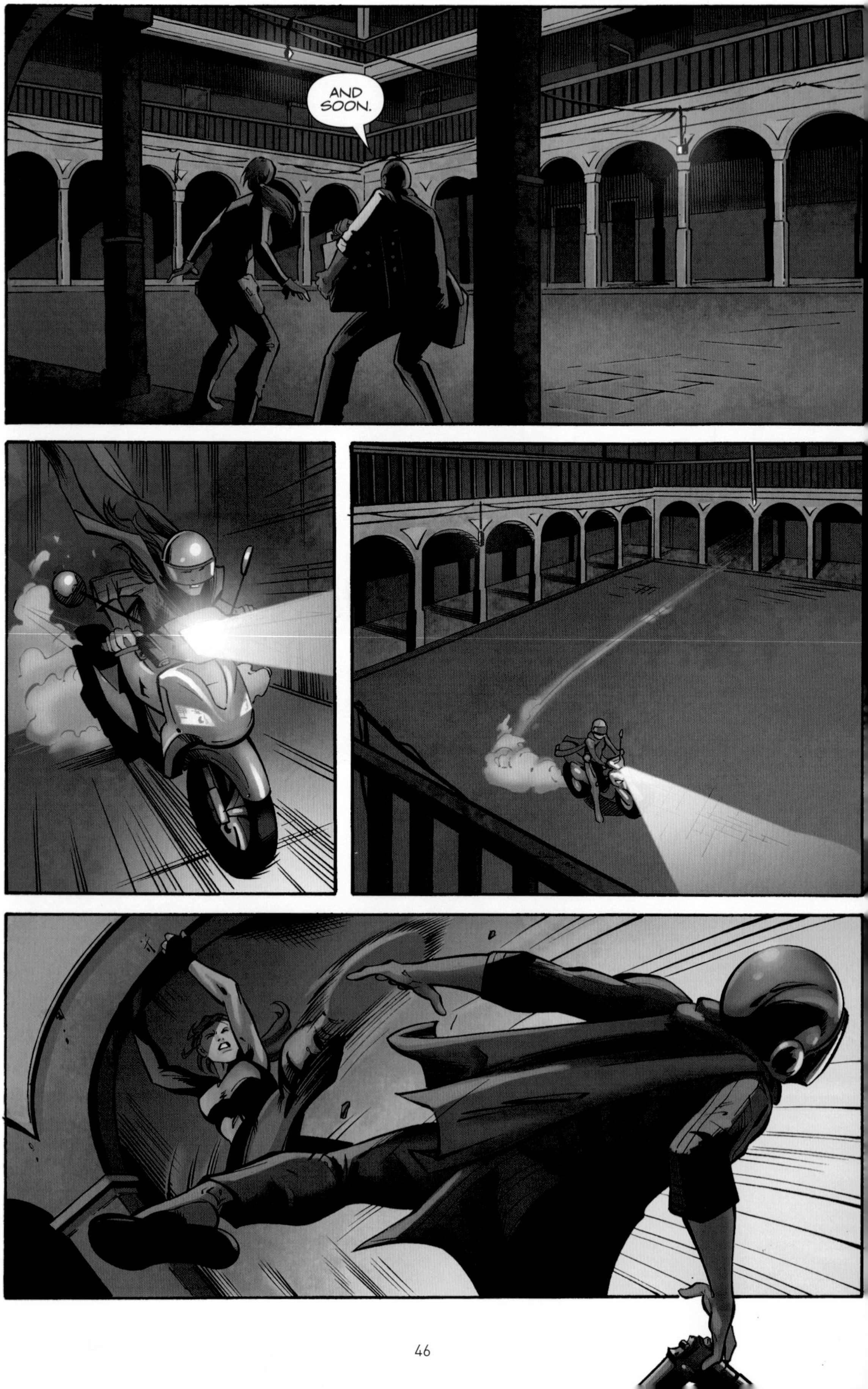
AND SOON.

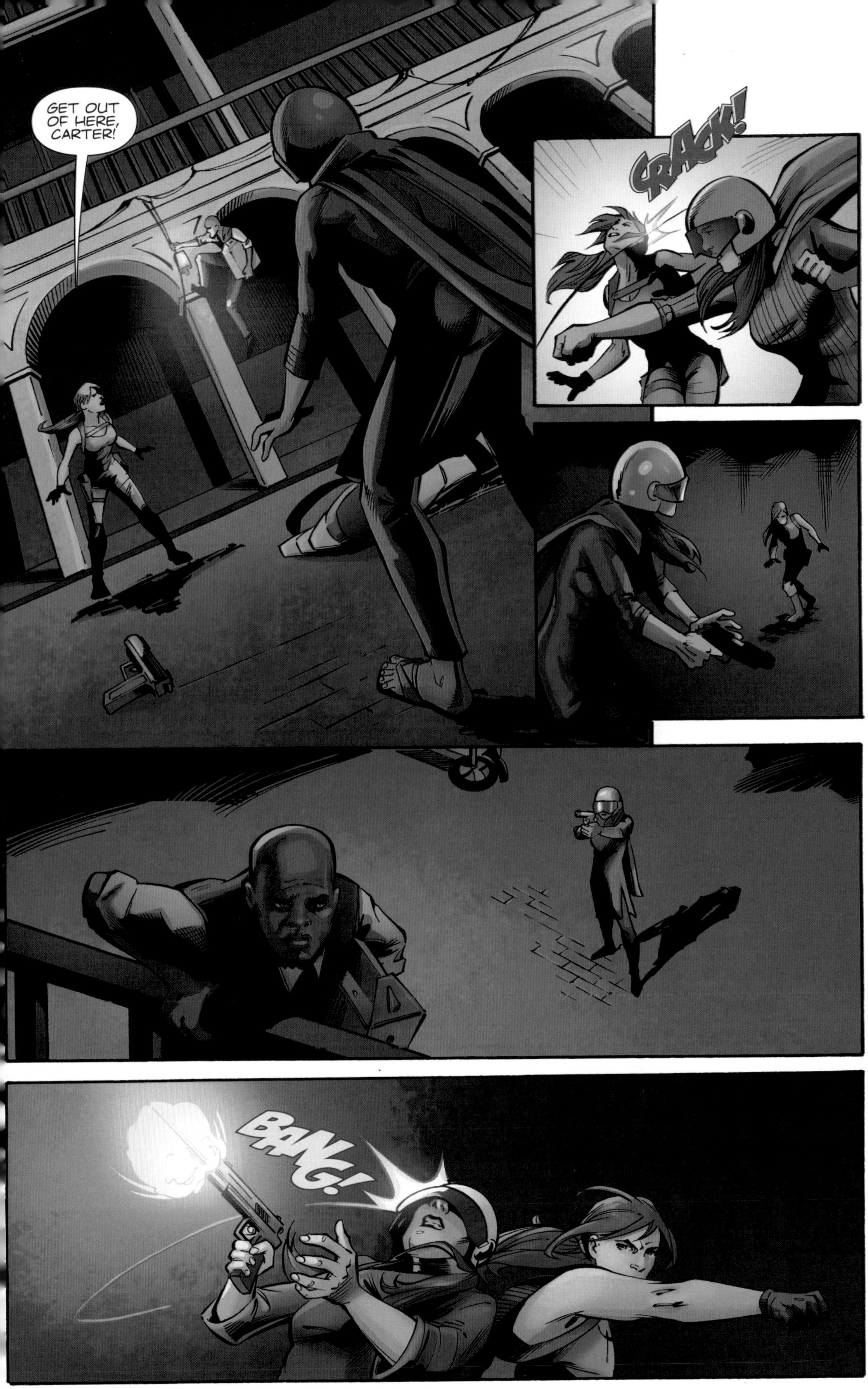
GET OUT OF HERE, CARTER!
CRACK!
BANG!

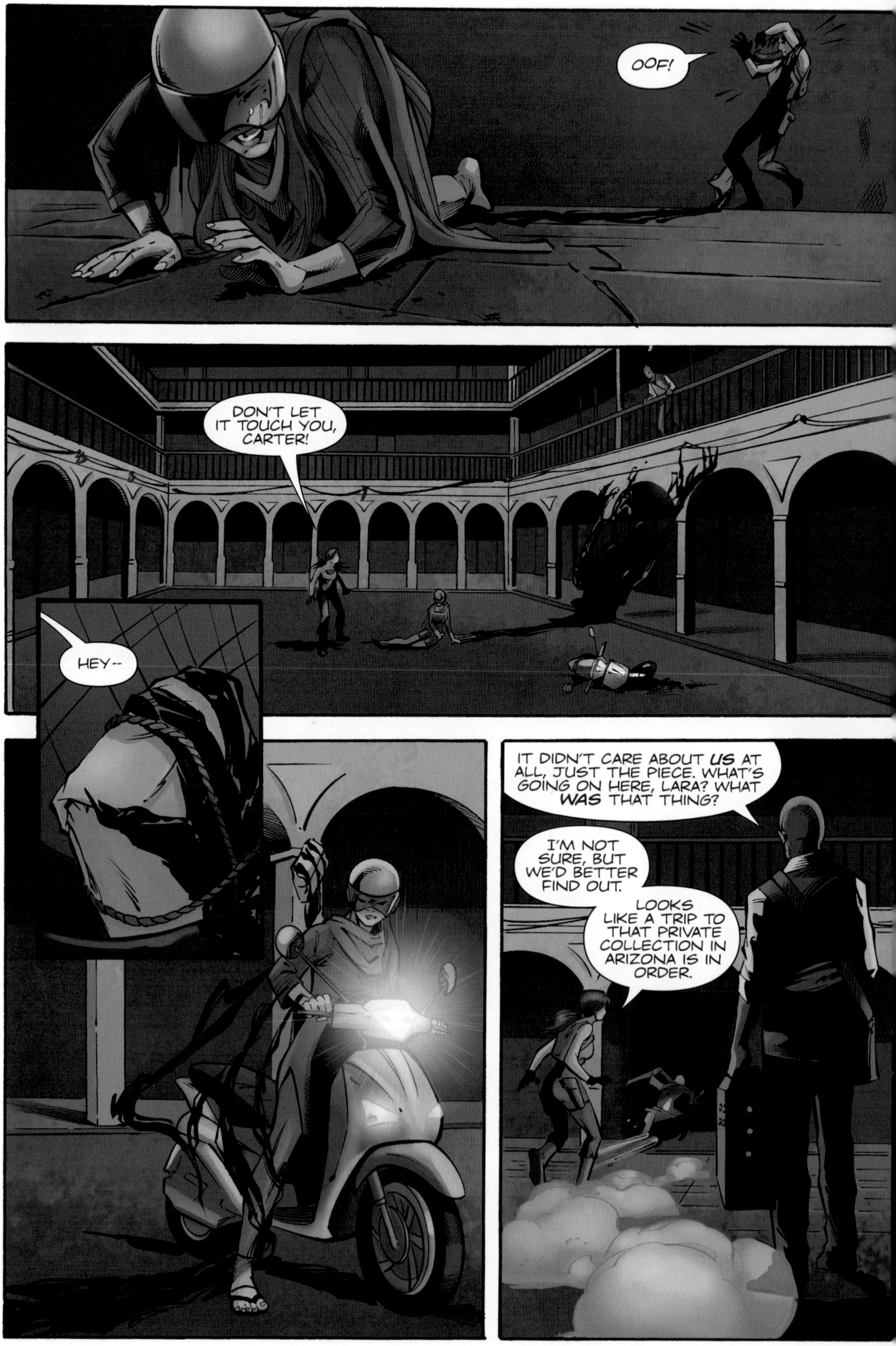
OOF!
DON'T LET IT TOUCH YOU, CARTER!
HEY--
IT DIDN'T CARE ABOUT US AT ALL, JUST THE PIECE. WHAT'S GOING ON HERE, LARA? WHAT WAS THAT THING?
I'M NOT SURE, BUT WE'D BETTER FIND OUT.
LOOKS LIKE A TRIP TO THAT PRIVATE COLLECTION IN ARIZONA IS IN ORDER.

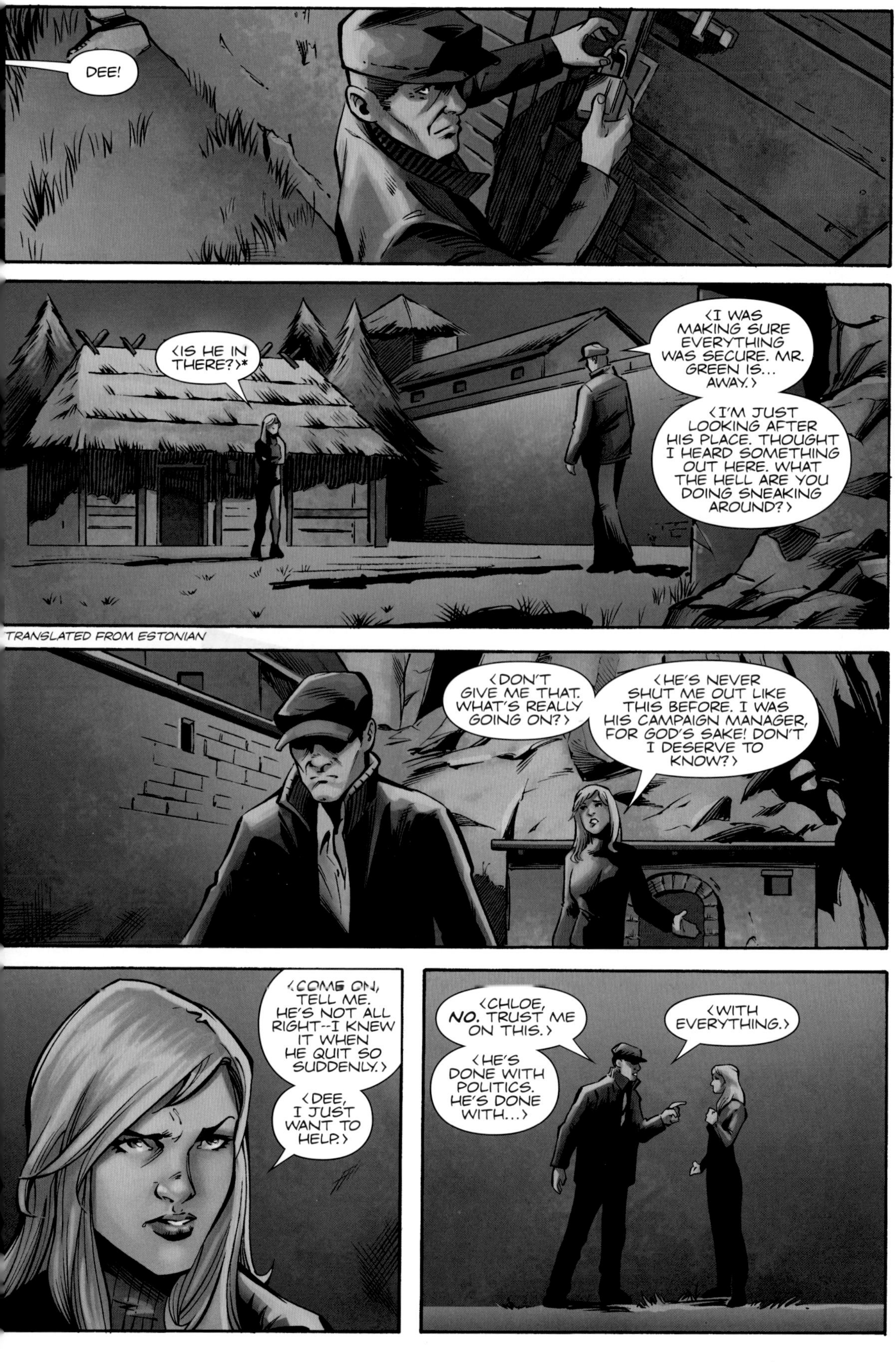
DEE!
<IS HE IN THERE?>*
<I WAS MAKING SURE EVERYTHING WAS SECURE. MR. GREEN IS... AWAY.>
<I'M JUST LOOKING AFTER HIS PLACE. THOUGHT I HEARD SOMETHING OUT HERE. WHAT THE HELL ARE YOU DOING SNEAKING AROUND?>
*TRANSLATED FROM ESTONIAN
<DON'T GIVE ME THAT. WHAT'S REALLY GOING ON?>
<HE'S NEVER SHUT ME OUT LIKE THIS BEFORE. I WAS HIS CAMPAIGN MANAGER, FOR GOD'S SAKE! DON'T I DESERVE TO KNOW?>
<COME ON, TELL ME. HE'S NOT ALL RIGHT--I KNEW IT WHEN HE QUIT SO SUDDENLY.>
<DEE, I JUST WANT TO HELP.>
<CHLOE, NO. TRUST ME ON THIS.>
<HE'S DONE WITH POLITICS. HE'S DONE WITH...>
<WITH EVERYTHING.>

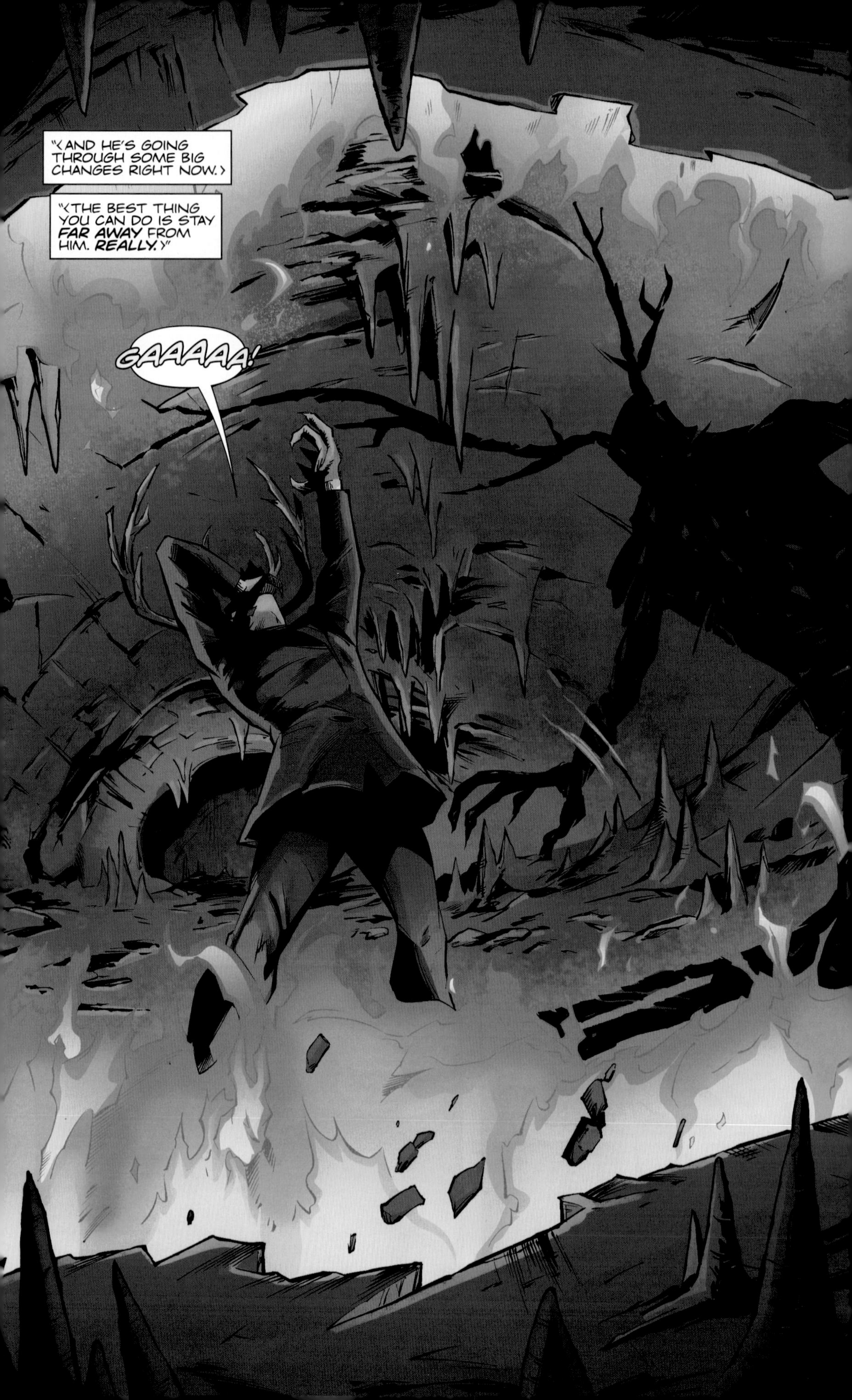
"‹AND HE'S GOING THROUGH SOME BIG CHANGES RIGHT NOW.›
"‹THE BEST THING YOU CAN DO IS STAY **FAR AWAY** FROM HIM. **REALLY.**›"
GAAAAA!

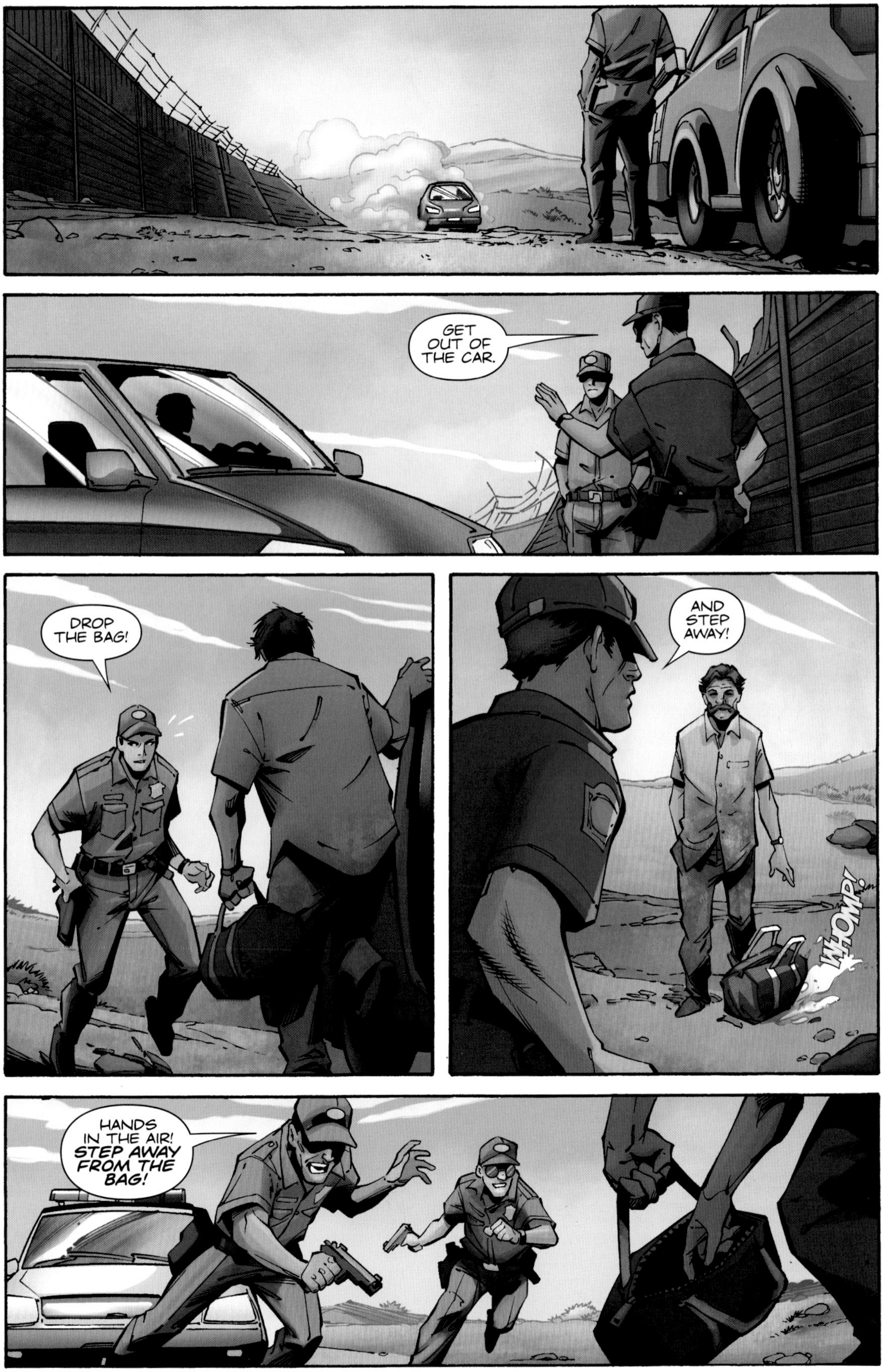
GET OUT OF THE CAR.
DROP THE BAG!
AND STEP AWAY!
WHOMP!
HANDS IN THE AIR! STEP AWAY FROM THE BAG!

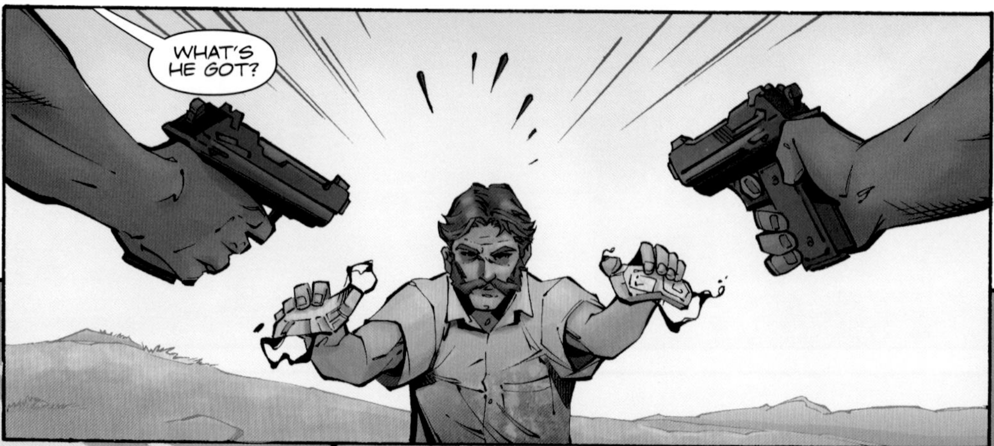
WHAT'S HE GOT?

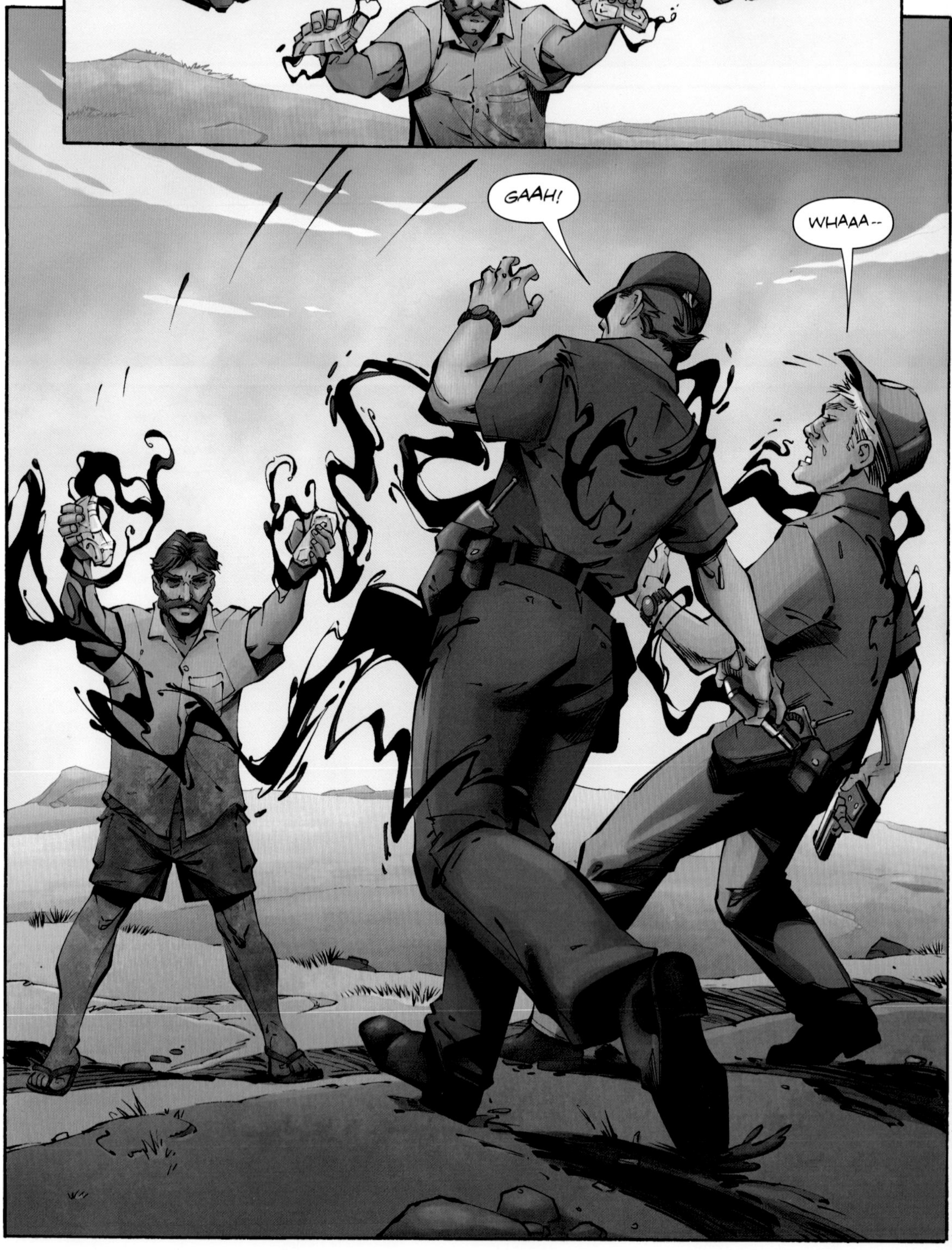
GAAH!
WHAAA--

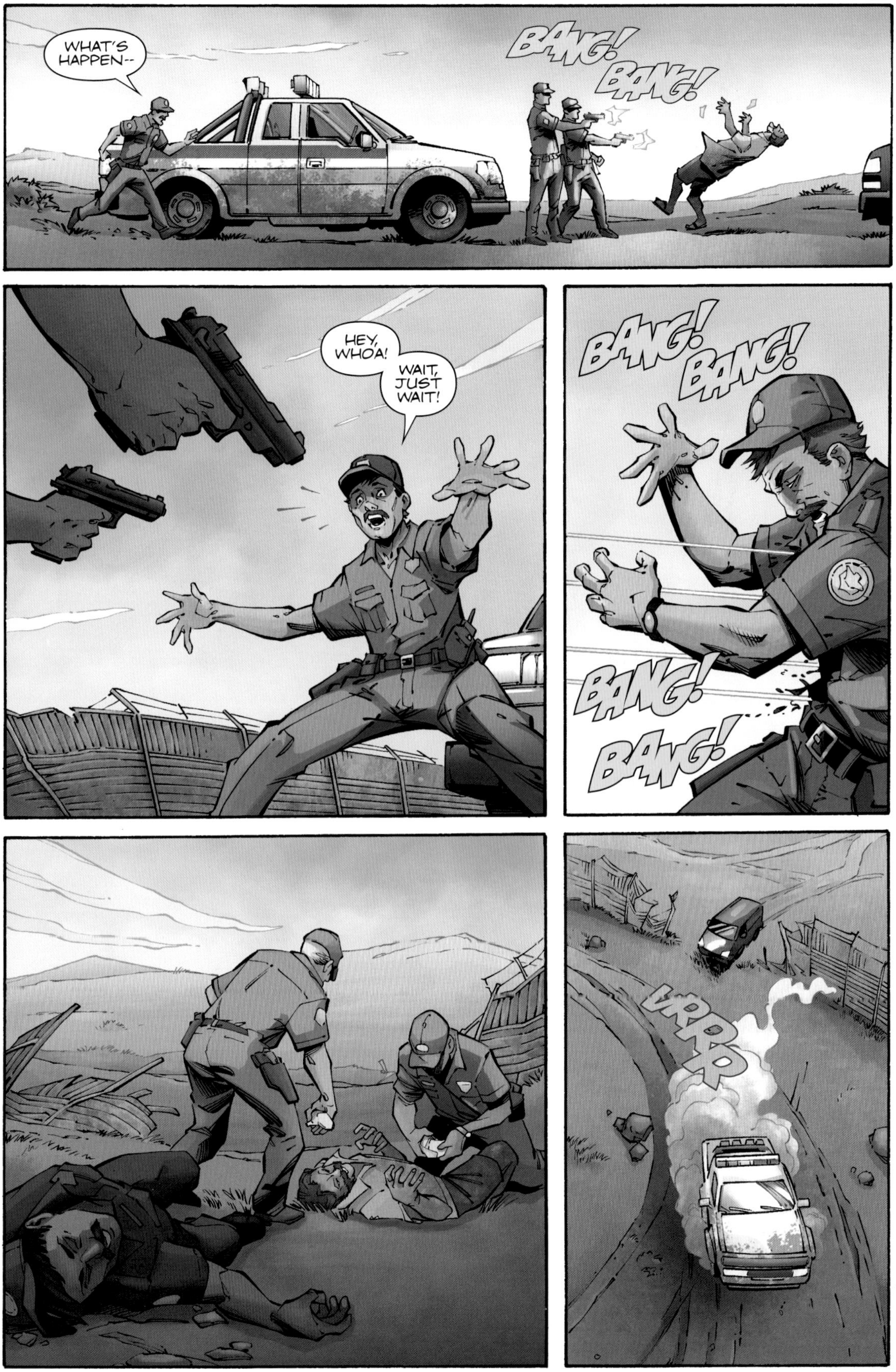
WHAT'S HAPPEN--
BANG!
BANG!
HEY, WHOA!
WAIT, JUST WAIT!
BANG!
BANG!
BANG!
BANG!
VRRR

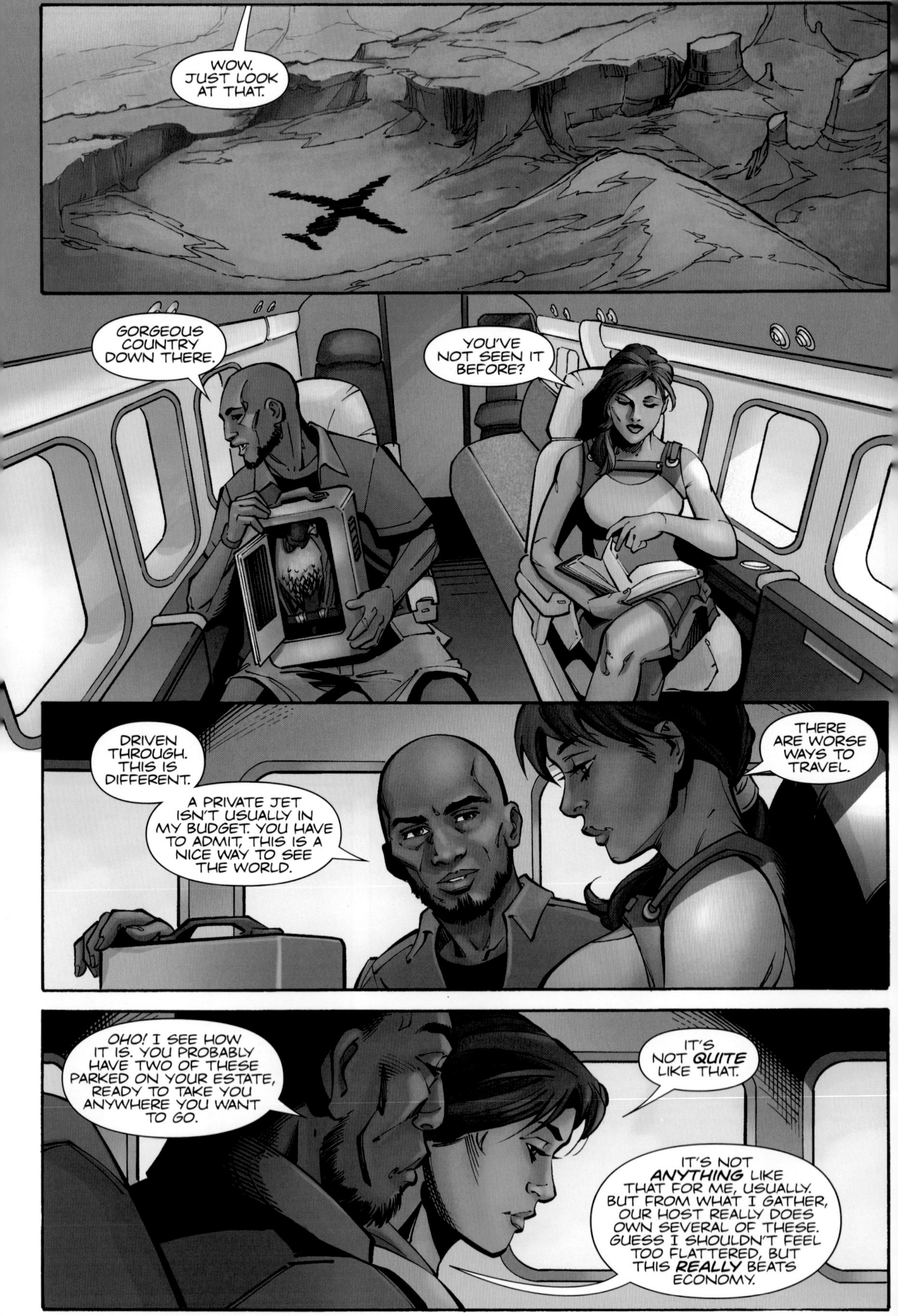
WOW. JUST LOOK AT THAT.
GORGEOUS COUNTRY DOWN THERE.
YOU'VE NOT SEEN IT BEFORE?
DRIVEN THROUGH. THIS IS DIFFERENT.
A PRIVATE JET ISN'T USUALLY IN MY BUDGET. YOU HAVE TO ADMIT, THIS IS A NICE WAY TO SEE THE WORLD.
THERE ARE WORSE WAYS TO TRAVEL.
OHO! I SEE HOW IT IS. YOU PROBABLY HAVE TWO OF THESE PARKED ON YOUR ESTATE, READY TO TAKE YOU ANYWHERE YOU WANT TO GO.
IT'S NOT QUITE LIKE THAT.
IT'S NOT ANYTHING LIKE THAT FOR ME, USUALLY. BUT FROM WHAT I GATHER, OUR HOST REALLY DOES OWN SEVERAL OF THESE. GUESS I SHOULDN'T FEEL TOO FLATTERED, BUT THIS REALLY BEATS ECONOMY.

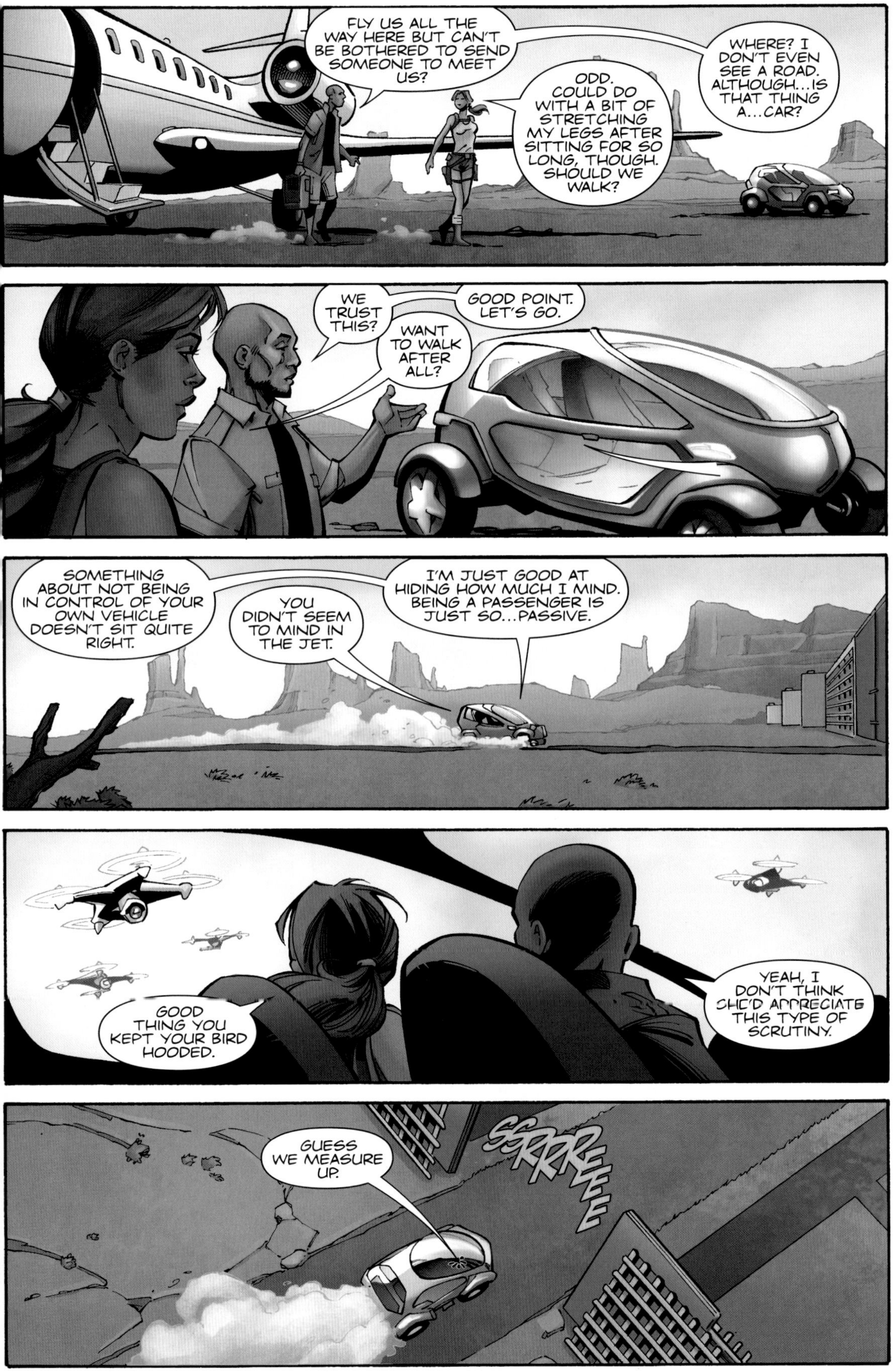
FLY US ALL THE WAY HERE BUT CAN'T BE BOTHERED TO SEND SOMEONE TO MEET US?
ODD. COULD DO WITH A BIT OF STRETCHING MY LEGS AFTER SITTING FOR SO LONG, THOUGH. SHOULD WE WALK?
WHERE? I DON'T EVEN SEE A ROAD. ALTHOUGH...IS THAT THING A...CAR?
WE TRUST THIS?
WANT TO WALK AFTER ALL?
GOOD POINT. LET'S GO.
SOMETHING ABOUT NOT BEING IN CONTROL OF YOUR OWN VEHICLE DOESN'T SIT QUITE RIGHT.
YOU DIDN'T SEEM TO MIND IN THE JET.
I'M JUST GOOD AT HIDING HOW MUCH I MIND. BEING A PASSENGER IS JUST SO...PASSIVE.
GOOD THING YOU KEPT YOUR BIRD HOODED.
YEAH, I DON'T THINK SHE'D APPRECIATE THIS TYPE OF SCRUTINY.
GUESS WE MEASURE UP.
SSRRREEE

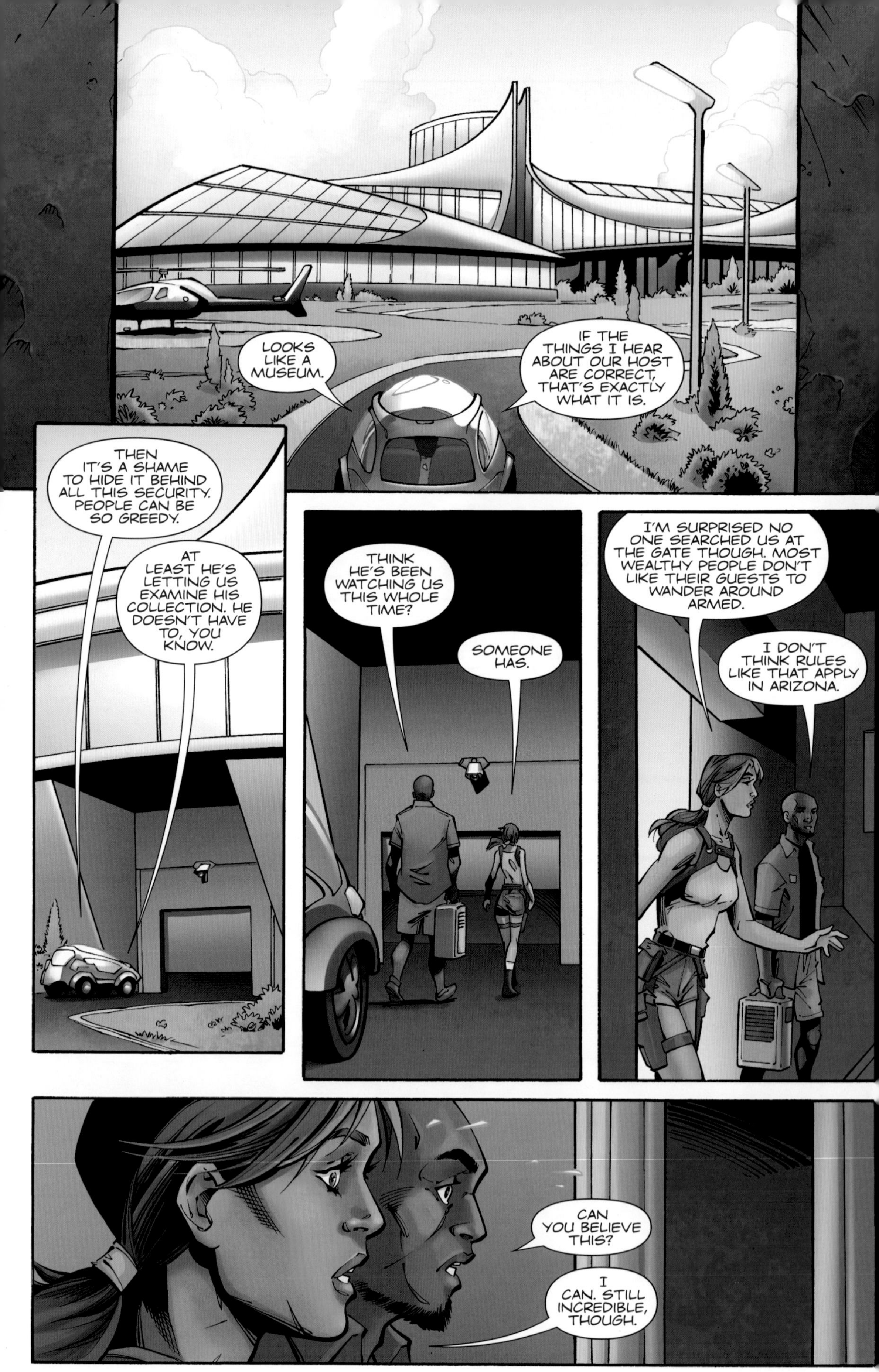
LOOKS LIKE A MUSEUM.
IF THE THINGS I HEAR ABOUT OUR HOST ARE CORRECT, THAT'S EXACTLY WHAT IT IS.
THEN IT'S A SHAME TO HIDE IT BEHIND ALL THIS SECURITY. PEOPLE CAN BE SO GREEDY.
AT LEAST HE'S LETTING US EXAMINE HIS COLLECTION. HE DOESN'T HAVE TO, YOU KNOW.
THINK HE'S BEEN WATCHING US THIS WHOLE TIME?
SOMEONE HAS.
I'M SURPRISED NO ONE SEARCHED US AT THE GATE THOUGH. MOST WEALTHY PEOPLE DON'T LIKE THEIR GUESTS TO WANDER AROUND ARMED.
I DON'T THINK RULES LIKE THAT APPLY IN ARIZONA.
CAN YOU BELIEVE THIS?
I CAN. STILL INCREDIBLE, THOUGH.

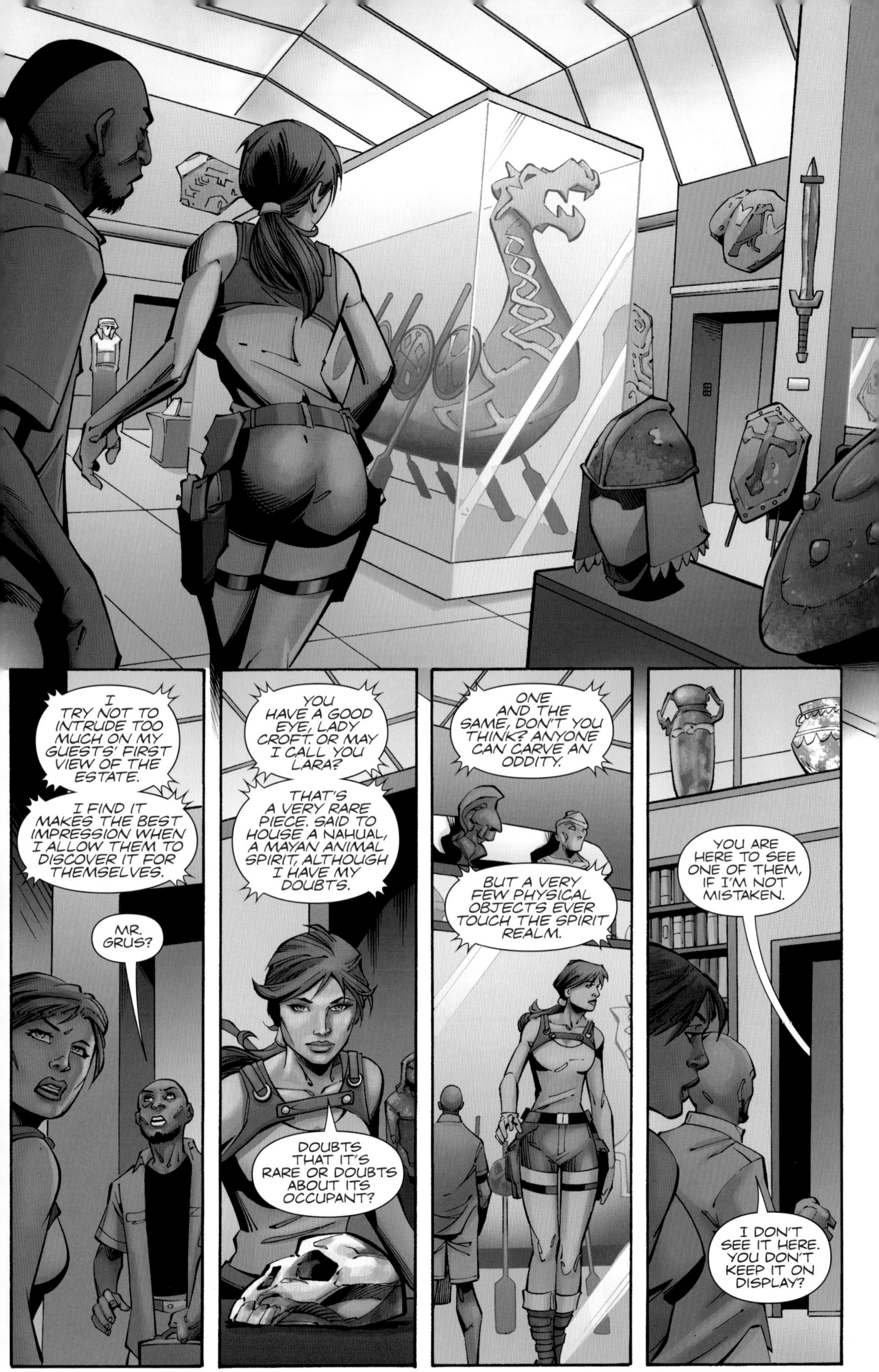
I TRY NOT TO INTRUDE TOO MUCH ON MY GUESTS' FIRST VIEW OF THE ESTATE.
I FIND IT MAKES THE BEST IMPRESSION WHEN I ALLOW THEM TO DISCOVER IT FOR THEMSELVES.
MR. GRUS?
YOU HAVE A GOOD EYE, LADY CROFT. OR MAY I CALL YOU LARA?
THAT'S A VERY RARE PIECE. SAID TO HOUSE A NAHUAL, A MAYAN ANIMAL SPIRIT, ALTHOUGH I HAVE MY DOUBTS.
DOUBTS THAT IT'S RARE OR DOUBTS ABOUT ITS OCCUPANT?
ONE AND THE SAME, DON'T YOU THINK? ANYONE CAN CARVE AN ODDITY.
BUT A VERY FEW PHYSICAL OBJECTS EVER TOUCH THE SPIRIT REALM.
YOU ARE HERE TO SEE ONE OF THEM, IF I'M NOT MISTAKEN.
I DON'T SEE IT HERE. YOU DON'T KEEP IT ON DISPLAY?

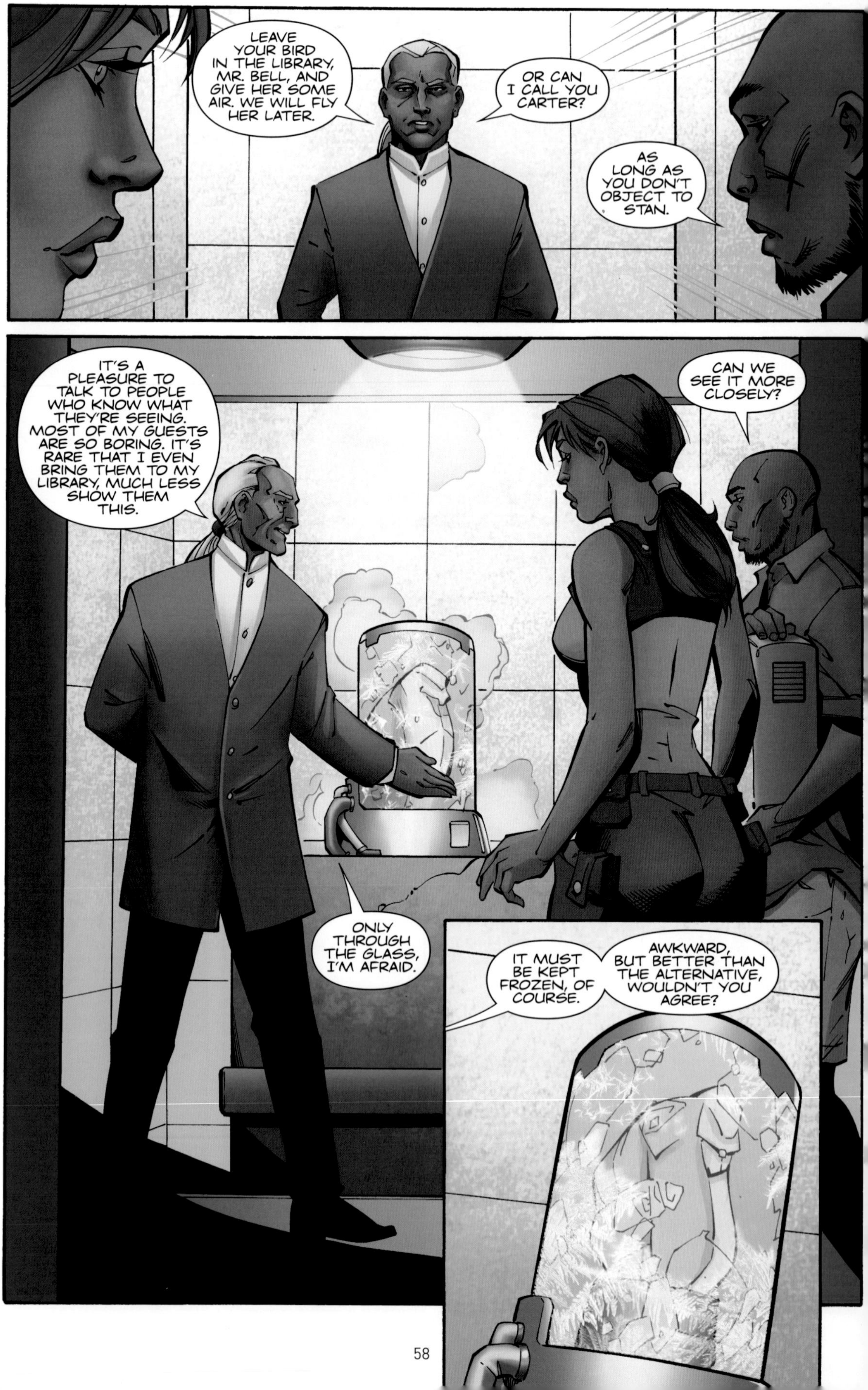

LEAVE YOUR BIRD IN THE LIBRARY, MR. BELL, AND GIVE HER SOME AIR. WE WILL FLY HER LATER.
OR CAN I CALL YOU CARTER?
AS LONG AS YOU DON'T OBJECT TO STAN.
IT'S A PLEASURE TO TALK TO PEOPLE WHO KNOW WHAT THEY'RE SEEING. MOST OF MY GUESTS ARE SO BORING. IT'S RARE THAT I EVEN BRING THEM TO MY LIBRARY, MUCH LESS SHOW THEM THIS.
CAN WE SEE IT MORE CLOSELY?
ONLY THROUGH THE GLASS, I'M AFRAID.
IT MUST BE KEPT FROZEN, OF COURSE.
AWKWARD, BUT BETTER THAN THE ALTERNATIVE, WOULDN'T YOU AGREE?

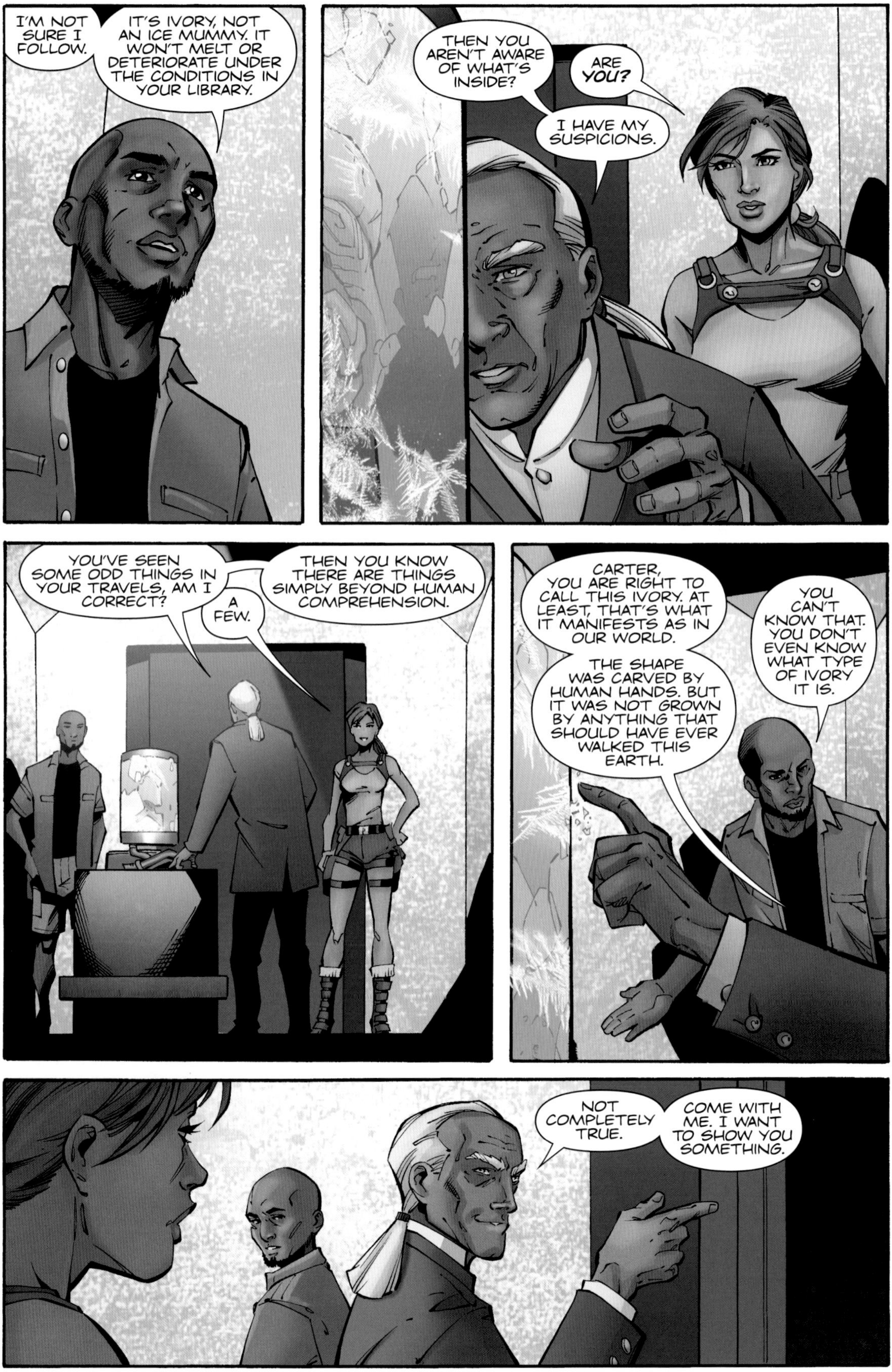

I'M NOT SURE I FOLLOW.
IT'S IVORY, NOT AN ICE MUMMY. IT WON'T MELT OR DETERIORATE UNDER THE CONDITIONS IN YOUR LIBRARY.
THEN YOU AREN'T AWARE OF WHAT'S INSIDE?
ARE *YOU?*
I HAVE MY SUSPICIONS.
YOU'VE SEEN SOME ODD THINGS IN YOUR TRAVELS, AM I CORRECT?
A FEW.
THEN YOU KNOW THERE ARE THINGS SIMPLY BEYOND HUMAN COMPREHENSION.
CARTER, YOU ARE RIGHT TO CALL THIS IVORY. AT LEAST, THAT'S WHAT IT MANIFESTS AS IN OUR WORLD.
THE SHAPE WAS CARVED BY HUMAN HANDS. BUT IT WAS NOT GROWN BY ANYTHING THAT SHOULD HAVE EVER WALKED THIS EARTH.
YOU CAN'T KNOW THAT. YOU DON'T EVEN KNOW WHAT TYPE OF IVORY IT IS.
NOT COMPLETELY TRUE.
COME WITH ME. I WANT TO SHOW YOU SOMETHING.

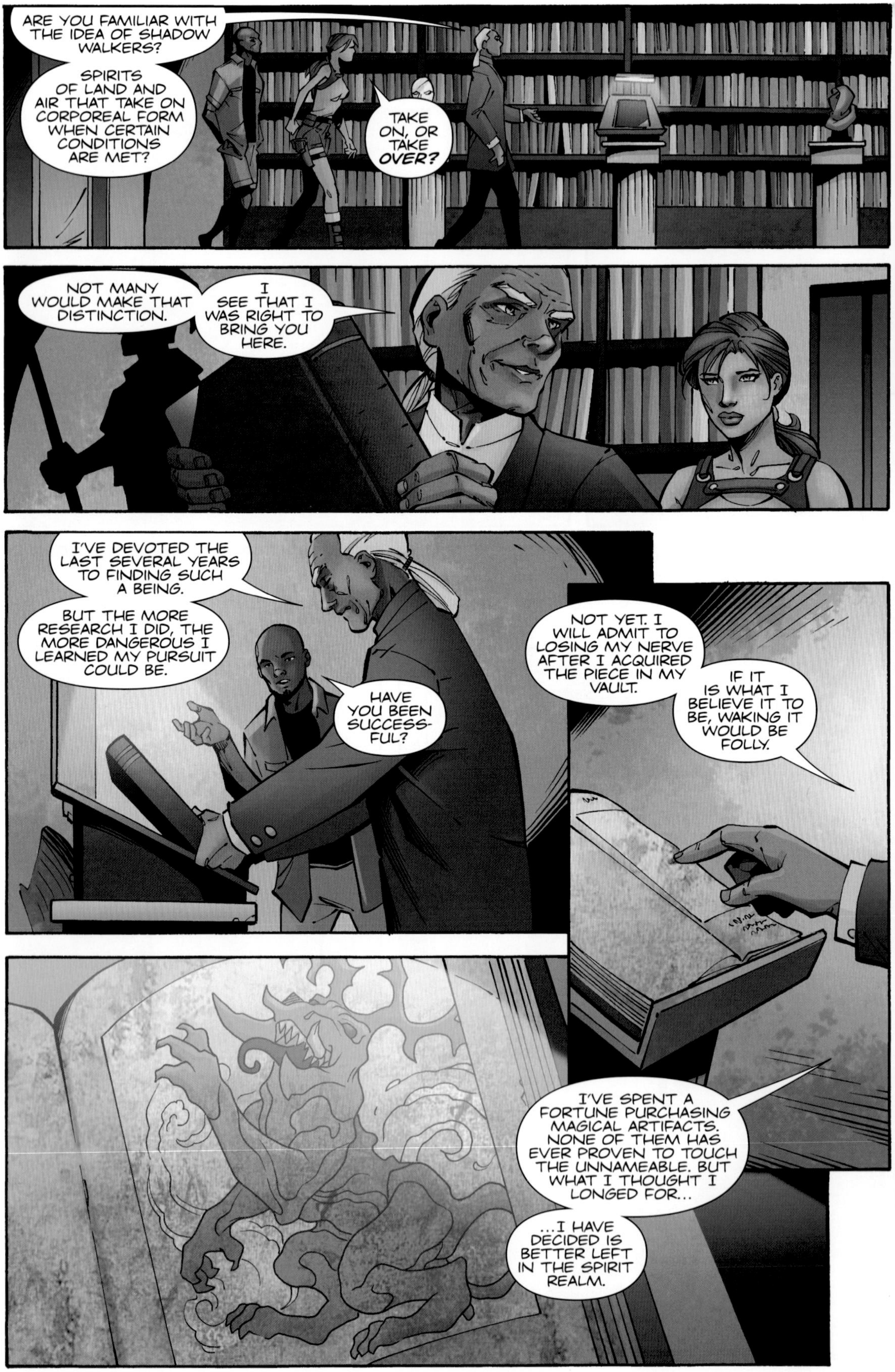
ARE YOU FAMILIAR WITH THE IDEA OF SHADOW WALKERS?
SPIRITS OF LAND AND AIR THAT TAKE ON CORPOREAL FORM WHEN CERTAIN CONDITIONS ARE MET?
TAKE ON, OR TAKE *OVER?*
NOT MANY WOULD MAKE THAT DISTINCTION.
I SEE THAT I WAS RIGHT TO BRING YOU HERE.
I'VE DEVOTED THE LAST SEVERAL YEARS TO FINDING SUCH A BEING.
BUT THE MORE RESEARCH I DID, THE MORE DANGEROUS I LEARNED MY PURSUIT COULD BE.
HAVE YOU BEEN SUCCESS-FUL?
NOT YET. I WILL ADMIT TO LOSING MY NERVE AFTER I ACQUIRED THE PIECE IN MY VAULT.
IF IT IS WHAT I BELIEVE IT TO BE, WAKING IT WOULD BE FOLLY.
I'VE SPENT A FORTUNE PURCHASING MAGICAL ARTIFACTS. NONE OF THEM HAS EVER PROVEN TO TOUCH THE UNNAMEABLE. BUT WHAT I THOUGHT I LONGED FOR...
...I HAVE DECIDED IS BETTER LEFT IN THE SPIRIT REALM.

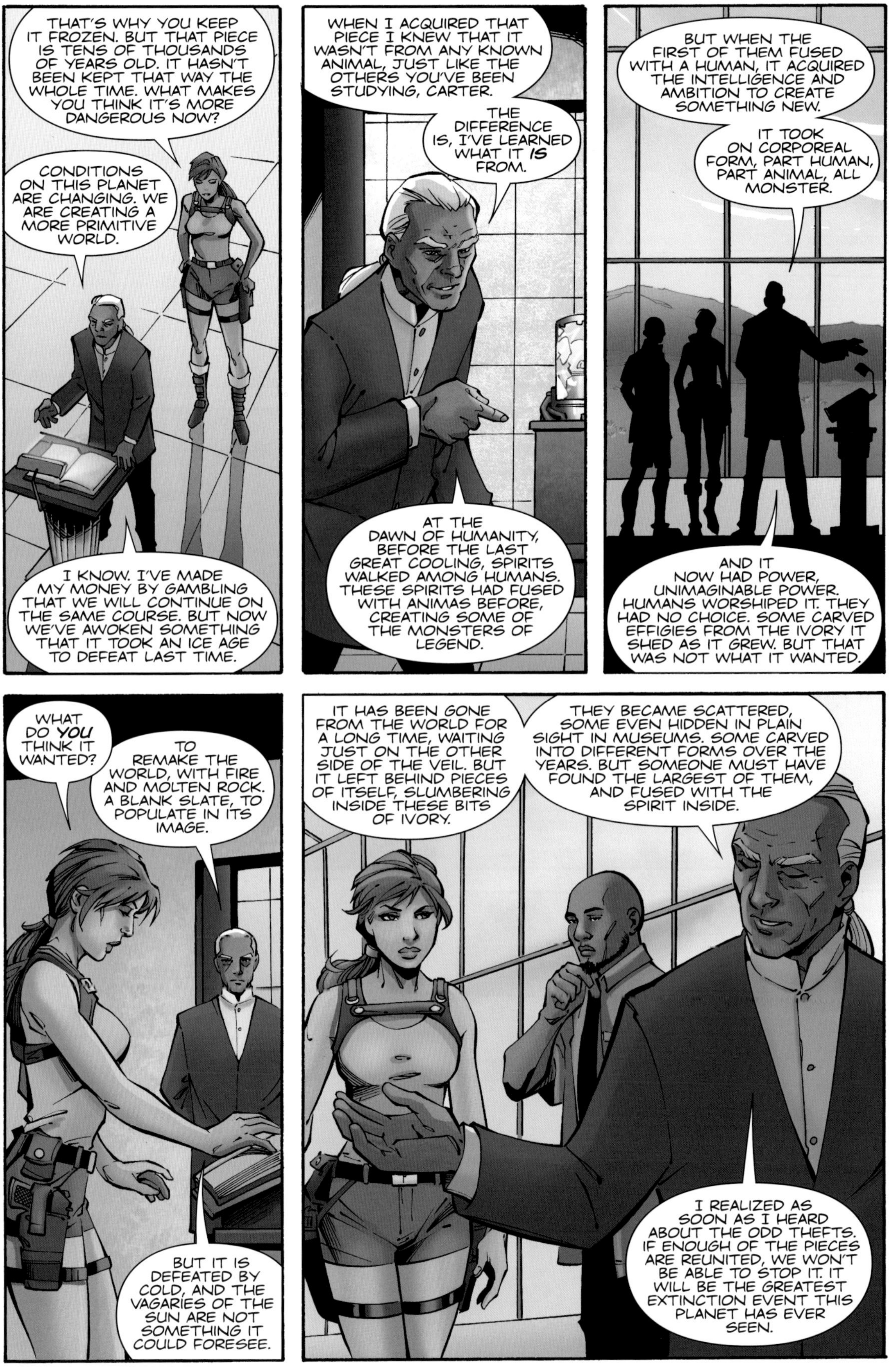
THAT'S WHY YOU KEEP IT FROZEN. BUT THAT PIECE IS TENS OF THOUSANDS OF YEARS OLD. IT HASN'T BEEN KEPT THAT WAY THE WHOLE TIME. WHAT MAKES YOU THINK IT'S MORE DANGEROUS NOW?
CONDITIONS ON THIS PLANET ARE CHANGING. WE ARE CREATING A MORE PRIMITIVE WORLD.
I KNOW. I'VE MADE MY MONEY BY GAMBLING THAT WE WILL CONTINUE ON THE SAME COURSE. BUT NOW WE'VE AWOKEN SOMETHING THAT IT TOOK AN ICE AGE TO DEFEAT LAST TIME.
WHEN I ACQUIRED THAT PIECE I KNEW THAT IT WASN'T FROM ANY KNOWN ANIMAL, JUST LIKE THE OTHERS YOU'VE BEEN STUDYING, CARTER.
THE DIFFERENCE IS, I'VE LEARNED WHAT IT IS FROM.
AT THE DAWN OF HUMANITY, BEFORE THE LAST GREAT COOLING, SPIRITS WALKED AMONG HUMANS. THESE SPIRITS HAD FUSED WITH ANIMAS BEFORE, CREATING SOME OF THE MONSTERS OF LEGEND.
BUT WHEN THE FIRST OF THEM FUSED WITH A HUMAN, IT ACQUIRED THE INTELLIGENCE AND AMBITION TO CREATE SOMETHING NEW.
IT TOOK ON CORPOREAL FORM, PART HUMAN, PART ANIMAL, ALL MONSTER.
AND IT NOW HAD POWER, UNIMAGINABLE POWER. HUMANS WORSHIPED IT. THEY HAD NO CHOICE. SOME CARVED EFFIGIES FROM THE IVORY IT SHED AS IT GREW. BUT THAT WAS NOT WHAT IT WANTED.
WHAT DO YOU THINK IT WANTED?
TO REMAKE THE WORLD, WITH FIRE AND MOLTEN ROCK. A BLANK SLATE, TO POPULATE IN ITS IMAGE.
BUT IT IS DEFEATED BY COLD, AND THE VAGARIES OF THE SUN ARE NOT SOMETHING IT COULD FORESEE.
IT HAS BEEN GONE FROM THE WORLD FOR A LONG TIME, WAITING JUST ON THE OTHER SIDE OF THE VEIL. BUT IT LEFT BEHIND PIECES OF ITSELF, SLUMBERING INSIDE THESE BITS OF IVORY.
THEY BECAME SCATTERED, SOME EVEN HIDDEN IN PLAIN SIGHT IN MUSEUMS. SOME CARVED INTO DIFFERENT FORMS OVER THE YEARS. BUT SOMEONE MUST HAVE FOUND THE LARGEST OF THEM, AND FUSED WITH THE SPIRIT INSIDE.
I REALIZED AS SOON AS I HEARD ABOUT THE ODD THEFTS. IF ENOUGH OF THE PIECES ARE REUNITED, WE WON'T BE ABLE TO STOP IT. IT WILL BE THE GREATEST EXTINCTION EVENT THIS PLANET HAS EVER SEEN.

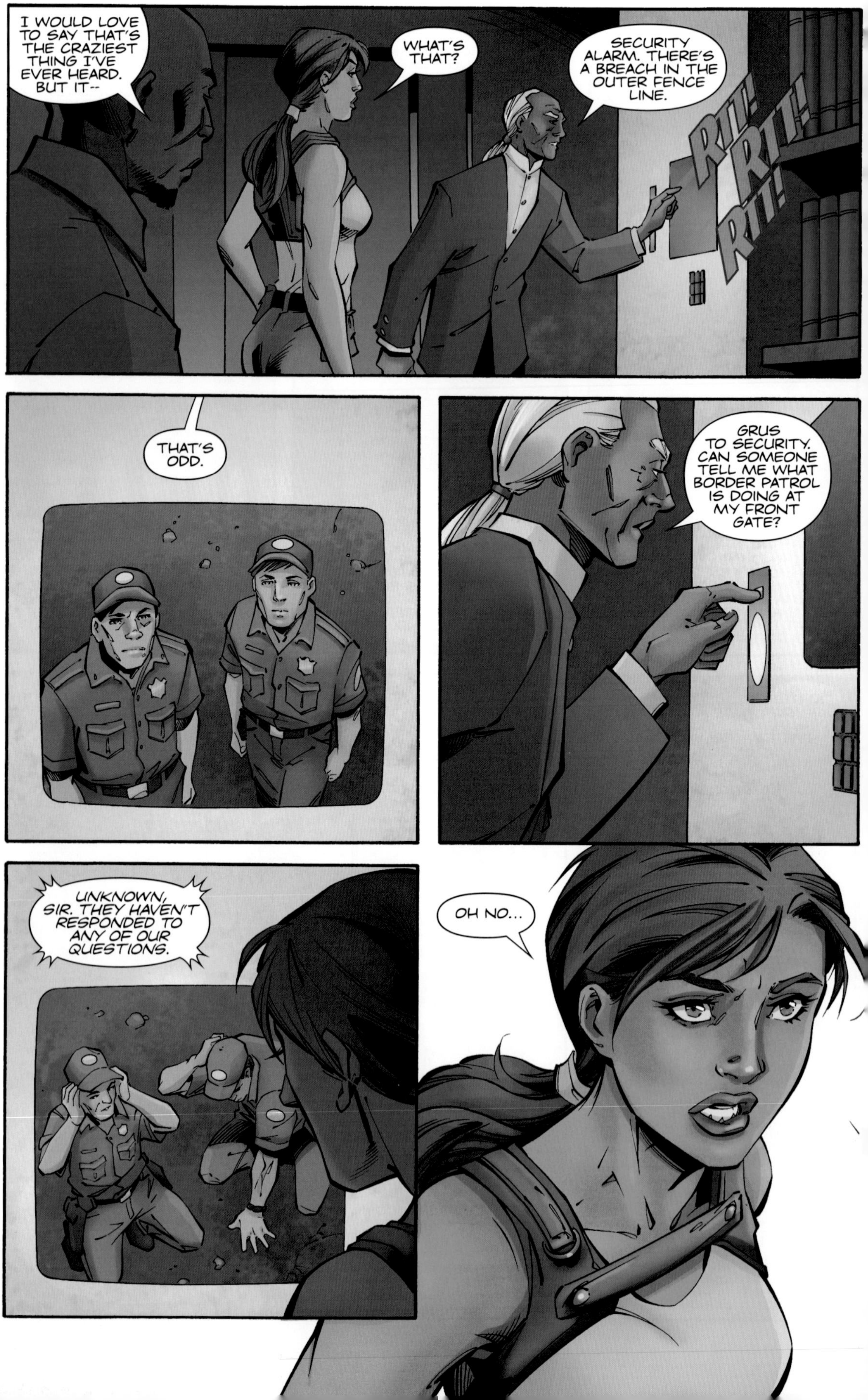
I WOULD LOVE TO SAY THAT'S THE CRAZIEST THING I'VE EVER HEARD. BUT IT--
WHAT'S THAT?
SECURITY ALARM. THERE'S A BREACH IN THE OUTER FENCE LINE.
RTT! RTT! RTT!
THAT'S ODD.
GRUS TO SECURITY. CAN SOMEONE TELL ME WHAT BORDER PATROL IS DOING AT MY FRONT GATE?
UNKNOWN, SIR. THEY HAVEN'T RESPONDED TO ANY OF OUR QUESTIONS.
OH NO...

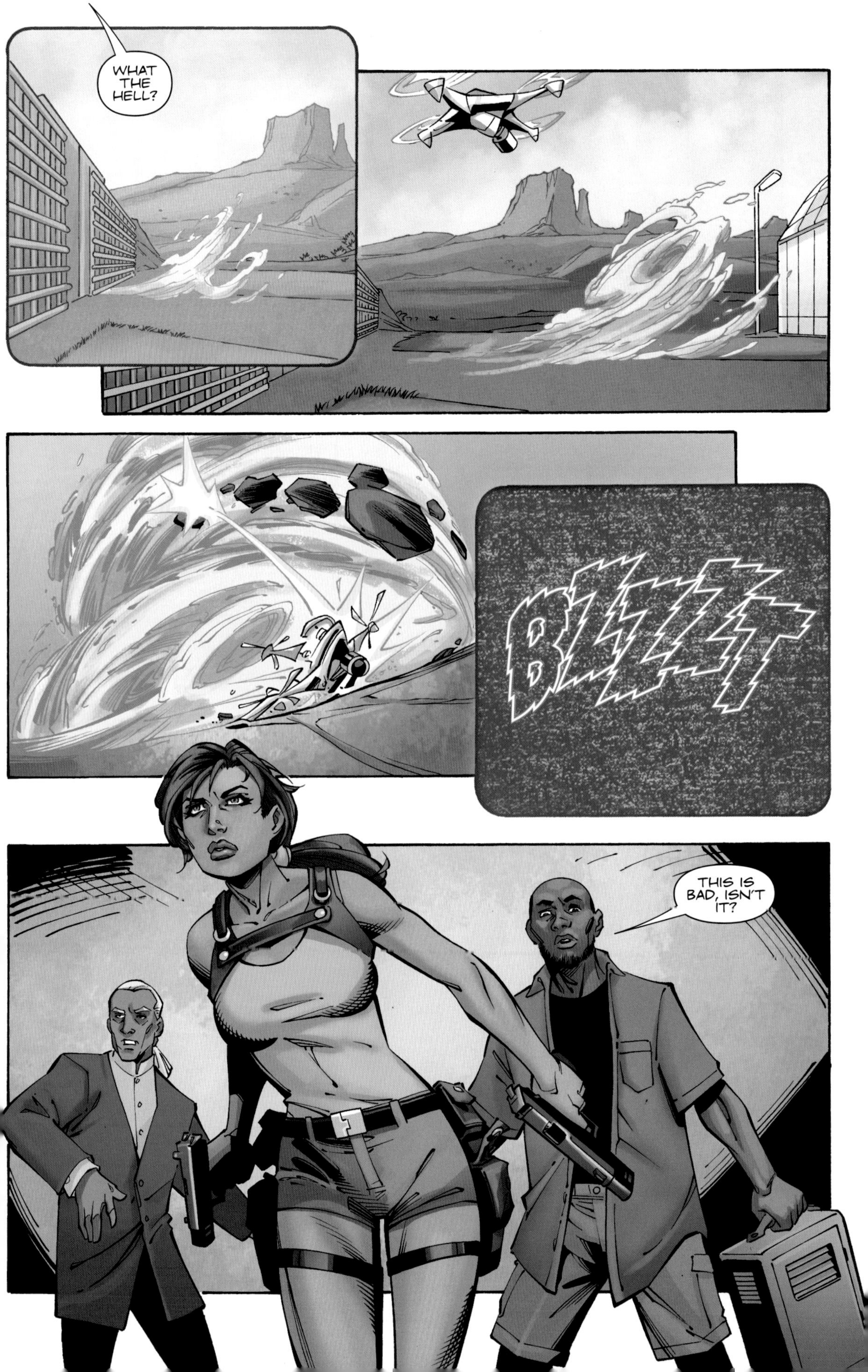
WHAT THE HELL?
BLZZT
THIS IS BAD, ISN'T IT?

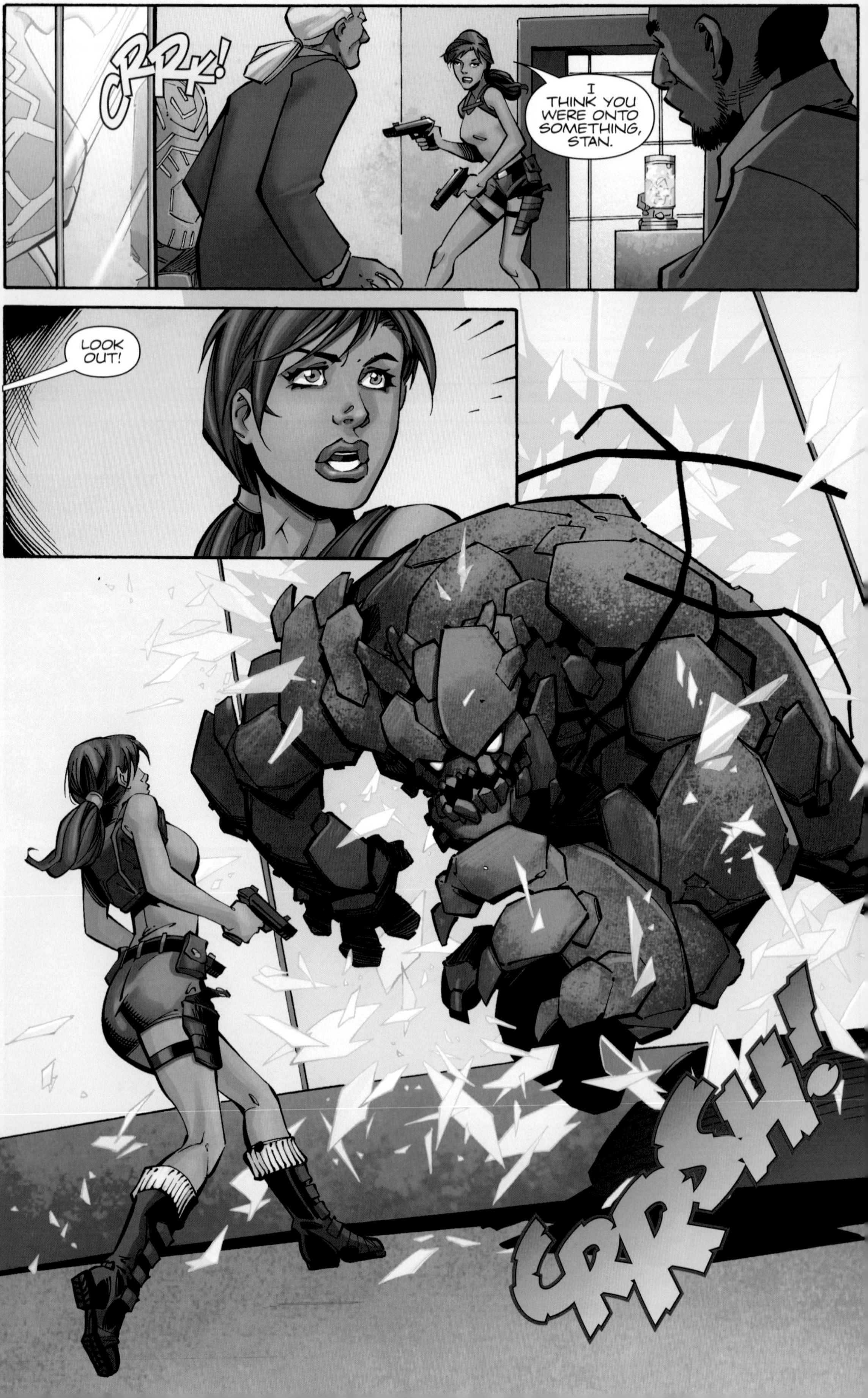
CRRK!
I THINK YOU WERE ONTO SOMETHING, STAN.
LOOK OUT!
CRASH!

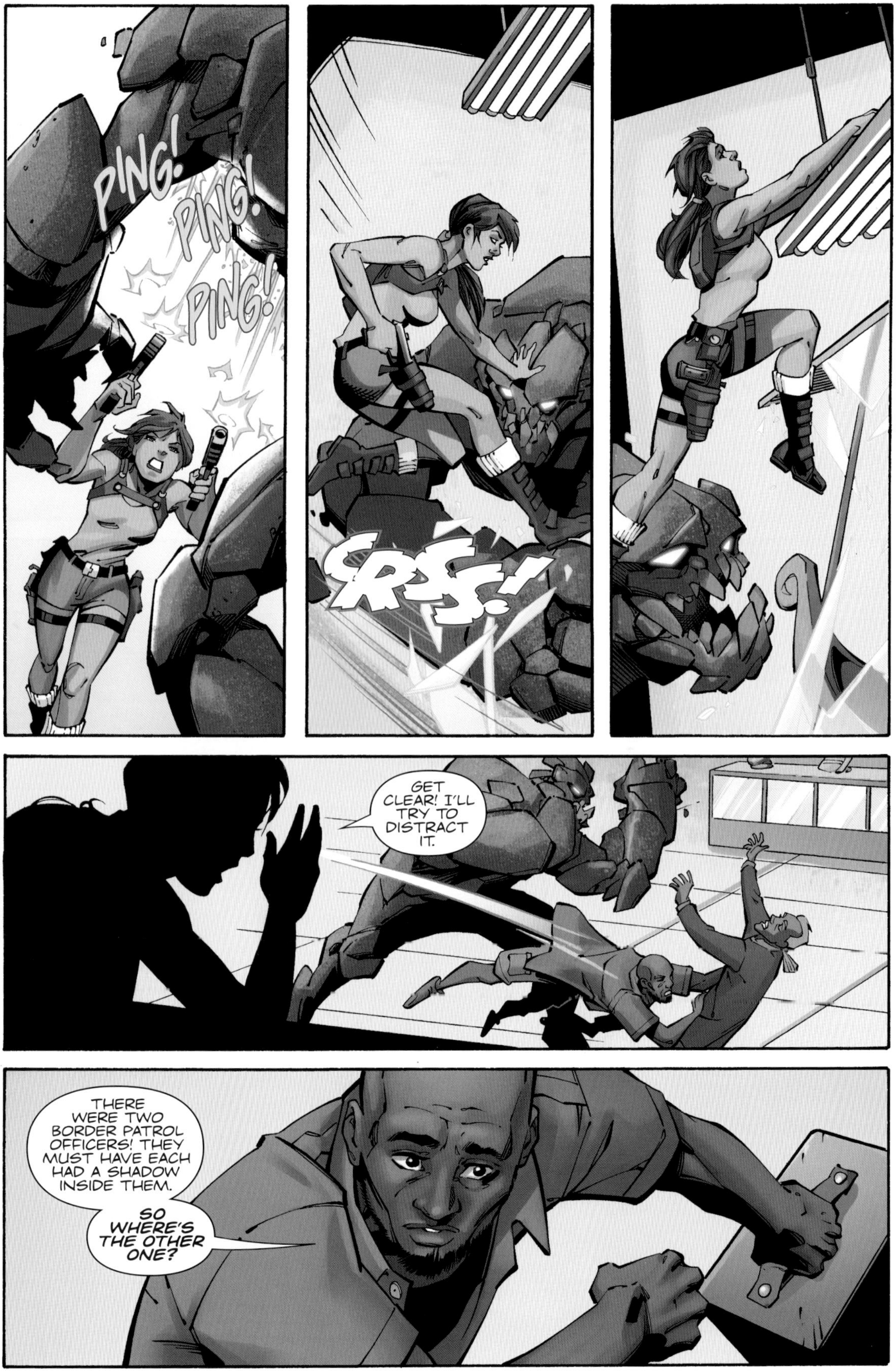
PING!
PING!
PING!
CRSS!
GET CLEAR! I'LL TRY TO DISTRACT IT.
THERE WERE TWO BORDER PATROL OFFICERS! THEY MUST HAVE EACH HAD A SHADOW INSIDE THEM.
SO WHERE'S THE OTHER ONE?

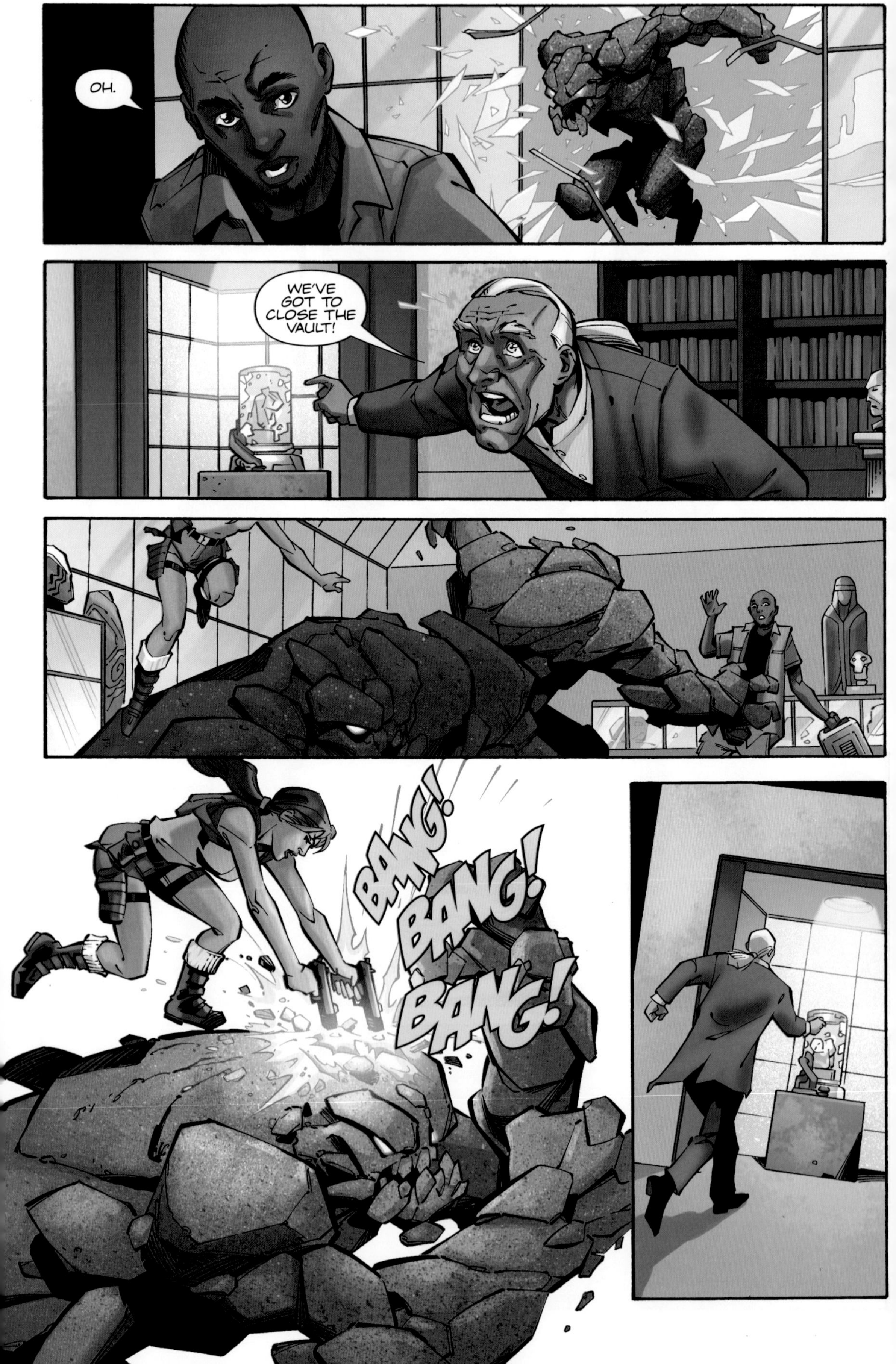
OH.
WE'VE GOT TO CLOSE THE VAULT!
BANG!
BANG!
BANG!

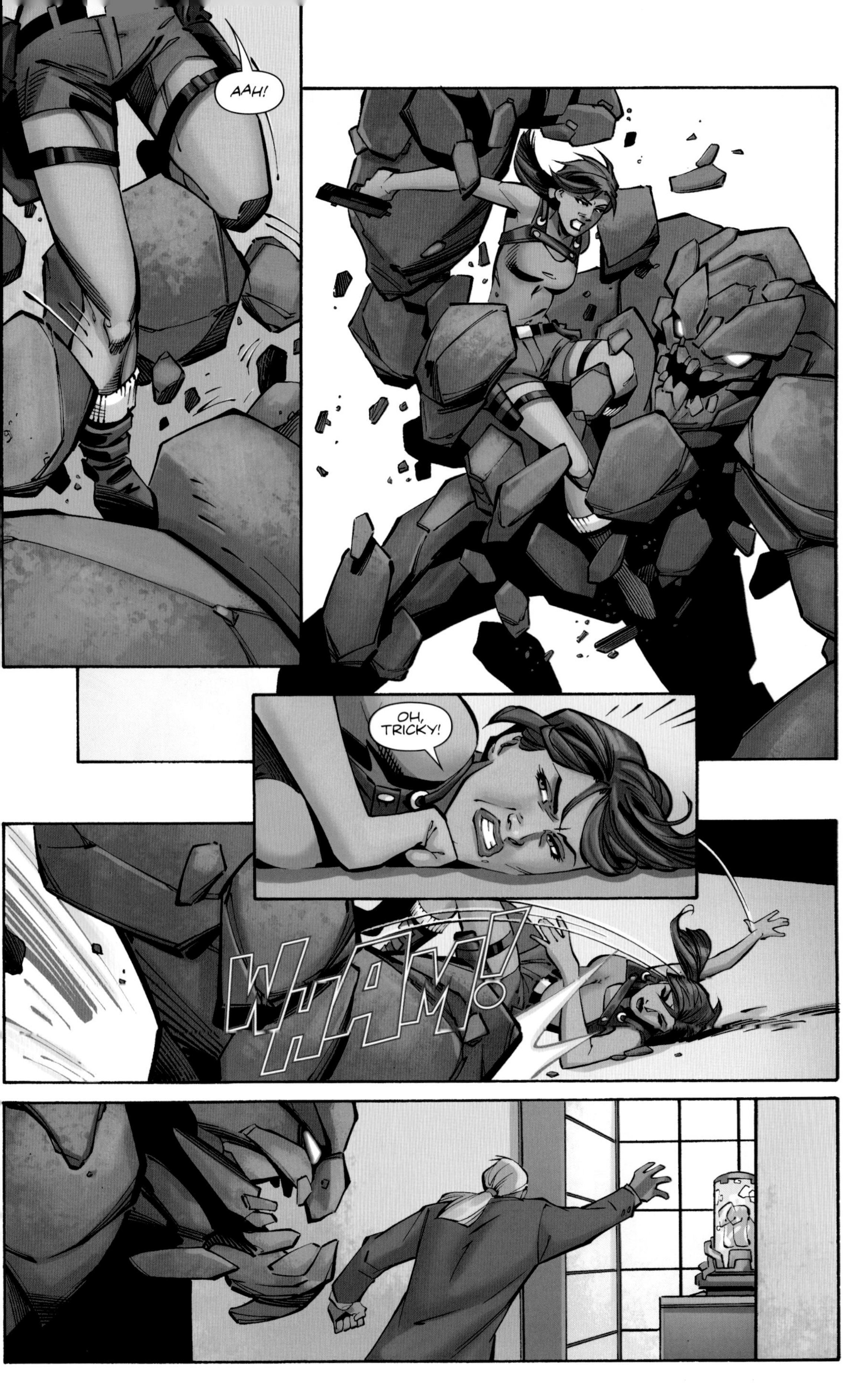
AAH!
OH, TRICKY!
WHAM!

WHAC!

OOF!

SMSH!

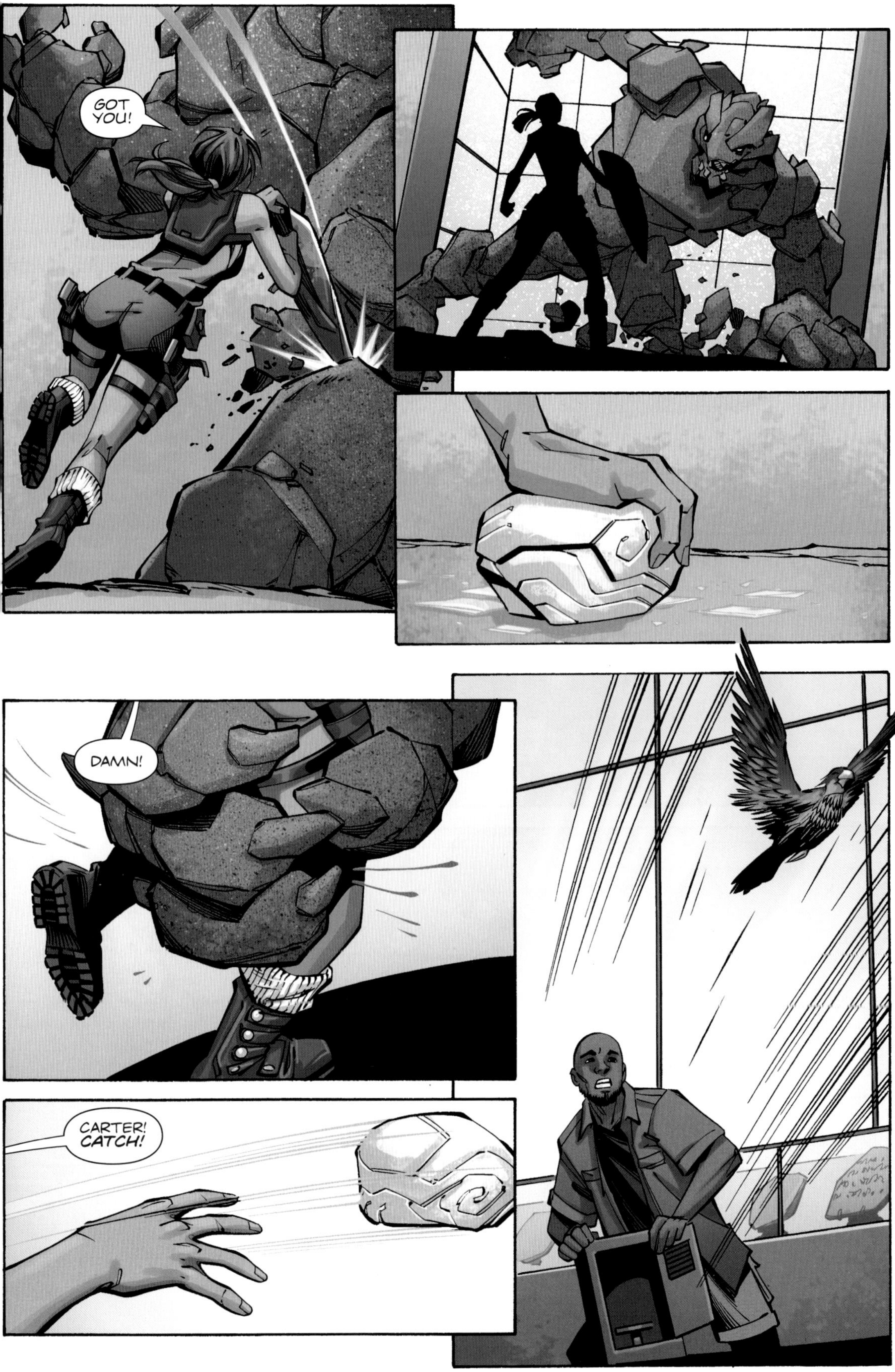
GOT YOU!
DAMN!
CARTER! CATCH!

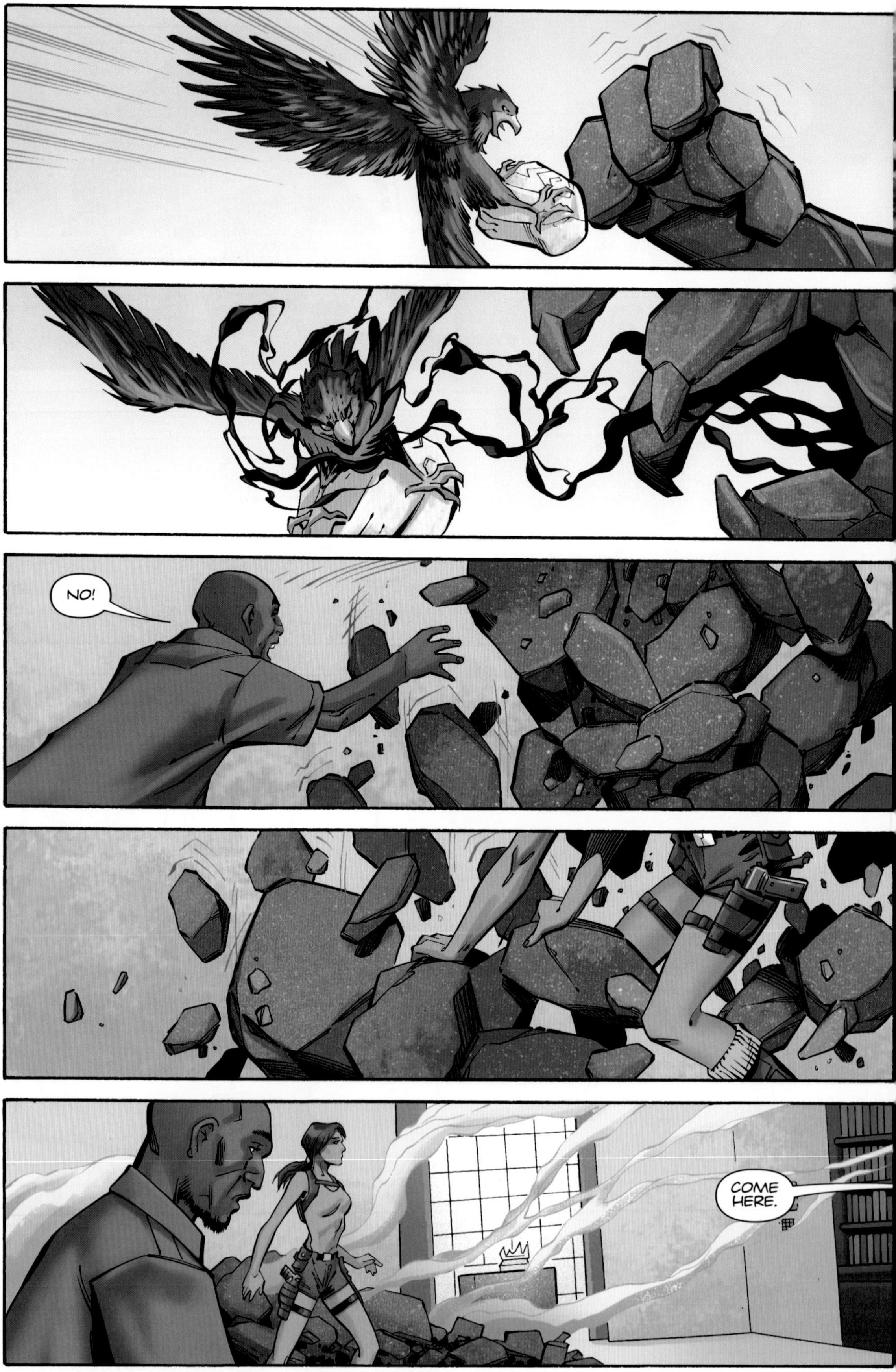
NO!
COME HERE.

MR. GRUS?

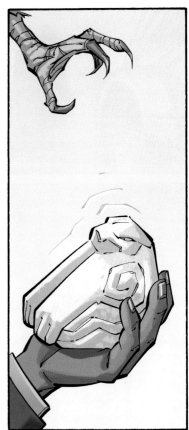

PUT THEM INTO THE VAULT.

SIR?

YOU HEARD ME. YOU WILL LOCK THEM IN THE *VAULT.*

NO, YOU DON'T UNDERSTAND!

THAT ISN'T REALLY GRUS! YOU HAVE TO LISTEN TO US!

UH-HUH.

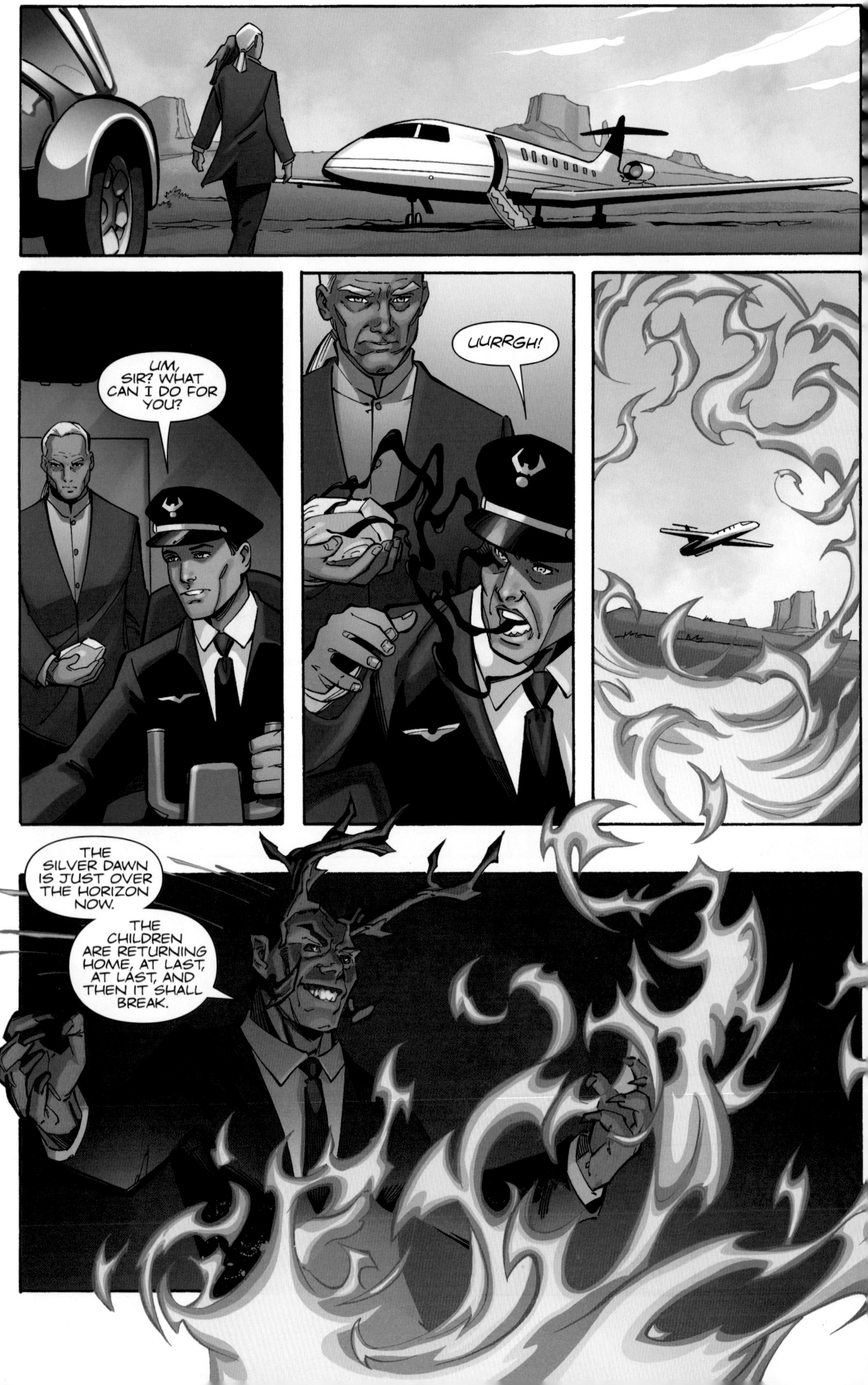
UM, SIR? WHAT CAN I DO FOR YOU?
UURRGH!
THE SILVER DAWN IS JUST OVER THE HORIZON NOW.
THE CHILDREN ARE RETURNING HOME, AT LAST, AT LAST, AND THEN IT SHALL BREAK.

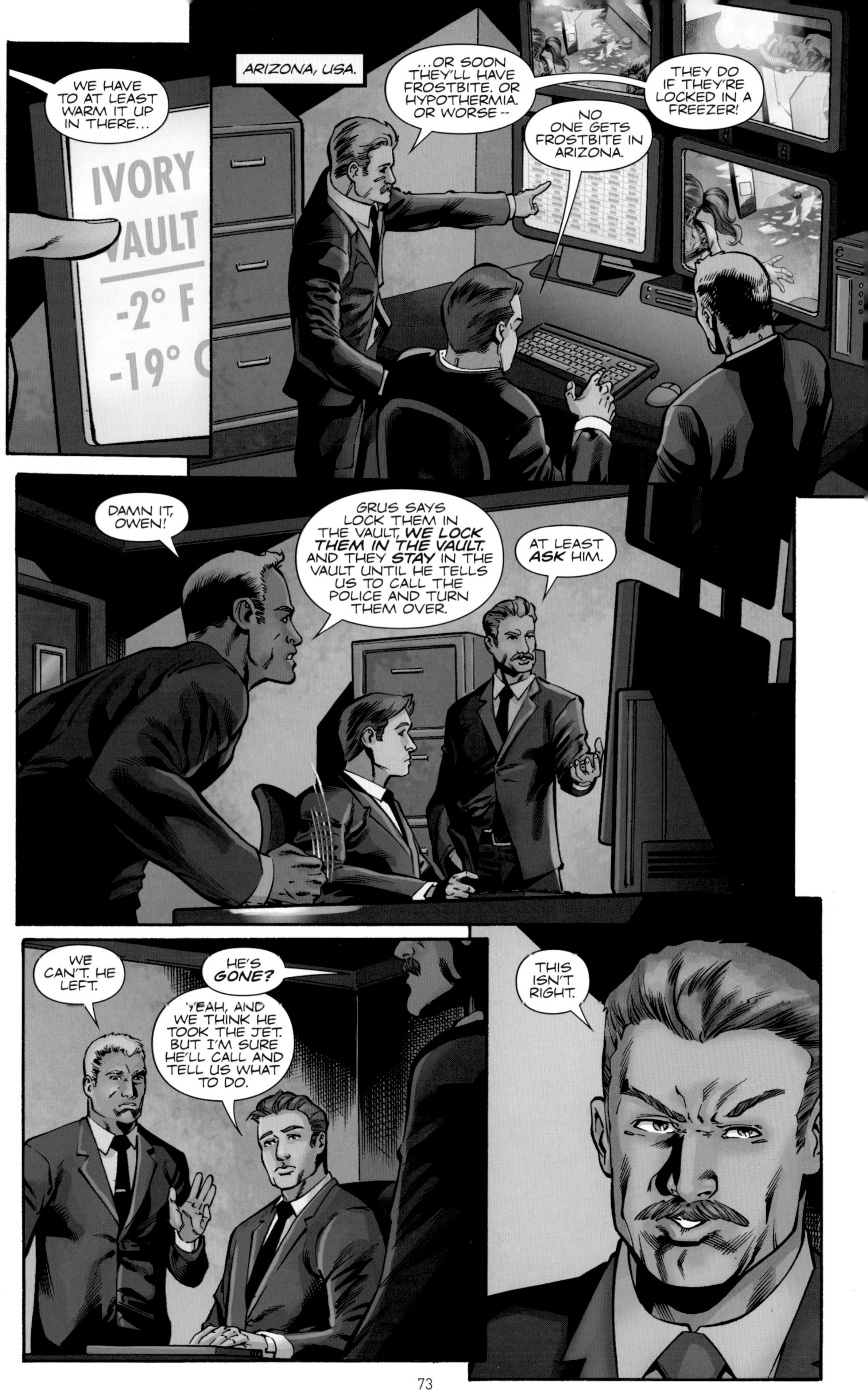
ARIZONA, USA.
WE HAVE TO AT LEAST WARM IT UP IN THERE...
...OR SOON THEY'LL HAVE FROSTBITE. OR HYPOTHERMIA. OR WORSE --
THEY DO IF THEY'RE LOCKED IN A FREEZER!
NO ONE GETS FROSTBITE IN ARIZONA.
IVORY VAULT
-2° F
-19° C
DAMN IT, OWEN!
GRUS SAYS LOCK THEM IN THE VAULT, WE LOCK THEM IN THE VAULT. AND THEY STAY IN THE VAULT UNTIL HE TELLS US TO CALL THE POLICE AND TURN THEM OVER.
AT LEAST ASK HIM.
WE CAN'T. HE LEFT.
HE'S GONE?
YEAH, AND WE THINK HE TOOK THE JET. BUT I'M SURE HE'LL CALL AND TELL US WHAT TO DO.
THIS ISN'T RIGHT.

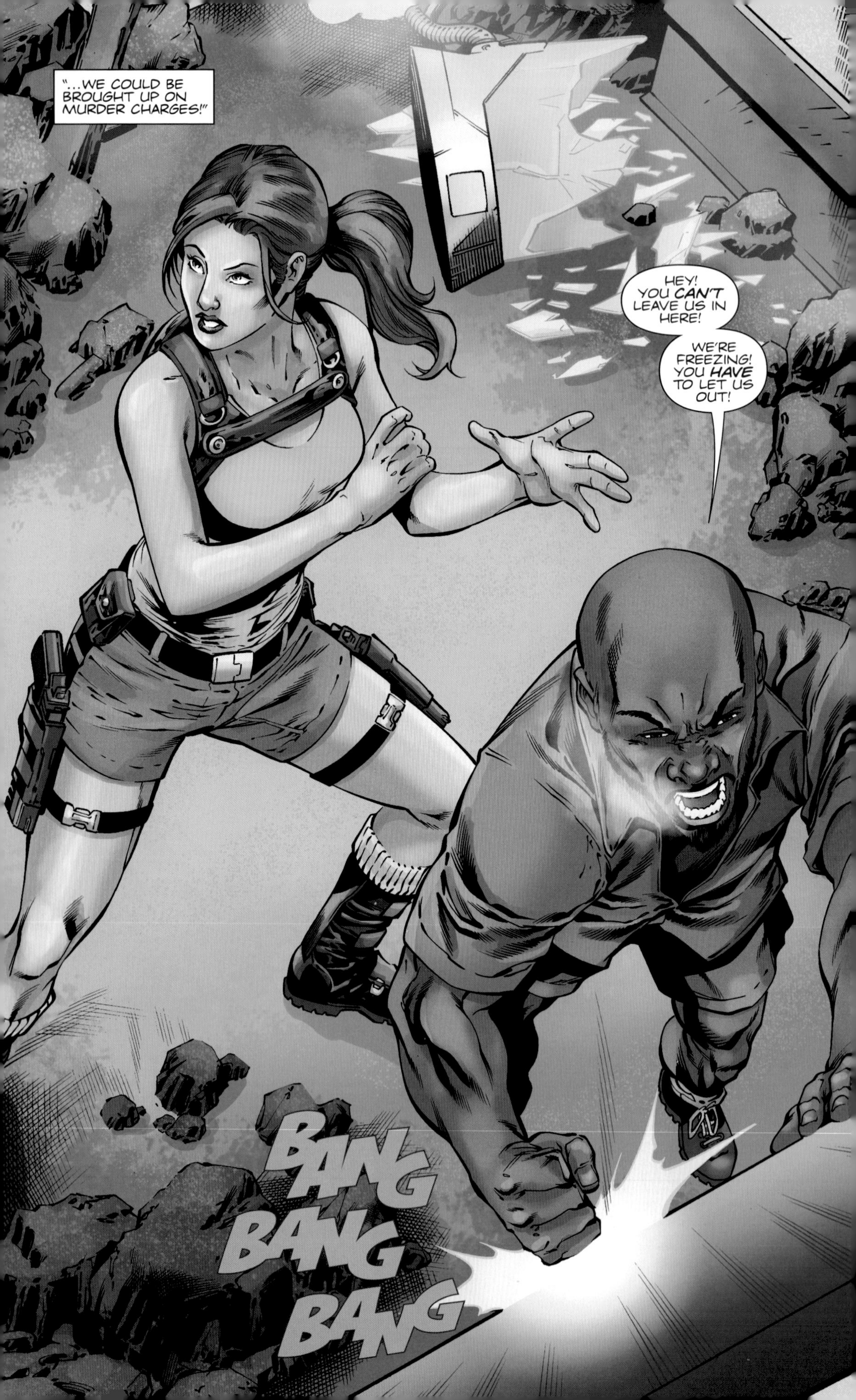
"...WE COULD BE BROUGHT UP ON MURDER CHARGES!"
HEY! YOU CAN'T LEAVE US IN HERE!
WE'RE FREEZING! YOU HAVE TO LET US OUT!
BANG BANG BANG

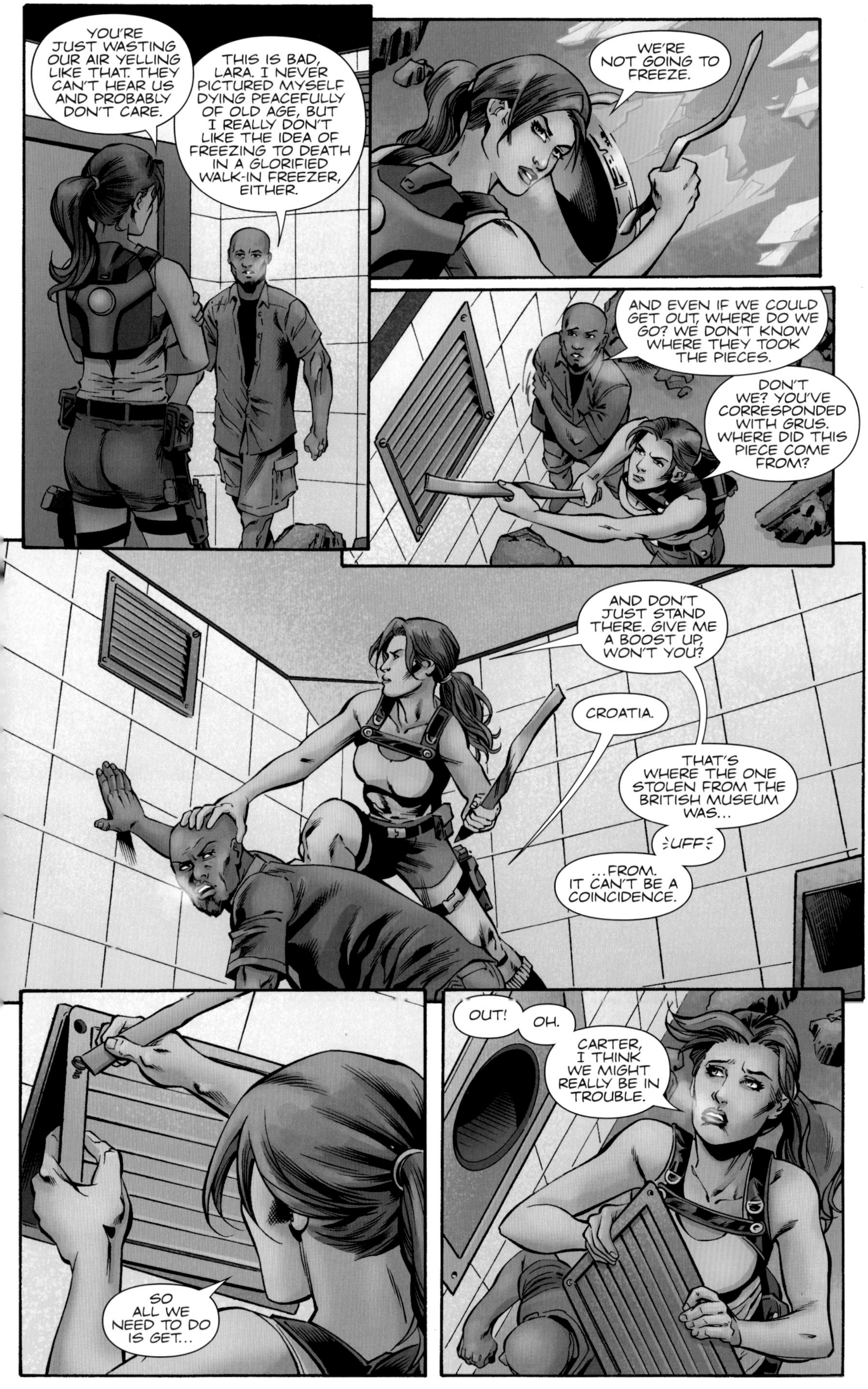
YOU'RE JUST WASTING OUR AIR YELLING LIKE THAT. THEY CAN'T HEAR US AND PROBABLY DON'T CARE.
THIS IS BAD, LARA. I NEVER PICTURED MYSELF DYING PEACEFULLY OF OLD AGE, BUT I REALLY DON'T LIKE THE IDEA OF FREEZING TO DEATH IN A GLORIFIED WALK-IN FREEZER, EITHER.
WE'RE NOT GOING TO FREEZE.
AND EVEN IF WE COULD GET OUT, WHERE DO WE GO? WE DON'T KNOW WHERE THEY TOOK THE PIECES.
DON'T WE? YOU'VE CORRESPONDED WITH GRUS. WHERE DID THIS PIECE COME FROM?
AND DON'T JUST STAND THERE. GIVE ME A BOOST UP, WON'T YOU?
CROATIA.
THAT'S WHERE THE ONE STOLEN FROM THE BRITISH MUSEUM WAS...
UFF
...FROM. IT CAN'T BE A COINCIDENCE.
SO ALL WE NEED TO DO IS GET...
OUT!
OH.
CARTER, I THINK WE MIGHT REALLY BE IN TROUBLE.

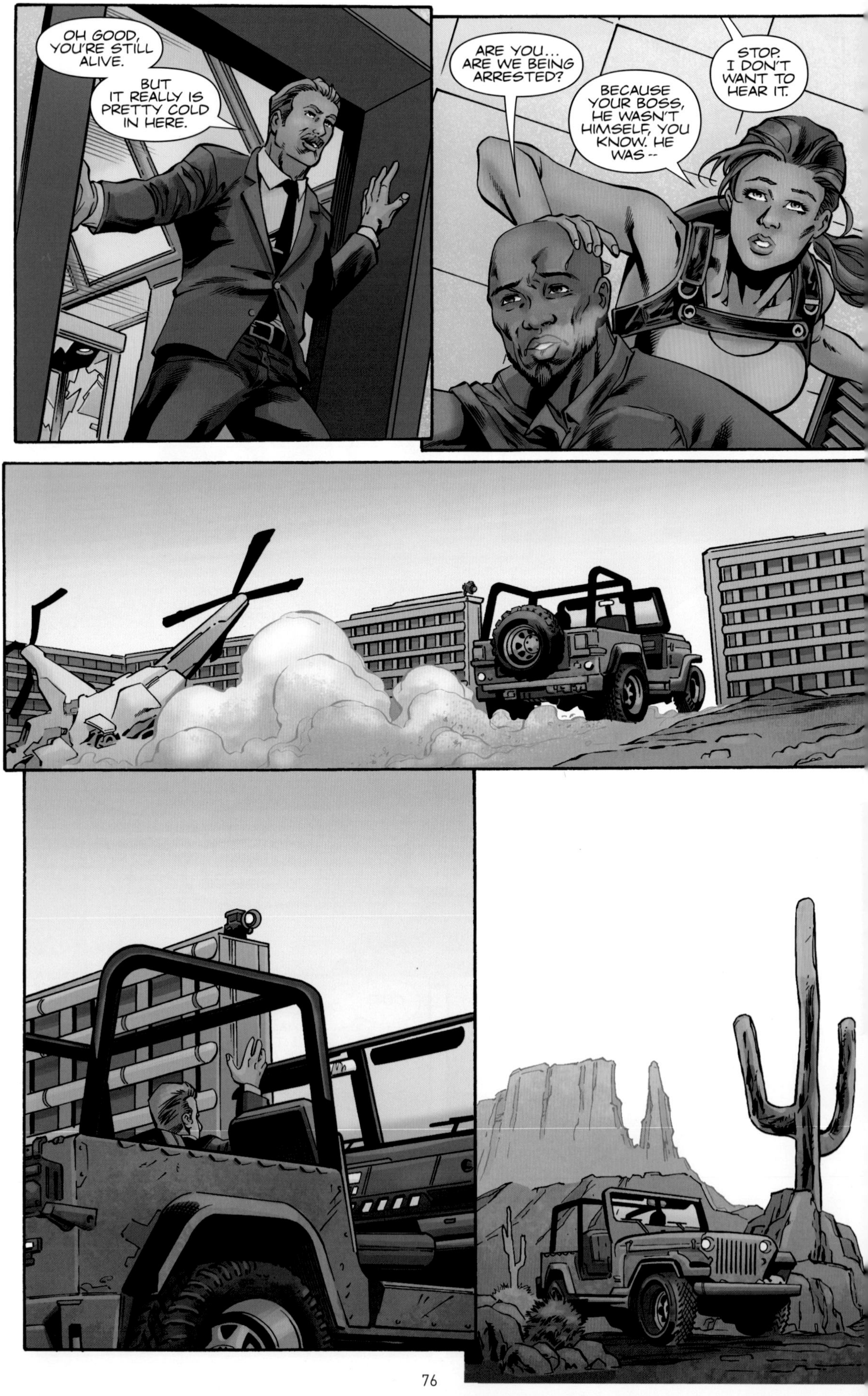
OH GOOD, YOU'RE STILL ALIVE.
BUT IT REALLY IS PRETTY COLD IN HERE.
ARE YOU... ARE WE BEING ARRESTED?
BECAUSE YOUR BOSS, HE WASN'T HIMSELF, YOU KNOW. HE WAS --
STOP. I DON'T WANT TO HEAR IT.

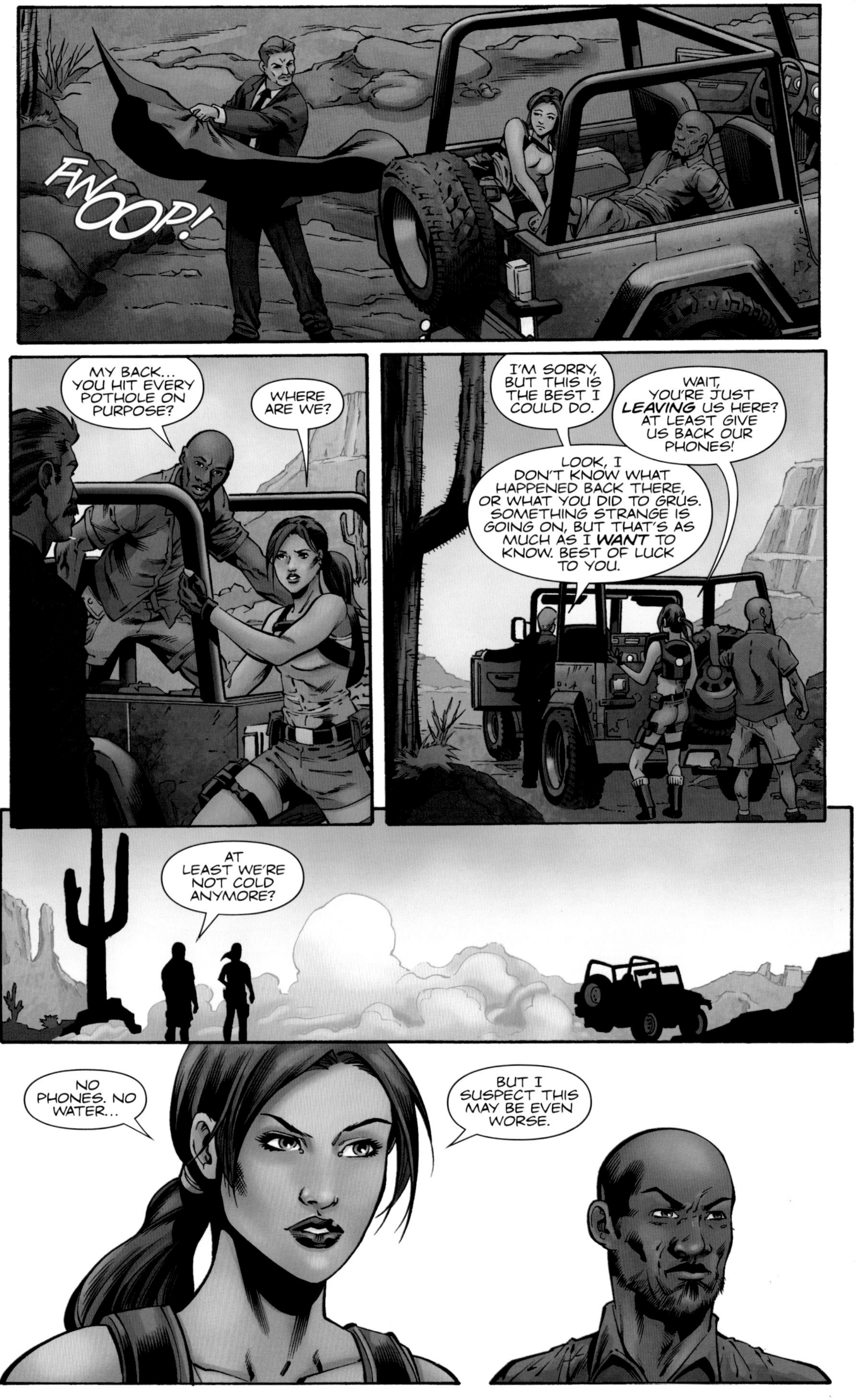
FWOOP!
MY BACK... YOU HIT EVERY POTHOLE ON PURPOSE?
WHERE ARE WE?
I'M SORRY, BUT THIS IS THE BEST I COULD DO.
WAIT, YOU'RE JUST **LEAVING** US HERE? AT LEAST GIVE US BACK OUR PHONES!
LOOK, I DON'T KNOW WHAT HAPPENED BACK THERE, OR WHAT YOU DID TO GRUS. SOMETHING STRANGE IS GOING ON, BUT THAT'S AS MUCH AS I **WANT** TO KNOW. BEST OF LUCK TO YOU.
AT LEAST WE'RE NOT COLD ANYMORE?
NO PHONES. NO WATER...
BUT I SUSPECT THIS MAY BE EVEN WORSE.

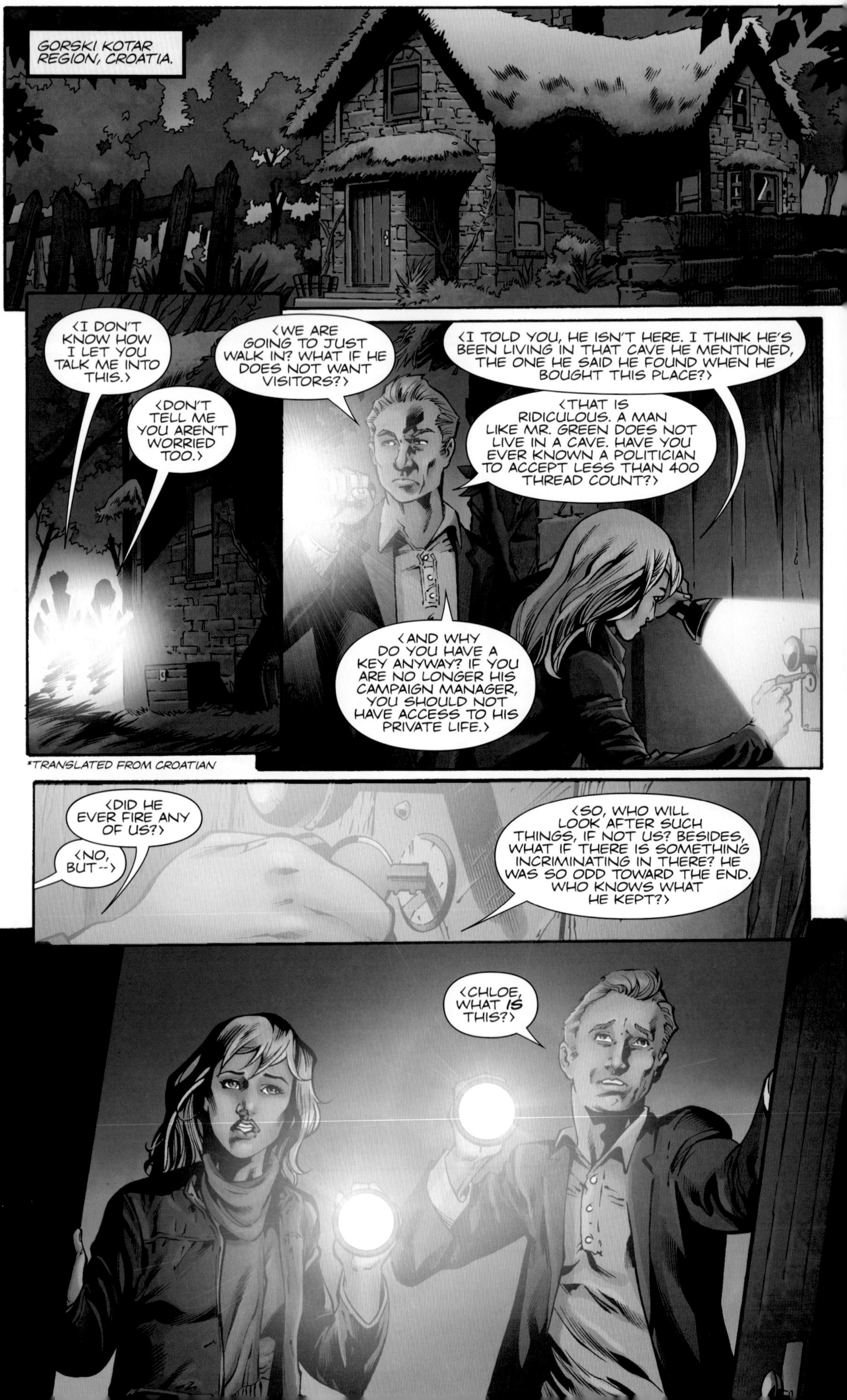
GORSKI KOTAR REGION, CROATIA.
‹I DON'T KNOW HOW I LET YOU TALK ME INTO THIS.›
‹DON'T TELL ME YOU AREN'T WORRIED TOO.›
‹WE ARE GOING TO JUST WALK IN? WHAT IF HE DOES NOT WANT VISITORS?›
‹I TOLD YOU, HE ISN'T HERE. I THINK HE'S BEEN LIVING IN THAT CAVE HE MENTIONED, THE ONE HE SAID HE FOUND WHEN HE BOUGHT THIS PLACE?›
‹THAT IS RIDICULOUS. A MAN LIKE MR. GREEN DOES NOT LIVE IN A CAVE. HAVE YOU EVER KNOWN A POLITICIAN TO ACCEPT LESS THAN 400 THREAD COUNT?›
‹AND WHY DO YOU HAVE A KEY ANYWAY? IF YOU ARE NO LONGER HIS CAMPAIGN MANAGER, YOU SHOULD NOT HAVE ACCESS TO HIS PRIVATE LIFE.›
*TRANSLATED FROM CROATIAN
‹DID HE EVER FIRE ANY OF US?›
‹NO, BUT --›
‹SO, WHO WILL LOOK AFTER SUCH THINGS, IF NOT US? BESIDES, WHAT IF THERE IS SOMETHING INCRIMINATING IN THERE? HE WAS SO ODD TOWARD THE END. WHO KNOWS WHAT HE KEPT?›
‹CHLOE, WHAT *IS* THIS?›

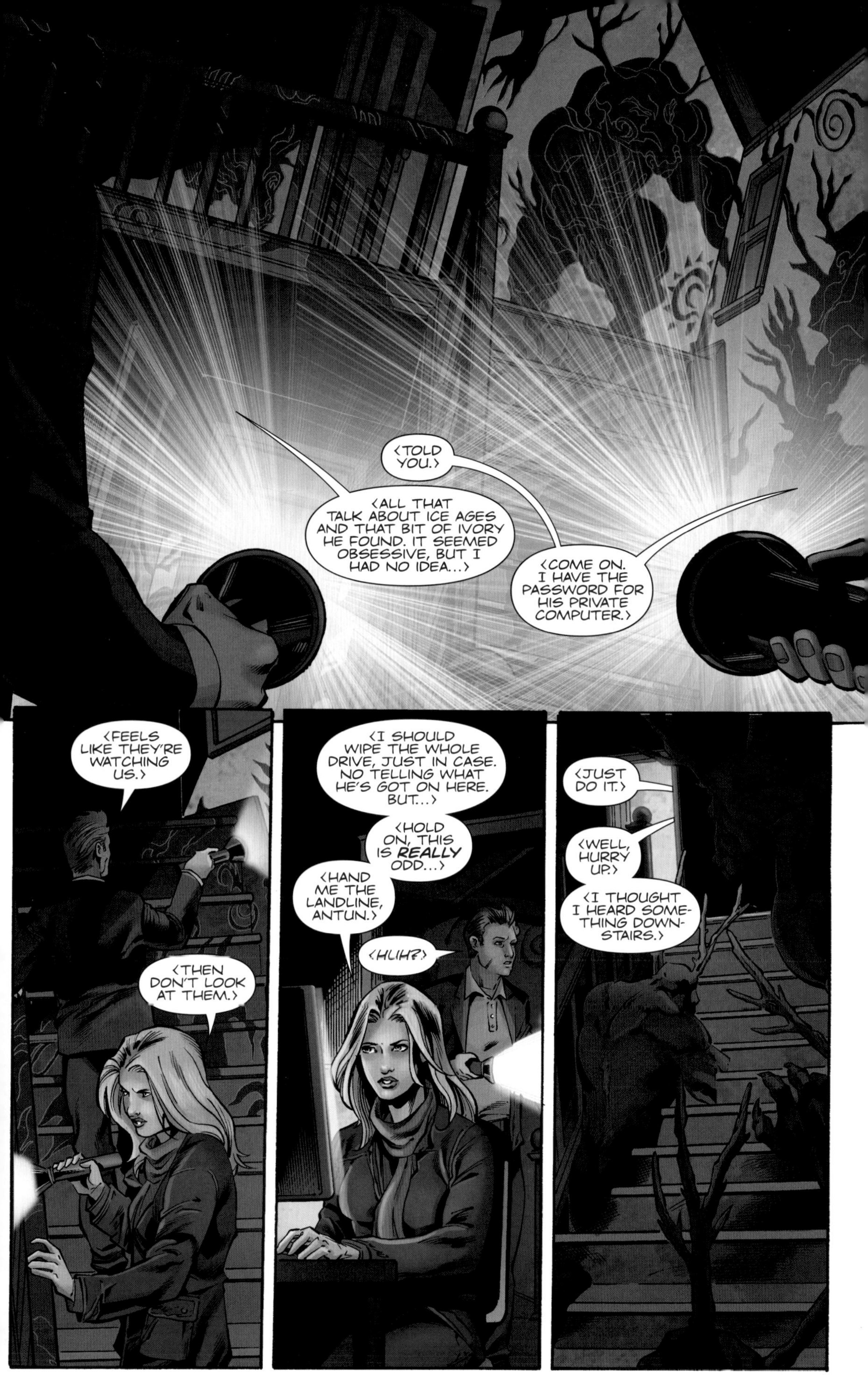

‹TOLD YOU.›
‹ALL THAT TALK ABOUT ICE AGES AND THAT BIT OF IVORY HE FOUND. IT SEEMED OBSESSIVE, BUT I HAD NO IDEA...›
‹COME ON. I HAVE THE PASSWORD FOR HIS PRIVATE COMPUTER.›
‹FEELS LIKE THEY'RE WATCHING US.›
‹THEN DON'T LOOK AT THEM.›
‹I SHOULD WIPE THE WHOLE DRIVE, JUST IN CASE. NO TELLING WHAT HE'S GOT ON HERE. BUT...›
‹HOLD ON, THIS IS **REALLY** ODD...›
‹HAND ME THE LANDLINE, ANTUN.›
‹HUH?›
‹JUST DO IT.›
‹WELL, HURRY UP.›
‹I THOUGHT I HEARD SOME-THING DOWN-STAIRS.›

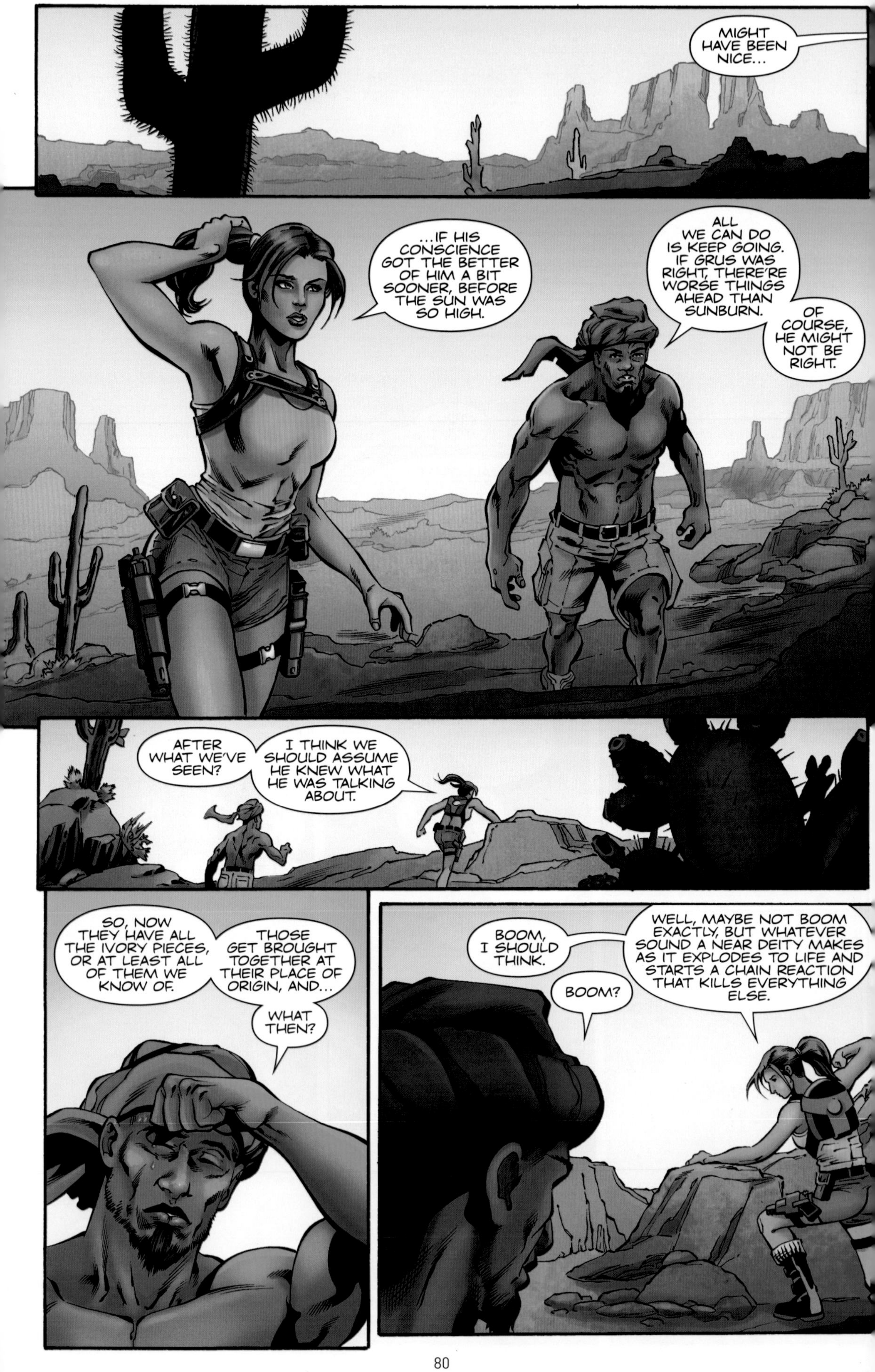

MIGHT HAVE BEEN NICE...
...IF HIS CONSCIENCE GOT THE BETTER OF HIM A BIT SOONER, BEFORE THE SUN WAS SO HIGH.
ALL WE CAN DO IS KEEP GOING. IF GRUS WAS RIGHT, THERE'RE WORSE THINGS AHEAD THAN SUNBURN.
OF COURSE, HE MIGHT NOT BE RIGHT.
AFTER WHAT WE'VE SEEN?
I THINK WE SHOULD ASSUME HE KNEW WHAT HE WAS TALKING ABOUT.
SO, NOW THEY HAVE ALL THE IVORY PIECES, OR AT LEAST ALL OF THEM WE KNOW OF.
THOSE GET BROUGHT TOGETHER AT THEIR PLACE OF ORIGIN, AND...
WHAT THEN?
BOOM, I SHOULD THINK.
BOOM?
WELL, MAYBE NOT BOOM EXACTLY, BUT WHATEVER SOUND A NEAR DEITY MAKES AS IT EXPLODES TO LIFE AND STARTS A CHAIN REACTION THAT KILLS EVERYTHING ELSE.

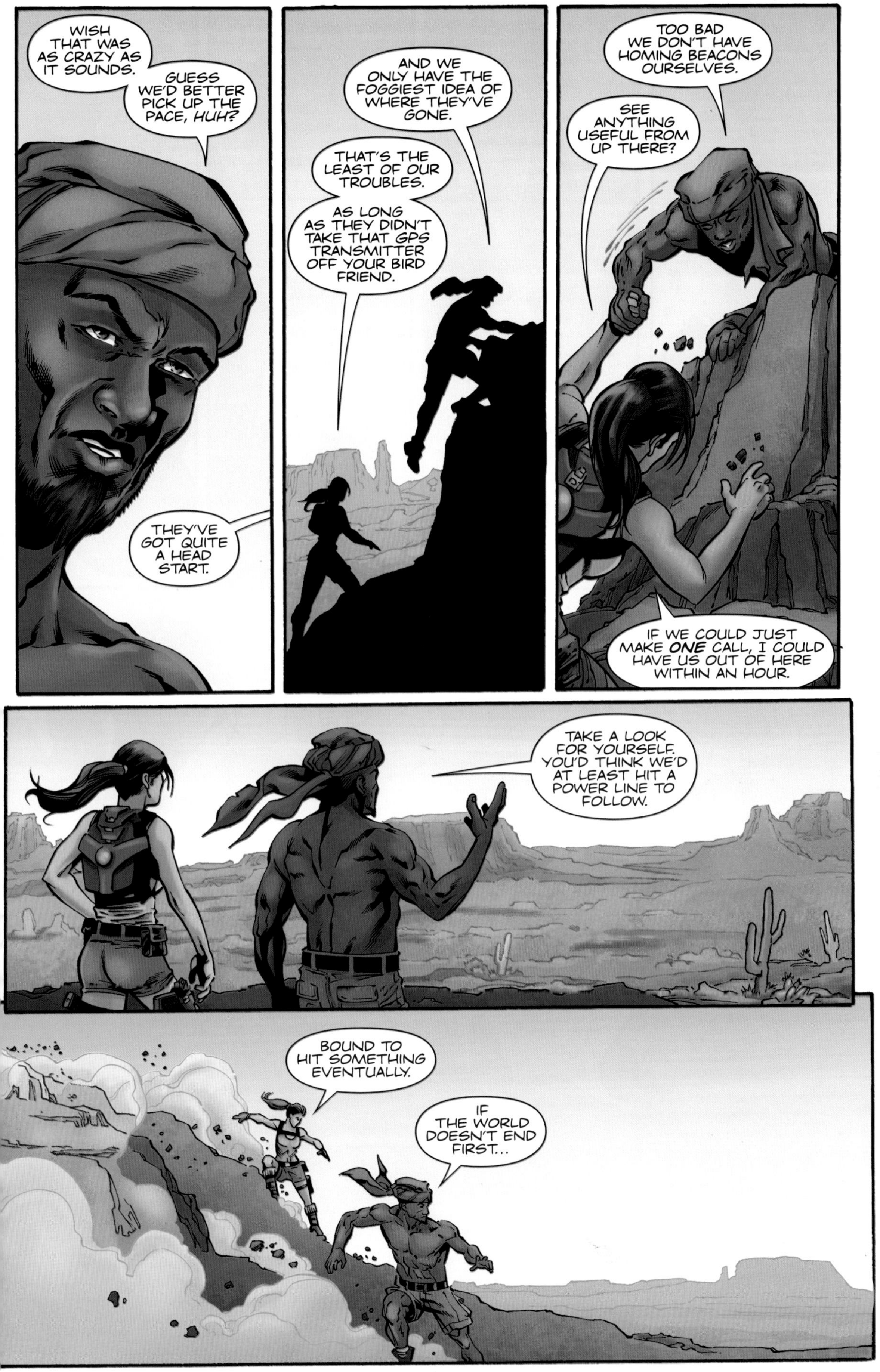

WISH THAT WAS AS CRAZY AS IT SOUNDS.
GUESS WE'D BETTER PICK UP THE PACE, HUH?
THEY'VE GOT QUITE A HEAD START.
AND WE ONLY HAVE THE FOGGIEST IDEA OF WHERE THEY'VE GONE.
THAT'S THE LEAST OF OUR TROUBLES.
AS LONG AS THEY DIDN'T TAKE THAT GPS TRANSMITTER OFF YOUR BIRD FRIEND.
TOO BAD WE DON'T HAVE HOMING BEACONS OURSELVES.
SEE ANYTHING USEFUL FROM UP THERE?
IF WE COULD JUST MAKE ***ONE*** CALL, I COULD HAVE US OUT OF HERE WITHIN AN HOUR.
TAKE A LOOK FOR YOURSELF. YOU'D THINK WE'D AT LEAST HIT A POWER LINE TO FOLLOW.
BOUND TO HIT SOMETHING EVENTUALLY.
IF THE WORLD DOESN'T END FIRST...

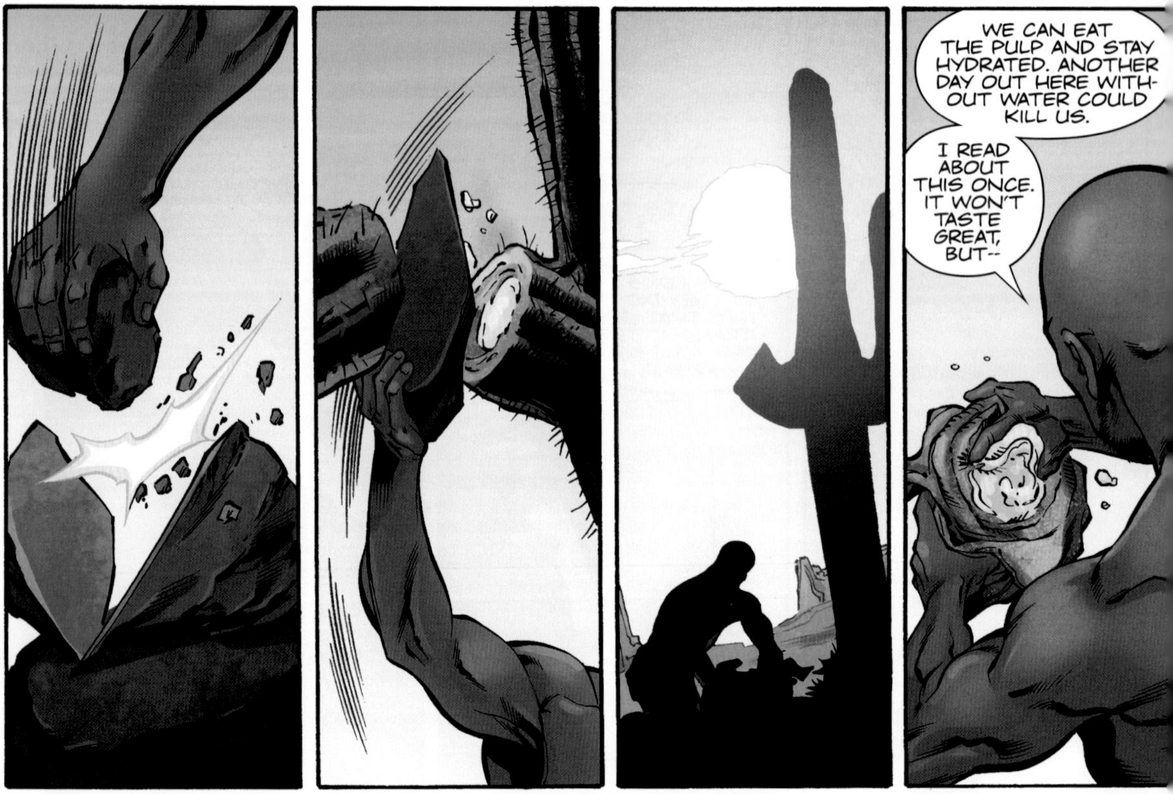
WE CAN EAT THE PULP AND STAY HYDRATED. ANOTHER DAY OUT HERE WITH-OUT WATER COULD KILL US.
I READ ABOUT THIS ONCE. IT WON'T TASTE GREAT, BUT--

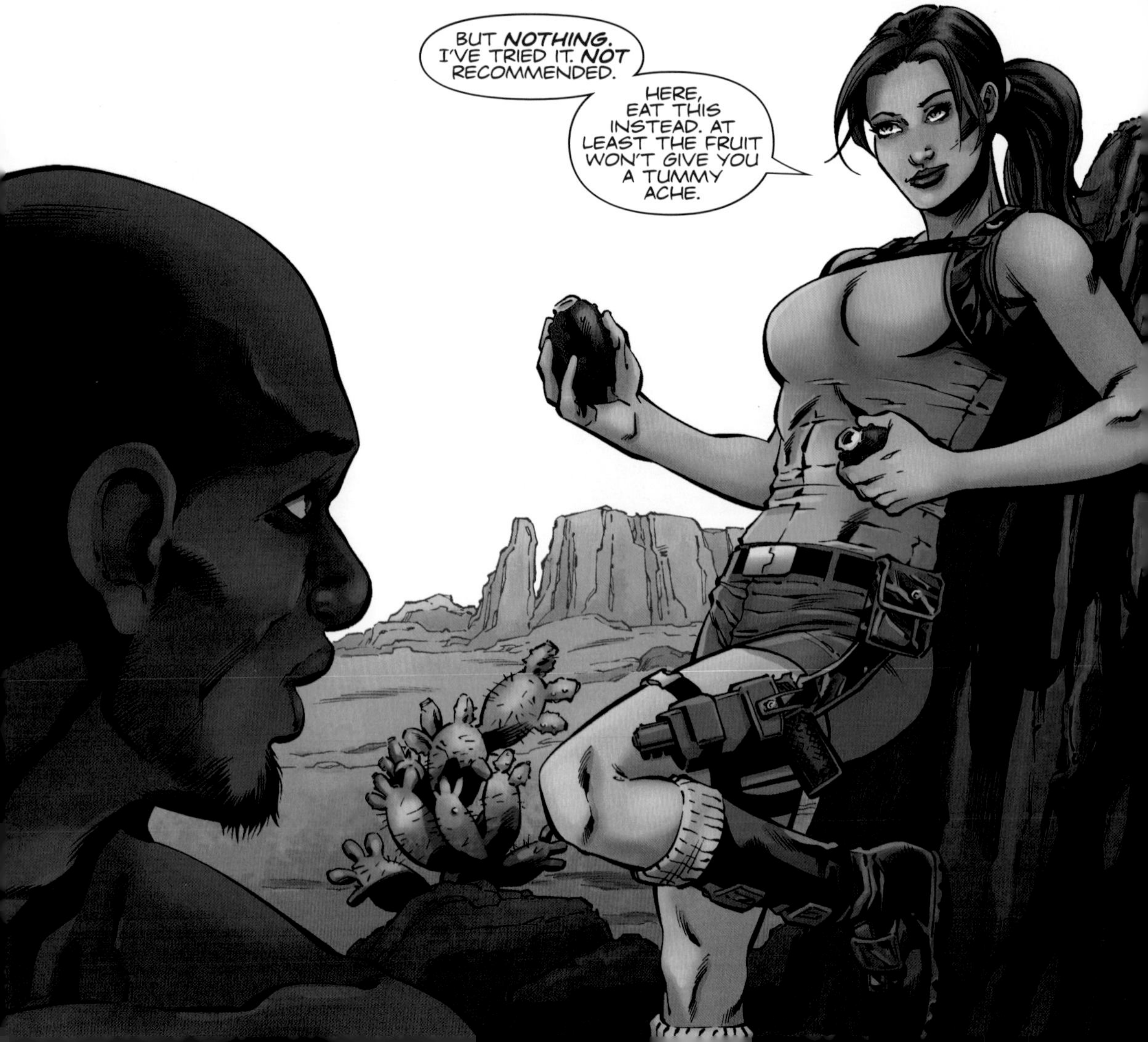
BUT NOTHING. I'VE TRIED IT. NOT RECOMMENDED.
HERE, EAT THIS INSTEAD. AT LEAST THE FRUIT WON'T GIVE YOU A TUMMY ACHE.

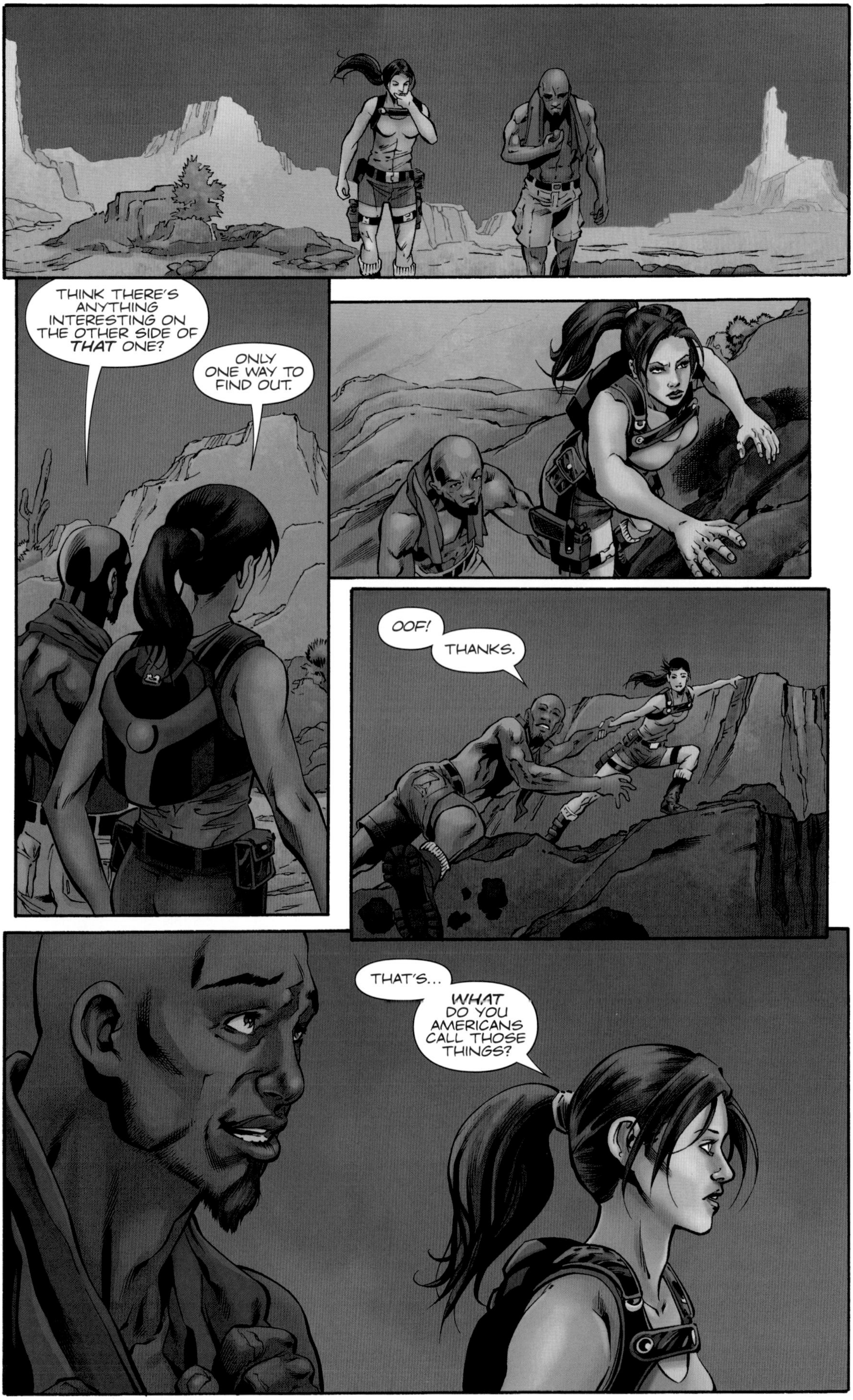
THINK THERE'S ANYTHING INTERESTING ON THE OTHER SIDE OF *THAT* ONE?
ONLY ONE WAY TO FIND OUT.
OOF!
THANKS.
THAT'S...
WHAT DO YOU AMERICANS CALL THOSE THINGS?

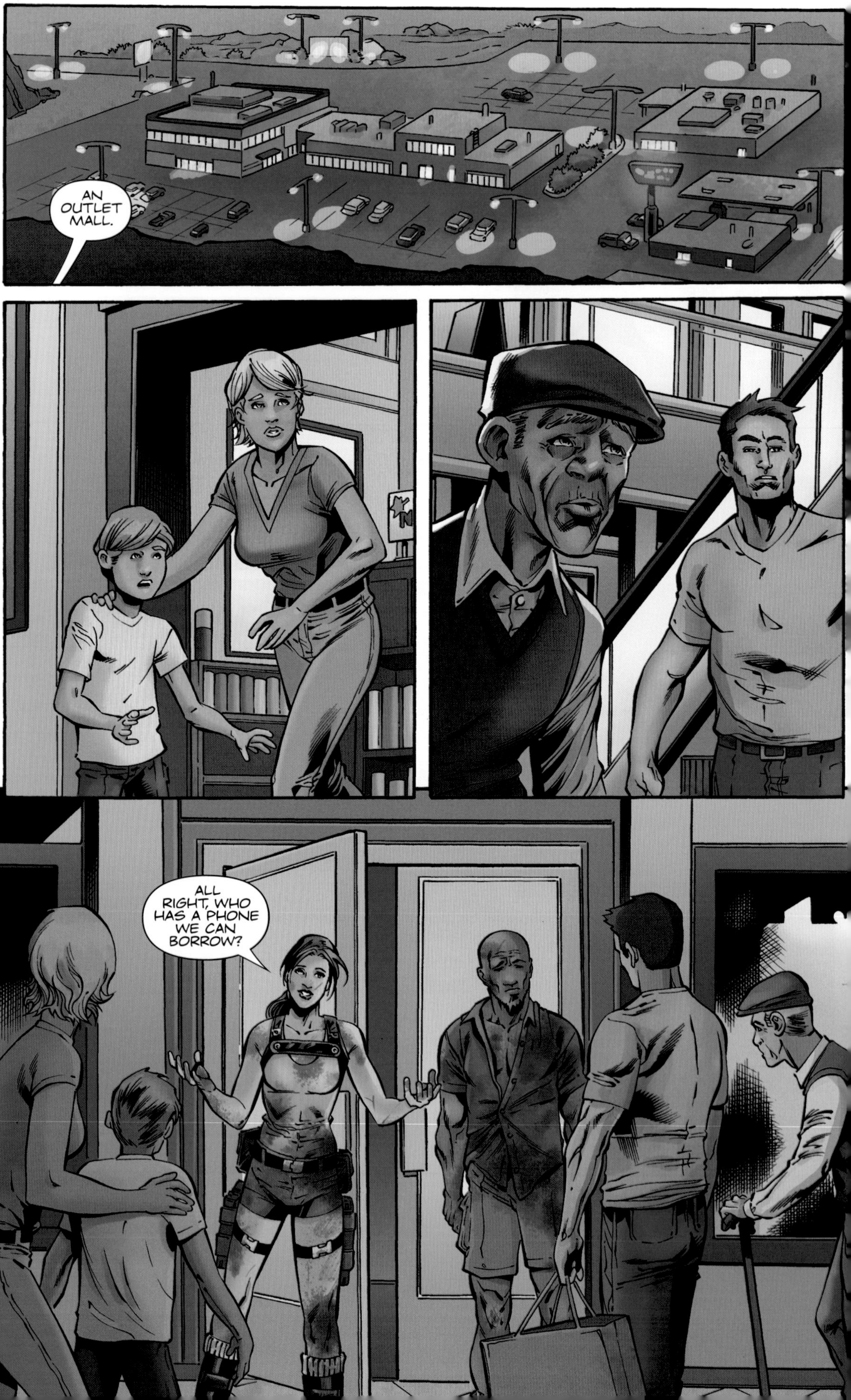
AN OUTLET MALL.
ALL RIGHT, WHO HAS A PHONE WE CAN BORROW?

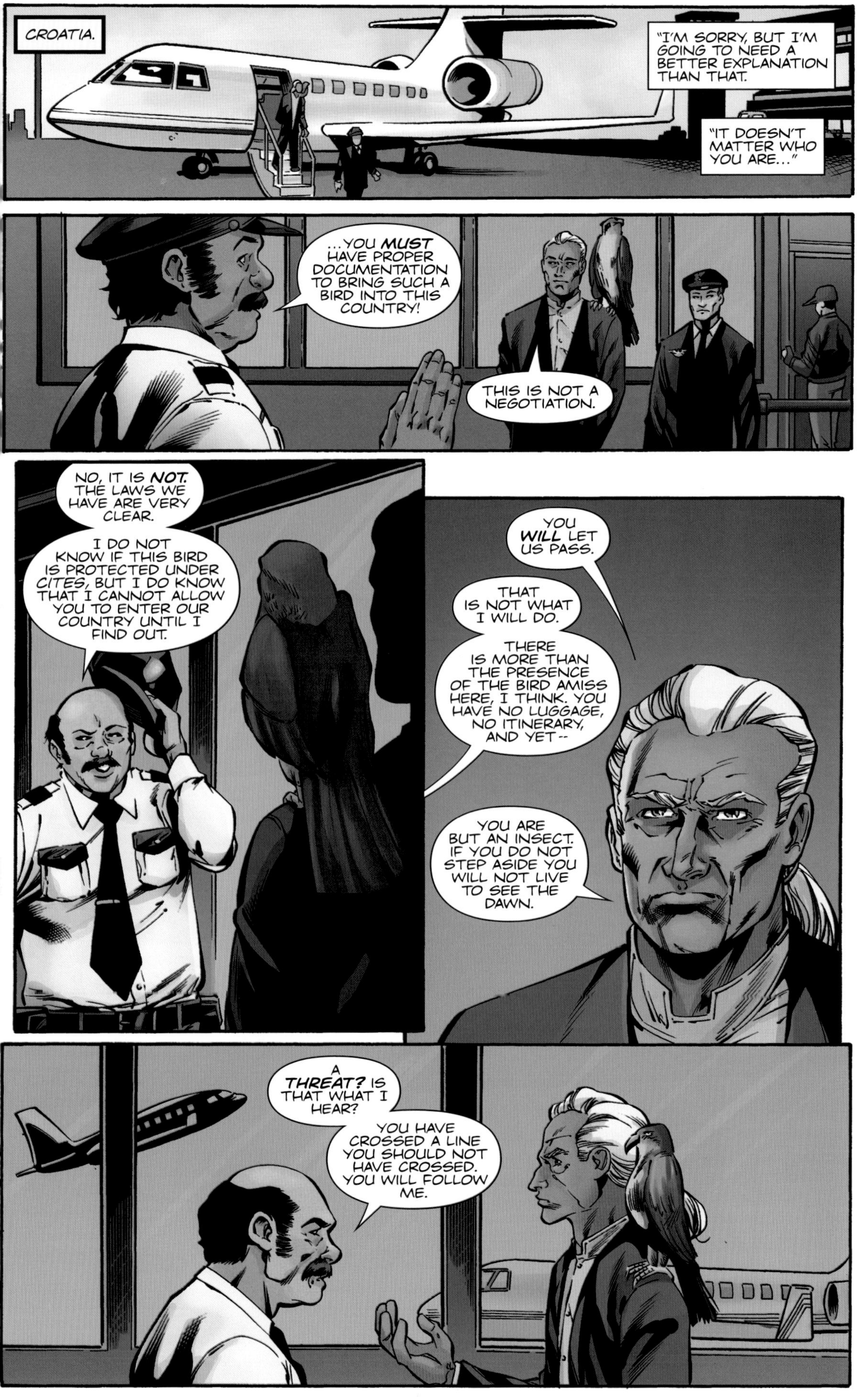
CROATIA.
"I'M SORRY, BUT I'M GOING TO NEED A BETTER EXPLANATION THAN THAT.
"IT DOESN'T MATTER WHO YOU ARE..."
...YOU MUST HAVE PROPER DOCUMENTATION TO BRING SUCH A BIRD INTO THIS COUNTRY!
THIS IS NOT A NEGOTIATION.
NO, IT IS NOT. THE LAWS WE HAVE ARE VERY CLEAR.
I DO NOT KNOW IF THIS BIRD IS PROTECTED UNDER CITES, BUT I DO KNOW THAT I CANNOT ALLOW YOU TO ENTER OUR COUNTRY UNTIL I FIND OUT.
YOU WILL LET US PASS.
THAT IS NOT WHAT I WILL DO.
THERE IS MORE THAN THE PRESENCE OF THE BIRD AMISS HERE, I THINK. YOU HAVE NO LUGGAGE, NO ITINERARY, AND YET--
YOU ARE BUT AN INSECT. IF YOU DO NOT STEP ASIDE YOU WILL NOT LIVE TO SEE THE DAWN.
A THREAT? IS THAT WHAT I HEAR?
YOU HAVE CROSSED A LINE YOU SHOULD NOT HAVE CROSSED. YOU WILL FOLLOW ME.

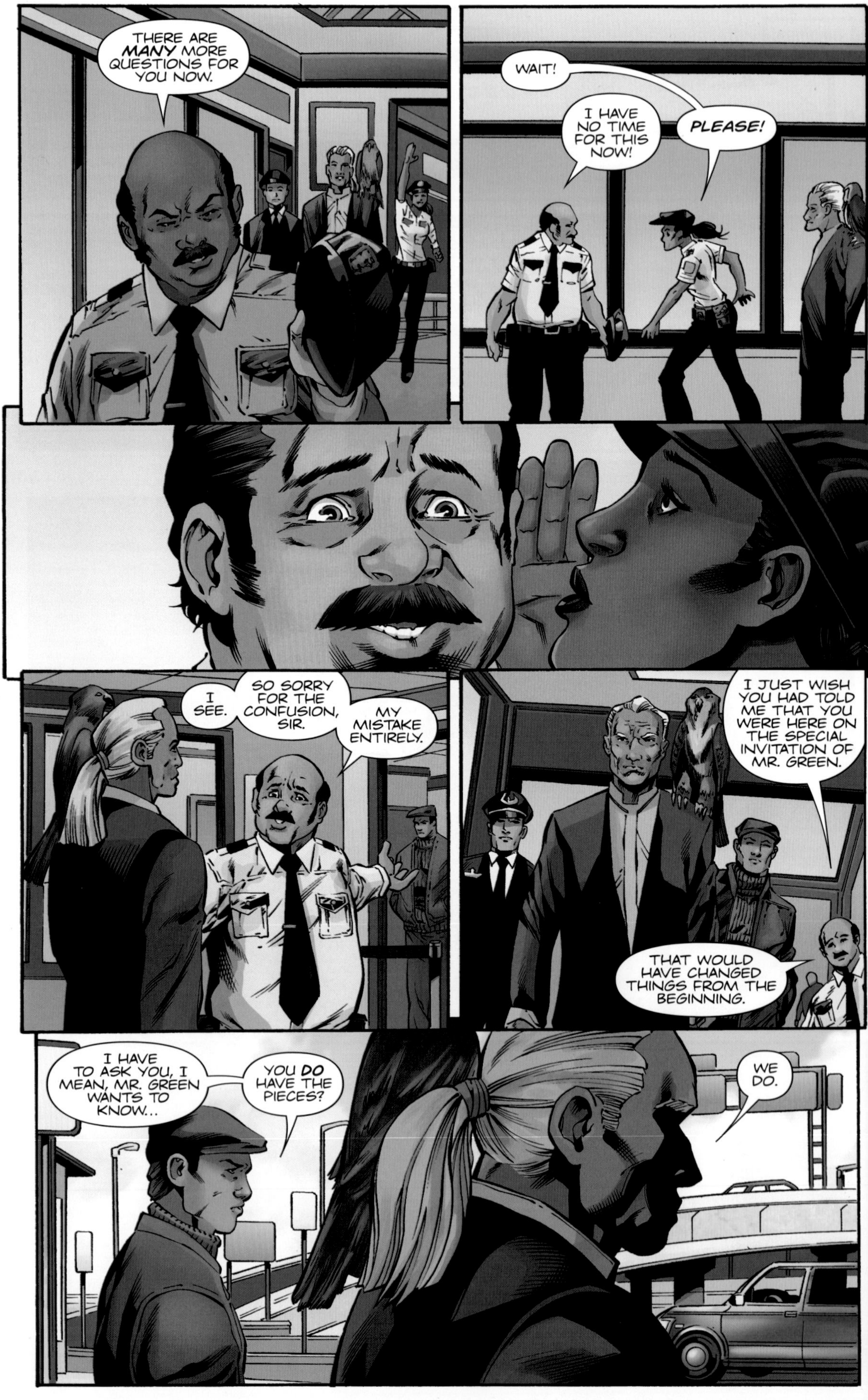
THERE ARE **MANY** MORE QUESTIONS FOR YOU NOW.
WAIT!
I HAVE NO TIME FOR THIS NOW!
PLEASE!
I SEE.
SO SORRY FOR THE CONFUSION, SIR.
MY MISTAKE ENTIRELY.
I JUST WISH YOU HAD TOLD ME THAT YOU WERE HERE ON THE SPECIAL INVITATION OF MR. GREEN.
THAT WOULD HAVE CHANGED THINGS FROM THE BEGINNING.
I HAVE TO ASK YOU, I MEAN, MR. GREEN WANTS TO KNOW...
YOU **DO** HAVE THE PIECES?
WE DO.

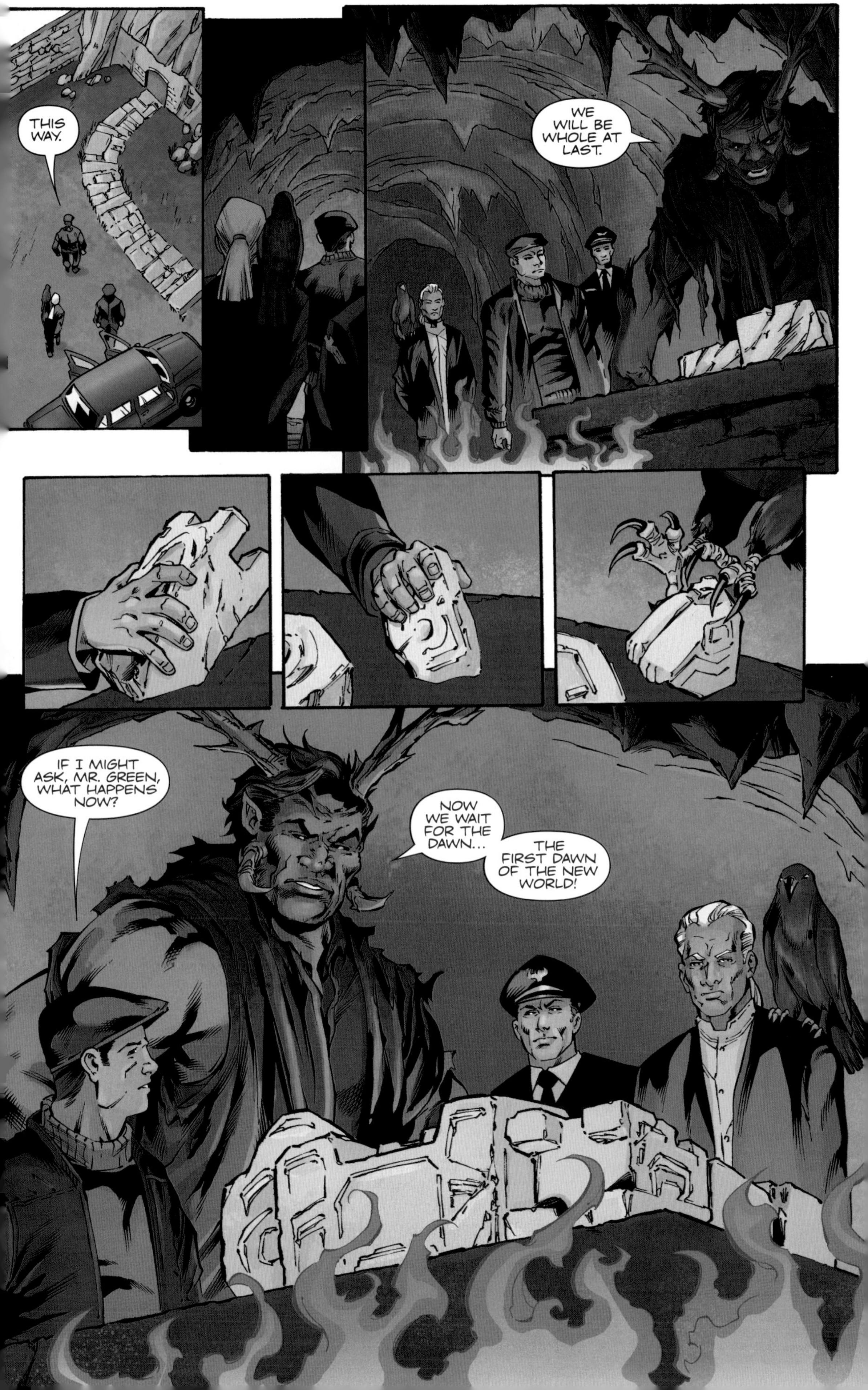
THIS WAY.
WE WILL BE WHOLE AT LAST.
IF I MIGHT ASK, MR. GREEN, WHAT HAPPENS NOW?
NOW WE WAIT FOR THE DAWN...
THE FIRST DAWN OF THE NEW WORLD!

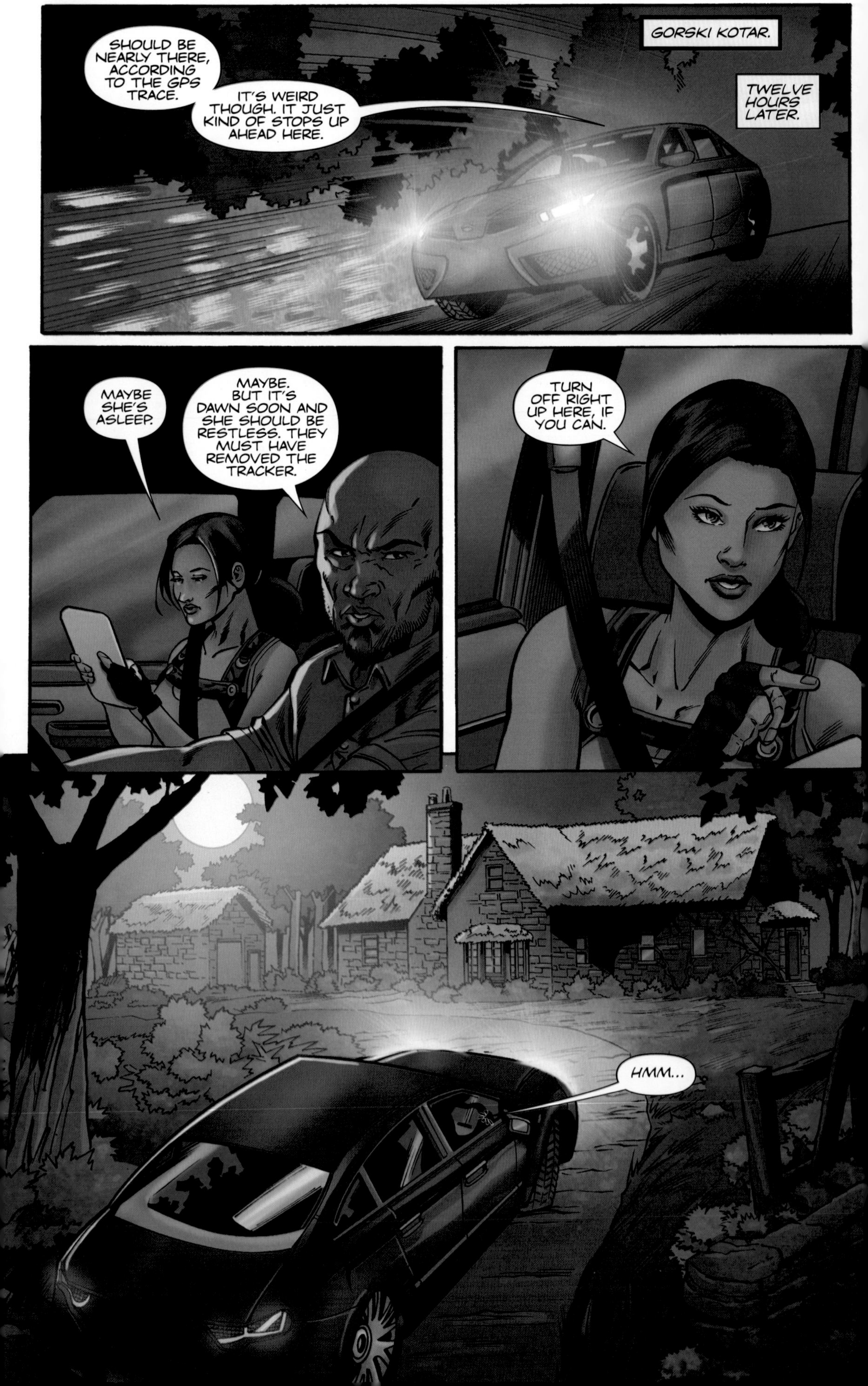
GORSKI KOTAR.
TWELVE HOURS LATER.
SHOULD BE NEARLY THERE, ACCORDING TO THE GPS TRACE.
IT'S WEIRD THOUGH. IT JUST KIND OF STOPS UP AHEAD HERE.
MAYBE SHE'S ASLEEP.
MAYBE. BUT IT'S DAWN SOON AND SHE SHOULD BE RESTLESS. THEY MUST HAVE REMOVED THE TRACKER.
TURN OFF RIGHT UP HERE, IF YOU CAN.
HMM...

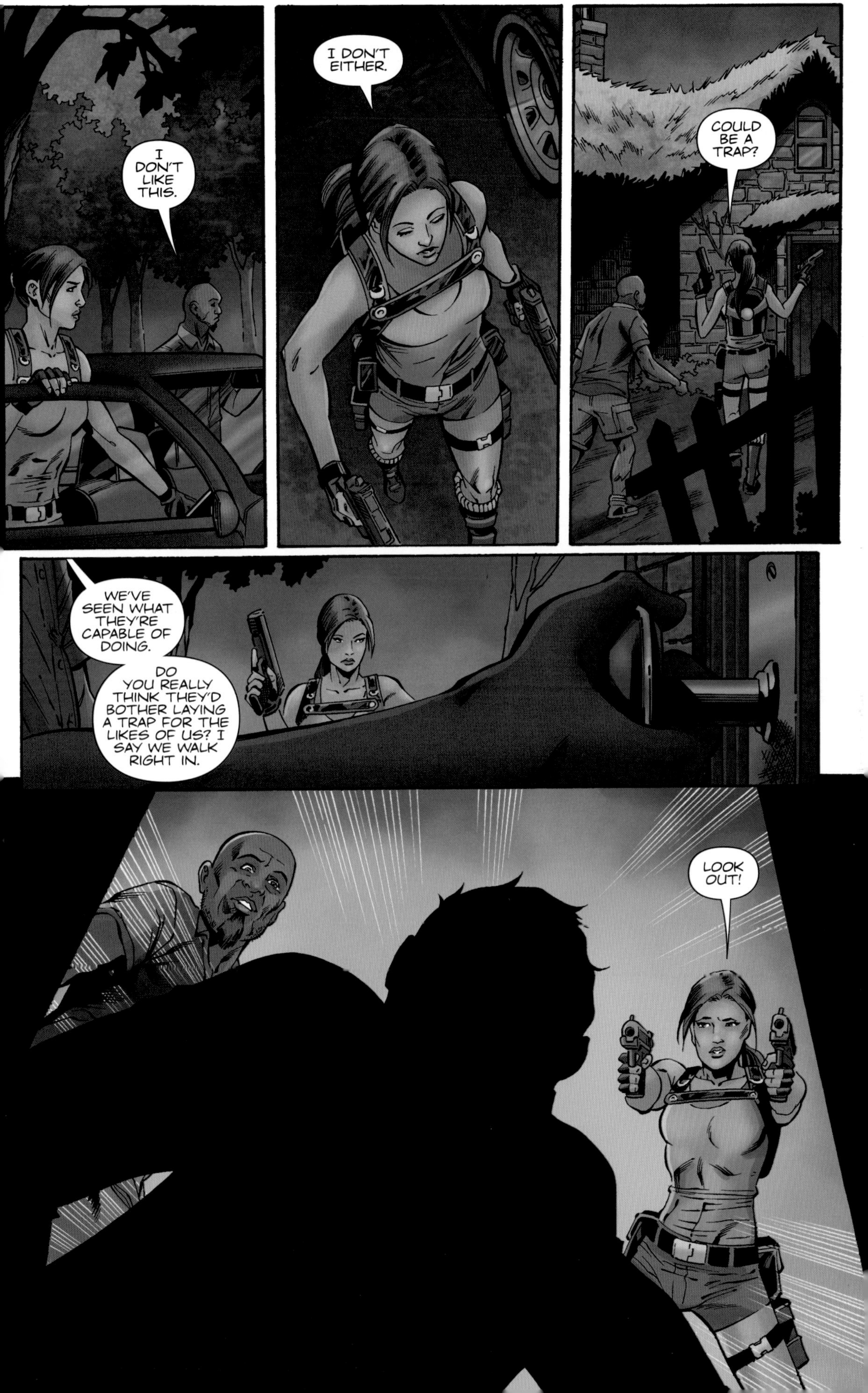
I DON'T LIKE THIS.
I DON'T EITHER.
COULD BE A TRAP?
WE'VE SEEN WHAT THEY'RE CAPABLE OF DOING.
DO YOU REALLY THINK THEY'D BOTHER LAYING A TRAP FOR THE LIKES OF US? I SAY WE WALK RIGHT IN.
LOOK OUT!

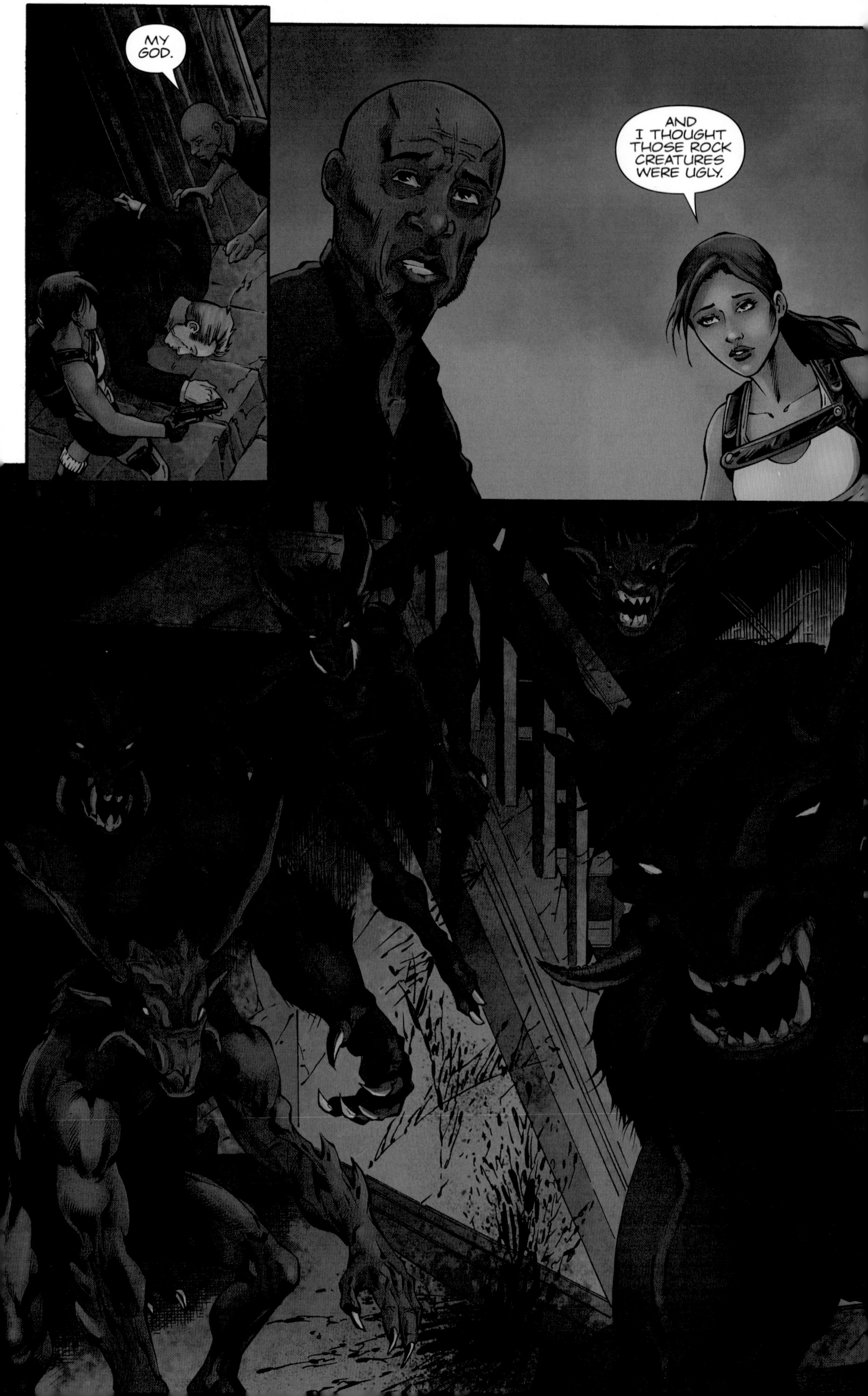
MY GOD.
AND I THOUGHT THOSE ROCK CREATURES WERE UGLY.

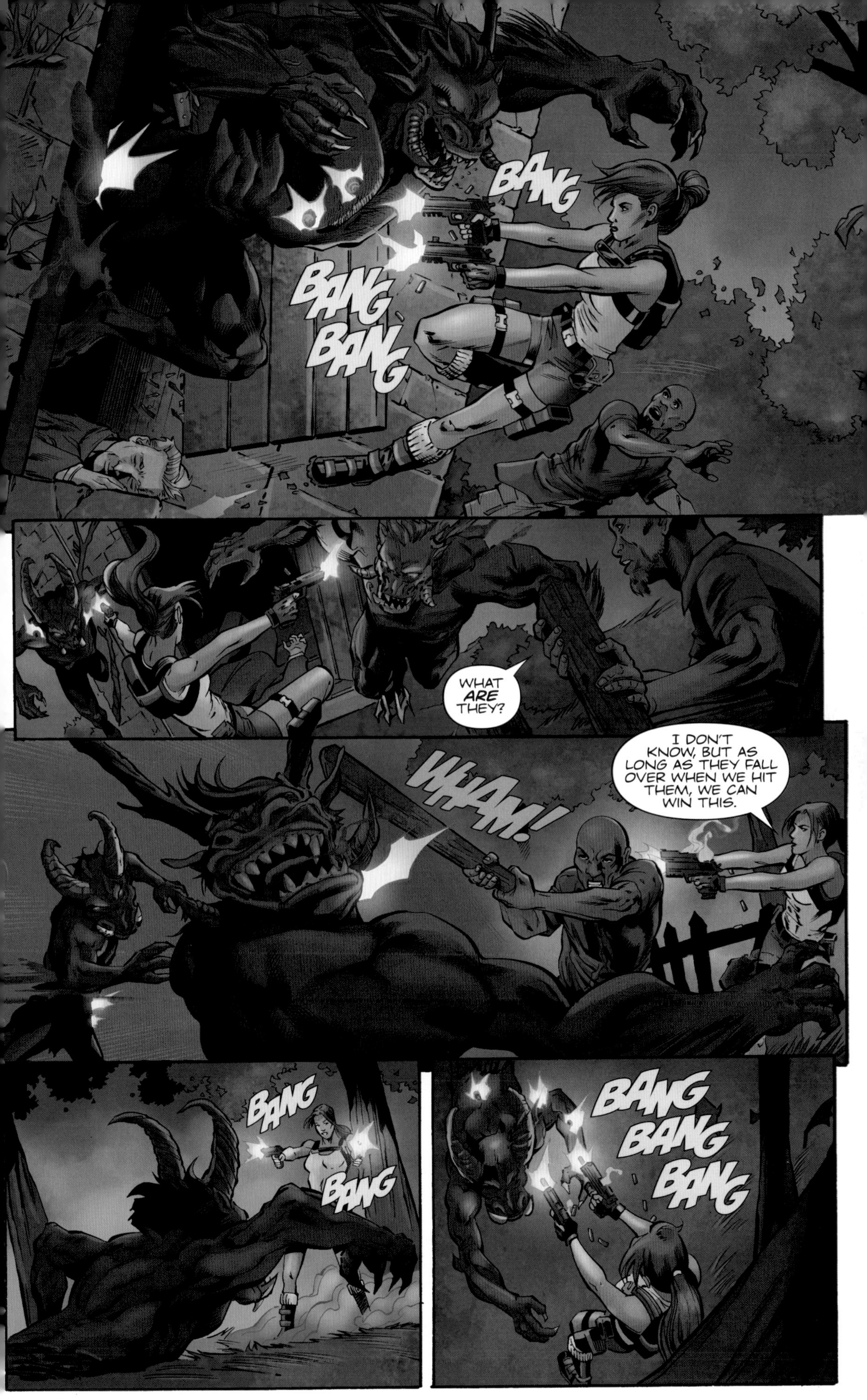
BANG
BANG BANG
BANG BANG
WHAT ARE THEY?
WHAM!
I DON'T KNOW, BUT AS LONG AS THEY FALL OVER WHEN WE HIT THEM, WE CAN WIN THIS.
BANG
BANG
BANG BANG BANG

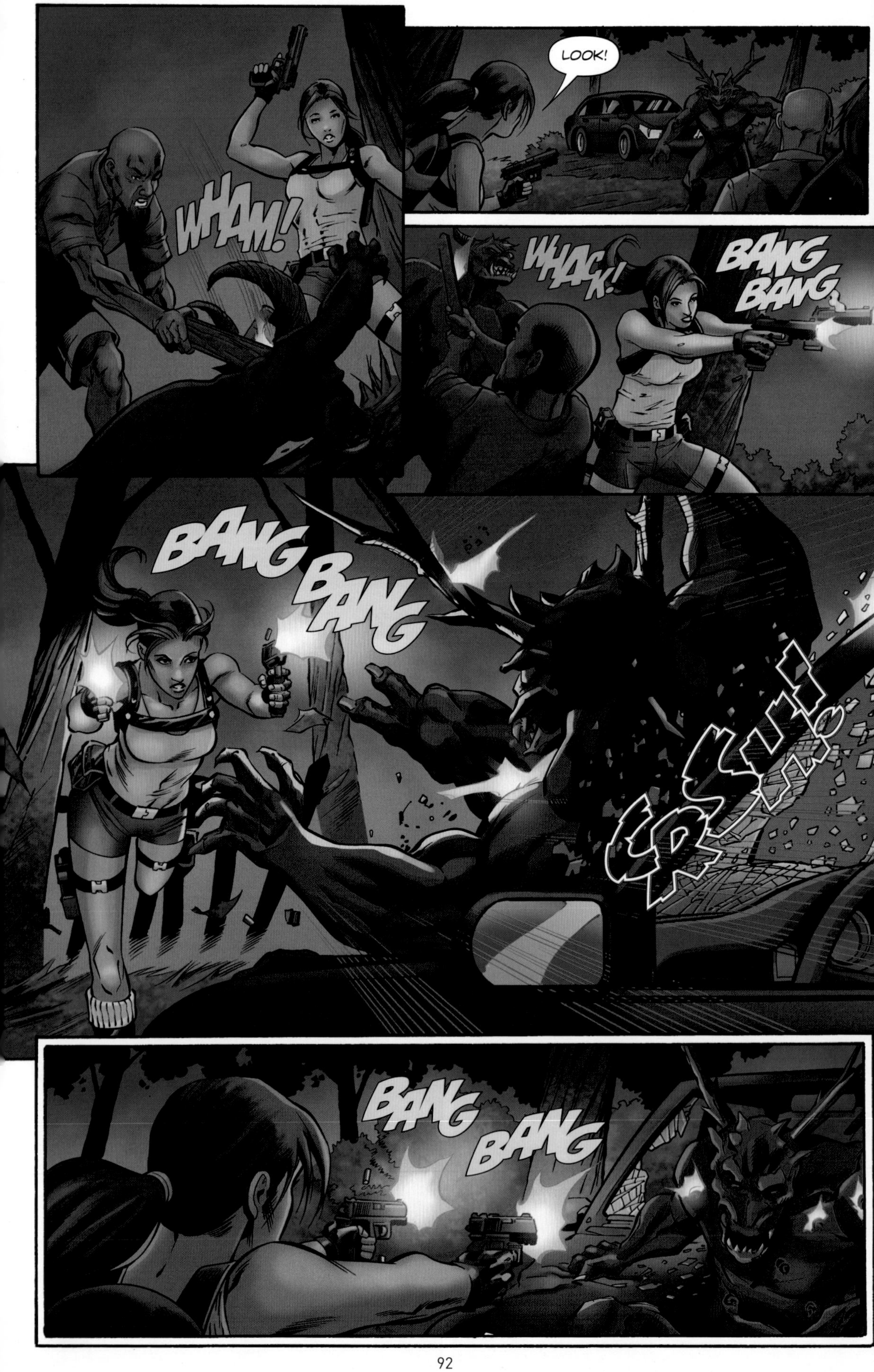
WHAM!
LOOK!
WHACK!
BANG BANG
BANG BANG
BANG BANG

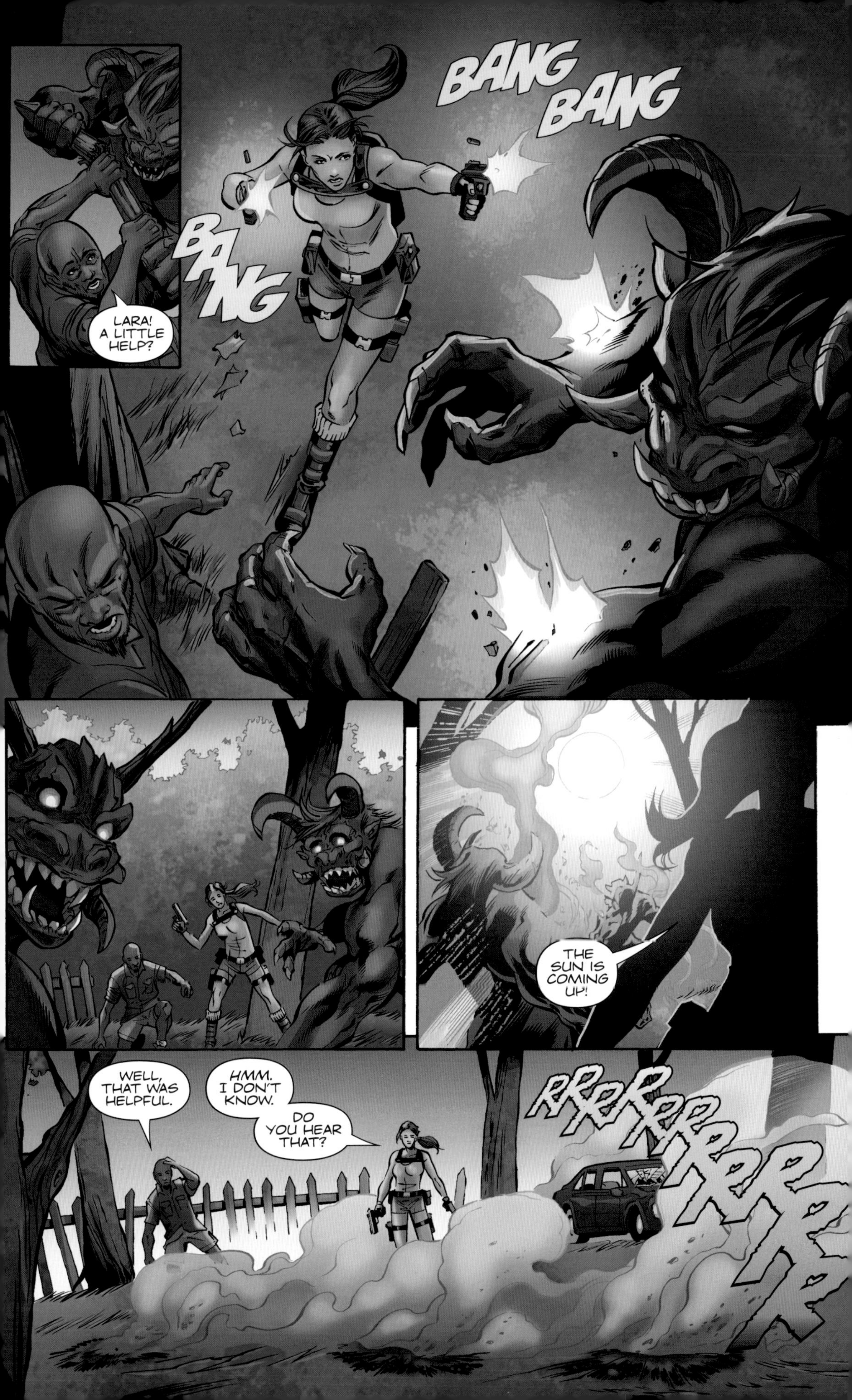
BANG
BANG
BANG
LARA! A LITTLE HELP?
BANG
THE SUN IS COMING UP!
WELL, THAT WAS HELPFUL.
HMM. I DON'T KNOW.
DO YOU HEAR THAT?
RRRRRRRRRRRRR

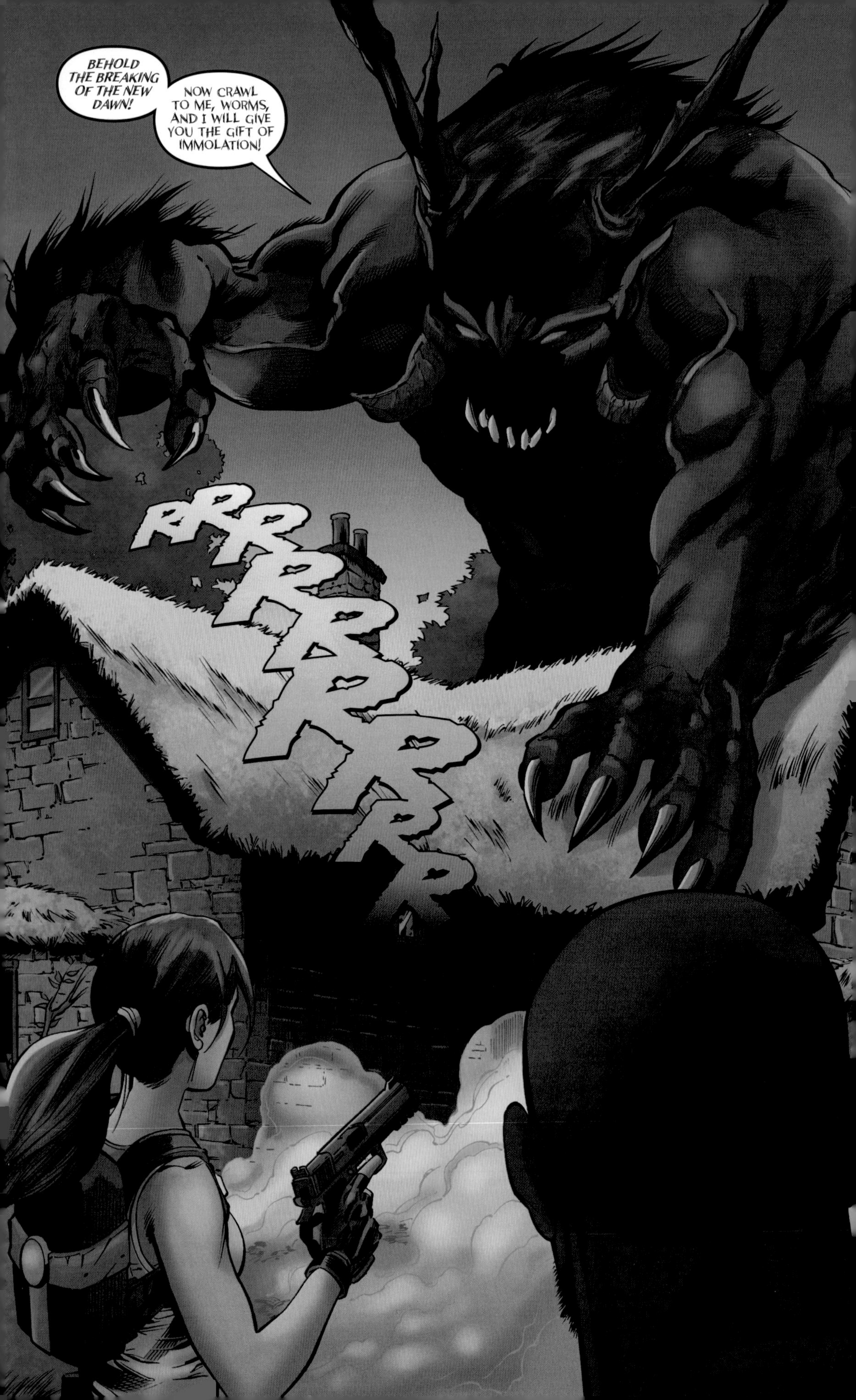
BEHOLD THE BREAKING OF THE NEW DAWN!
NOW CRAWL TO ME, WORMS, AND I WILL GIVE YOU THE GIFT OF IMMOLATION!
RRRRRRRR

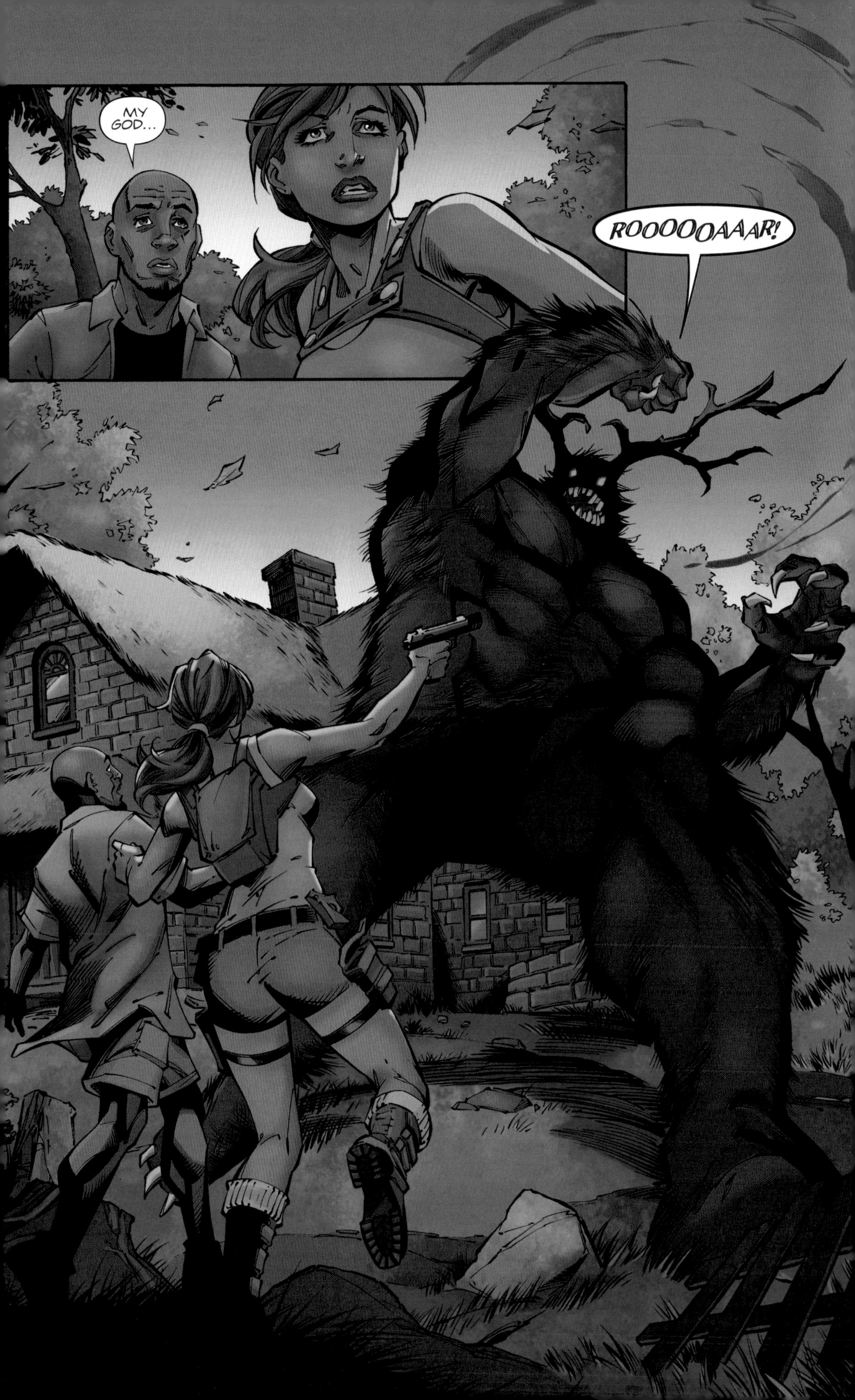
MY GOD...
ROOOOOAAAR!

CRRRKK

WATCH OUT!

WHOA!

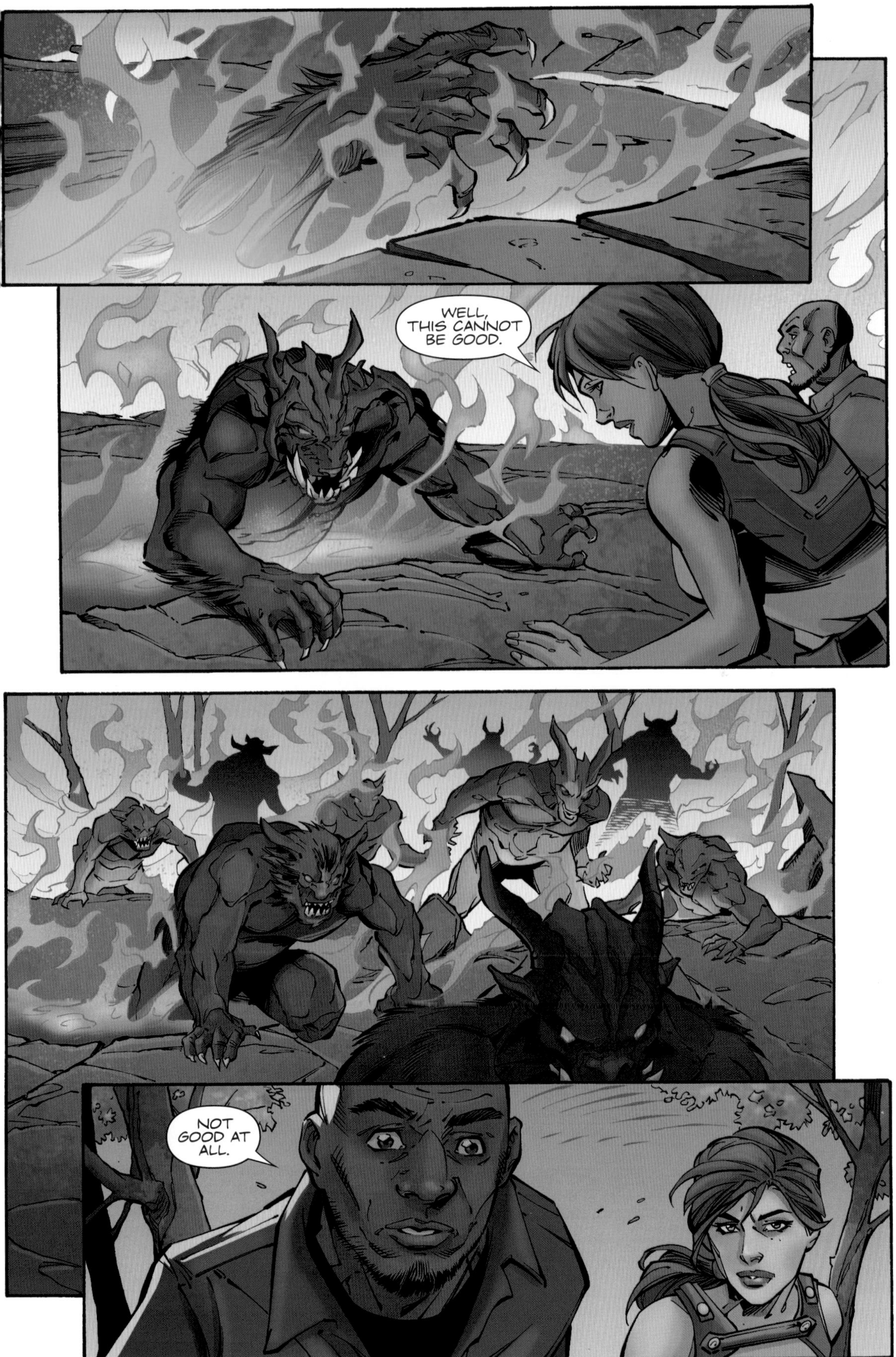
WELL, THIS CANNOT BE GOOD.
NOT GOOD AT ALL.

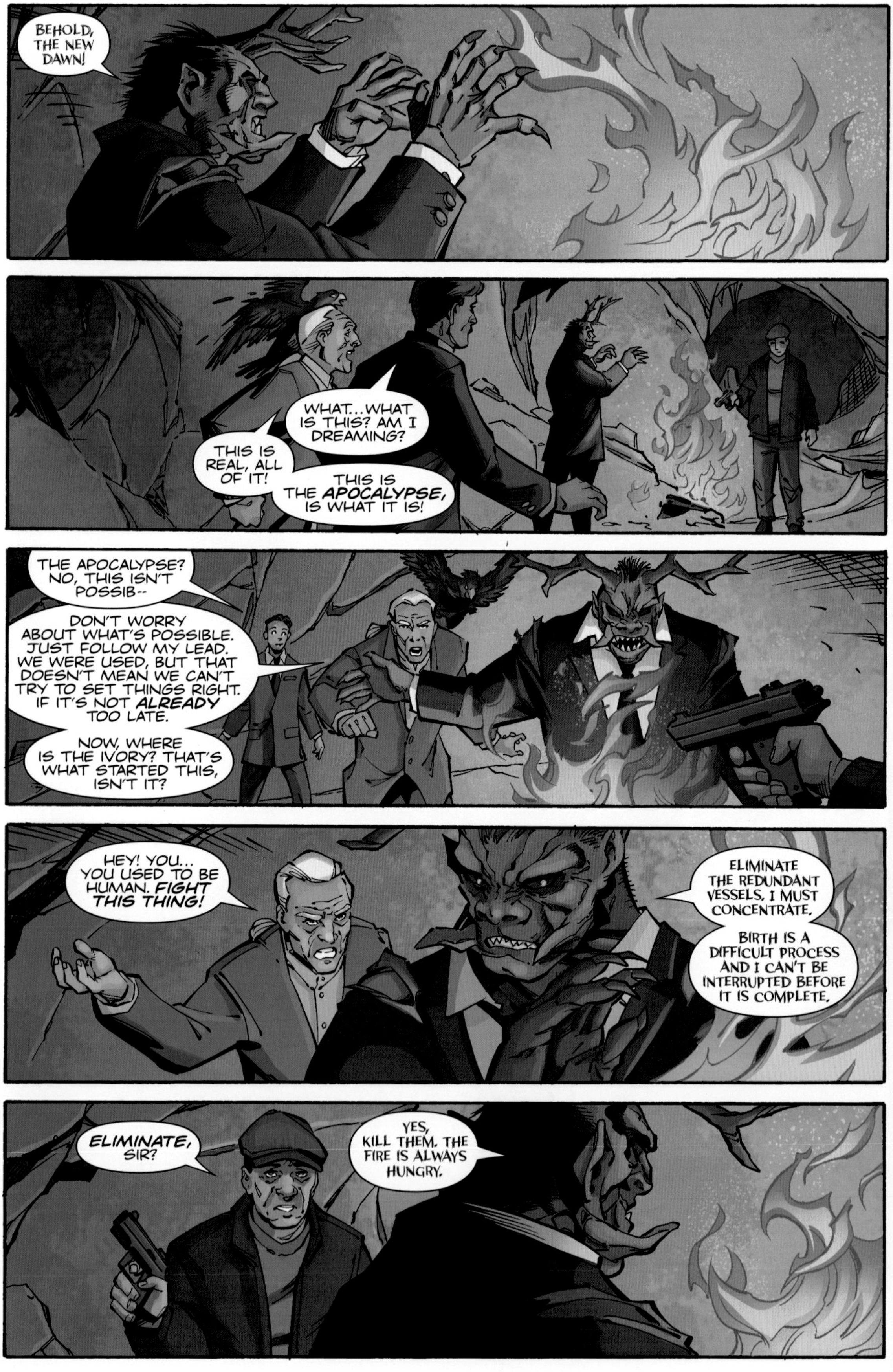
BEHOLD, THE NEW DAWN!
WHAT...WHAT IS THIS? AM I DREAMING?
THIS IS REAL, ALL OF IT!
THIS IS THE APOCALYPSE, IS WHAT IT IS!
THE APOCALYPSE? NO, THIS ISN'T POSSIB--
DON'T WORRY ABOUT WHAT'S POSSIBLE. JUST FOLLOW MY LEAD. WE WERE USED, BUT THAT DOESN'T MEAN WE CAN'T TRY TO SET THINGS RIGHT. IF IT'S NOT ALREADY TOO LATE.
NOW, WHERE IS THE IVORY? THAT'S WHAT STARTED THIS, ISN'T IT?
HEY! YOU... YOU USED TO BE HUMAN. FIGHT THIS THING!
ELIMINATE THE REDUNDANT VESSELS. I MUST CONCENTRATE.
BIRTH IS A DIFFICULT PROCESS AND I CAN'T BE INTERRUPTED BEFORE IT IS COMPLETE.
ELIMINATE, SIR?
YES, KILL THEM. THE FIRE IS ALWAYS HUNGRY.

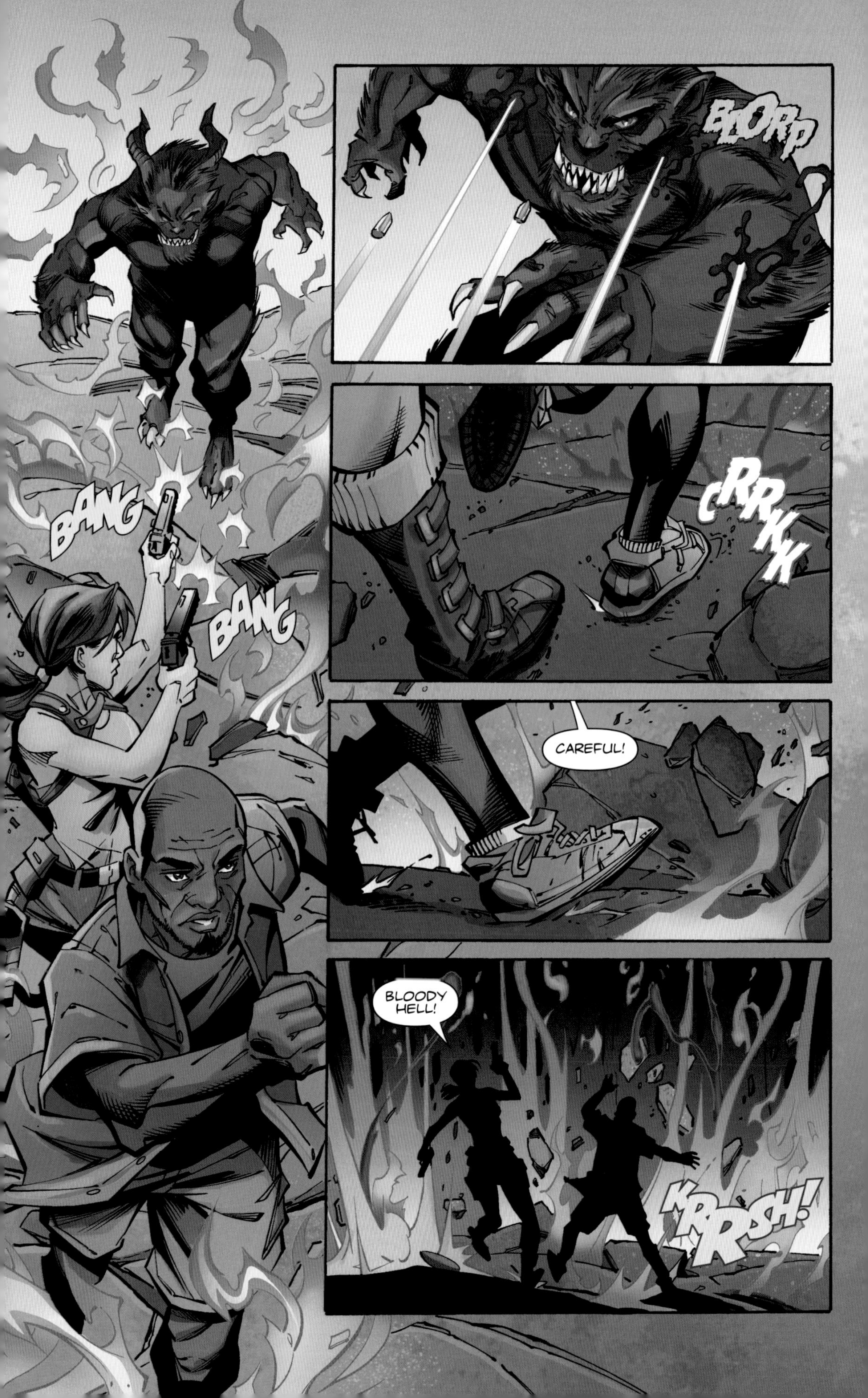
BANG
BANG
BLORP
CRRKK
CAREFUL!
BLOODY HELL!
KRRSH!

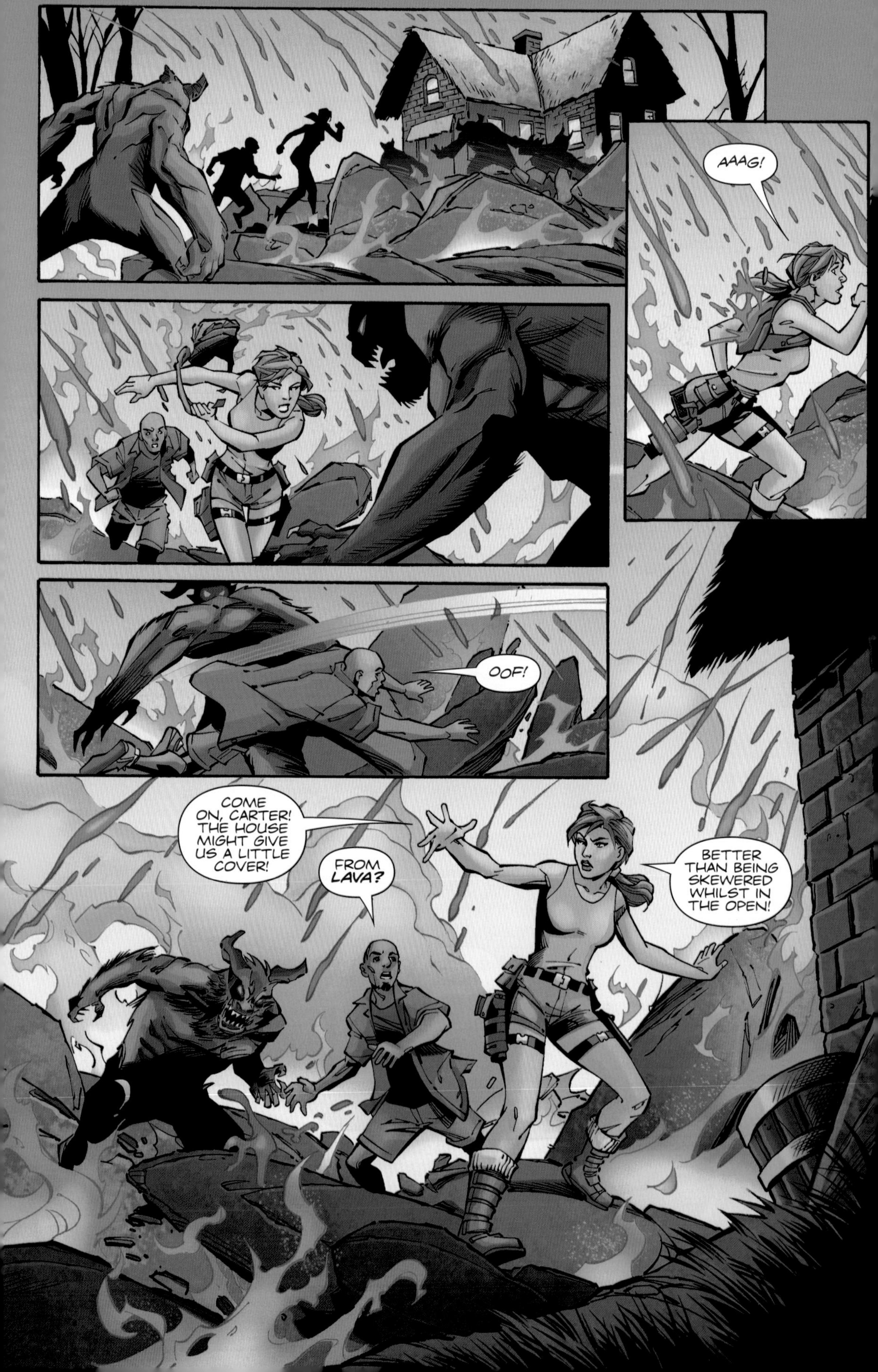
AAAG!
OOF!
COME ON, CARTER! THE HOUSE MIGHT GIVE US A LITTLE COVER!
FROM LAVA?
BETTER THAN BEING SKEWERED WHILST IN THE OPEN!

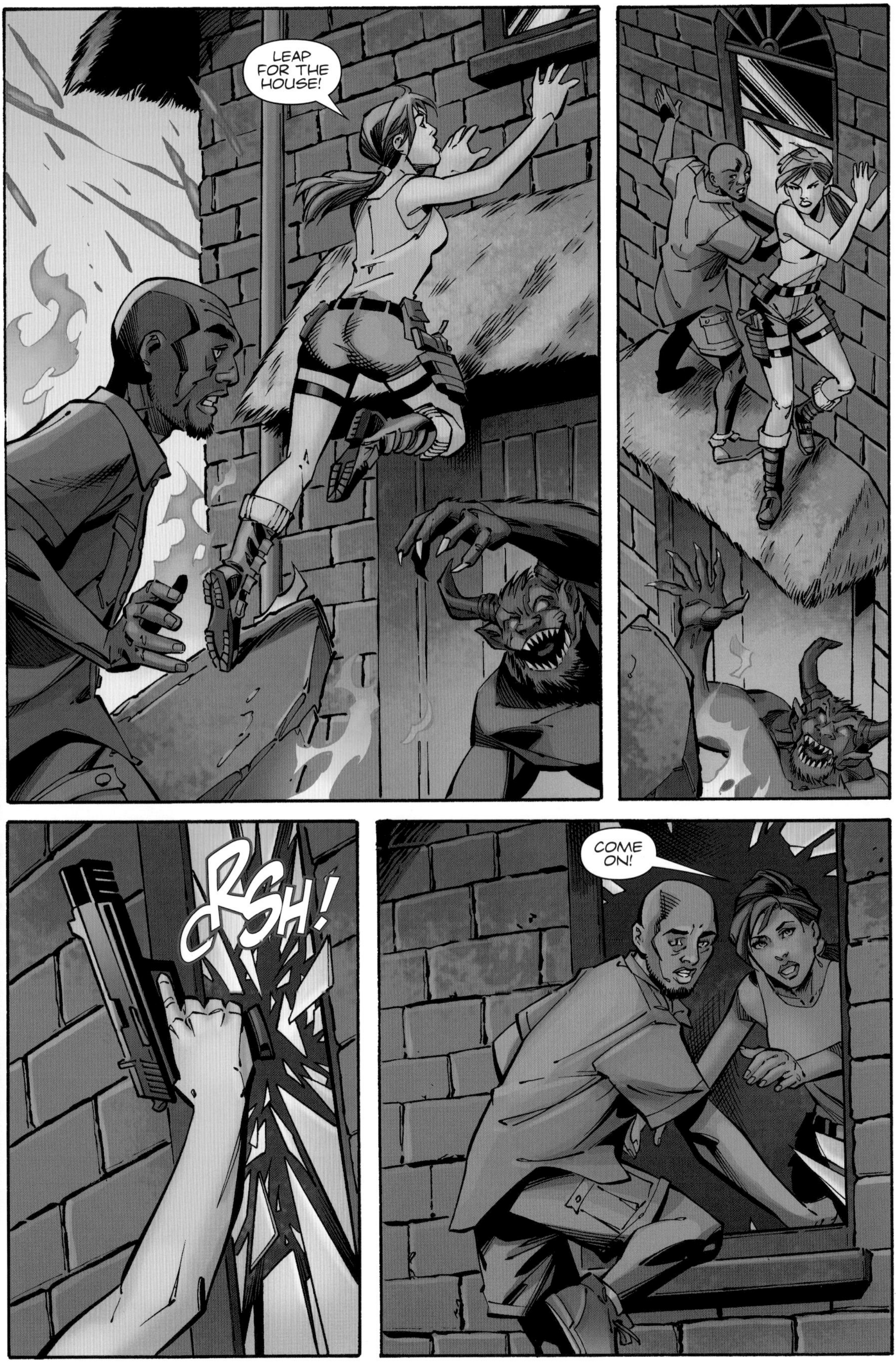
LEAP FOR THE HOUSE!
CRSH!
COME ON!

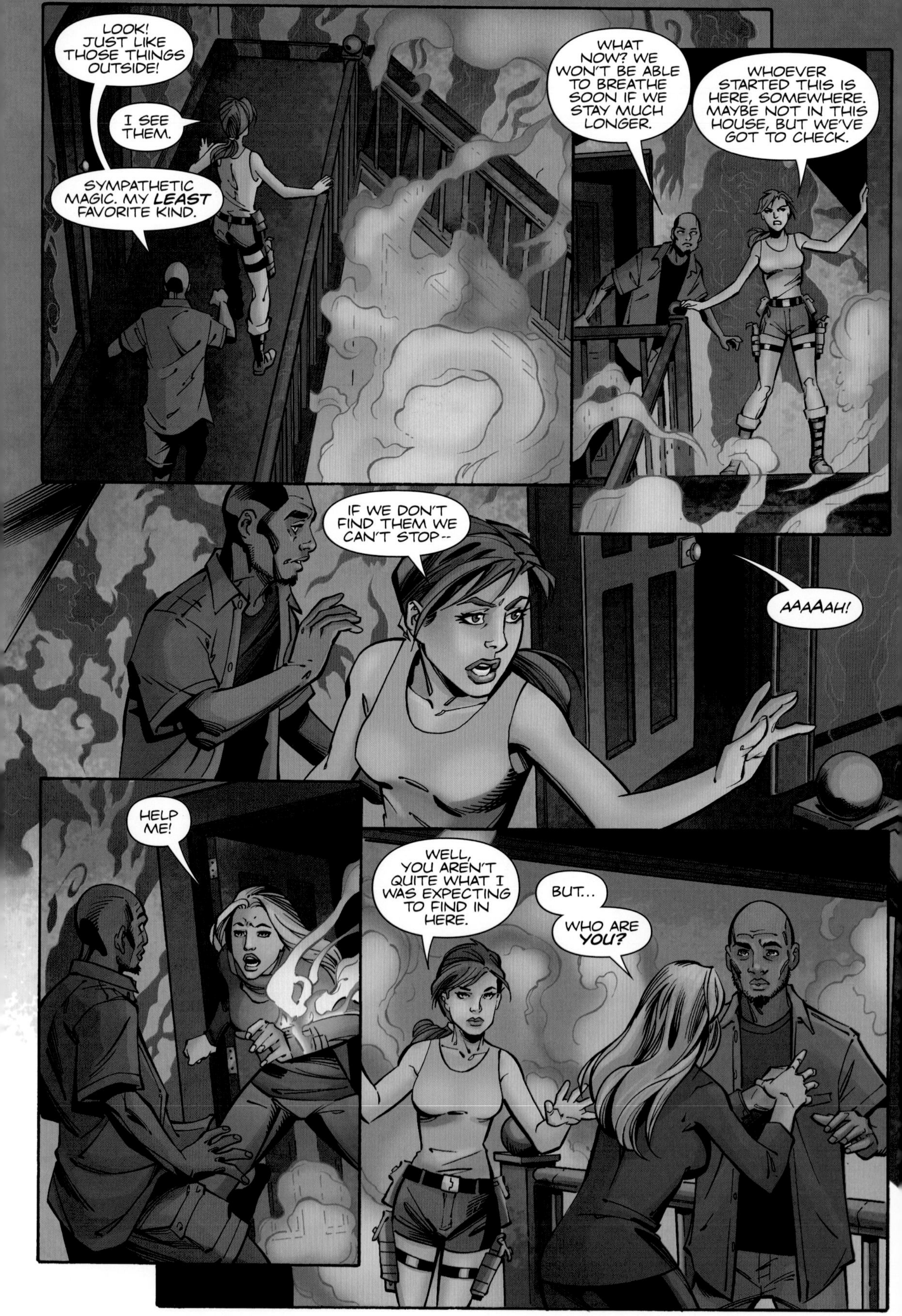
LOOK! JUST LIKE THOSE THINGS OUTSIDE!
I SEE THEM.
SYMPATHETIC MAGIC. MY **LEAST** FAVORITE KIND.
WHAT NOW? WE WON'T BE ABLE TO BREATHE SOON IF WE STAY MUCH LONGER.
WHOEVER STARTED THIS IS HERE, SOMEWHERE. MAYBE NOT IN THIS HOUSE, BUT WE'VE GOT TO CHECK.
IF WE DON'T FIND THEM WE CAN'T STOP--
AAAAAH!
HELP ME!
WELL, YOU AREN'T QUITE WHAT I WAS EXPECTING TO FIND IN HERE.
BUT...
WHO ARE ***YOU?***

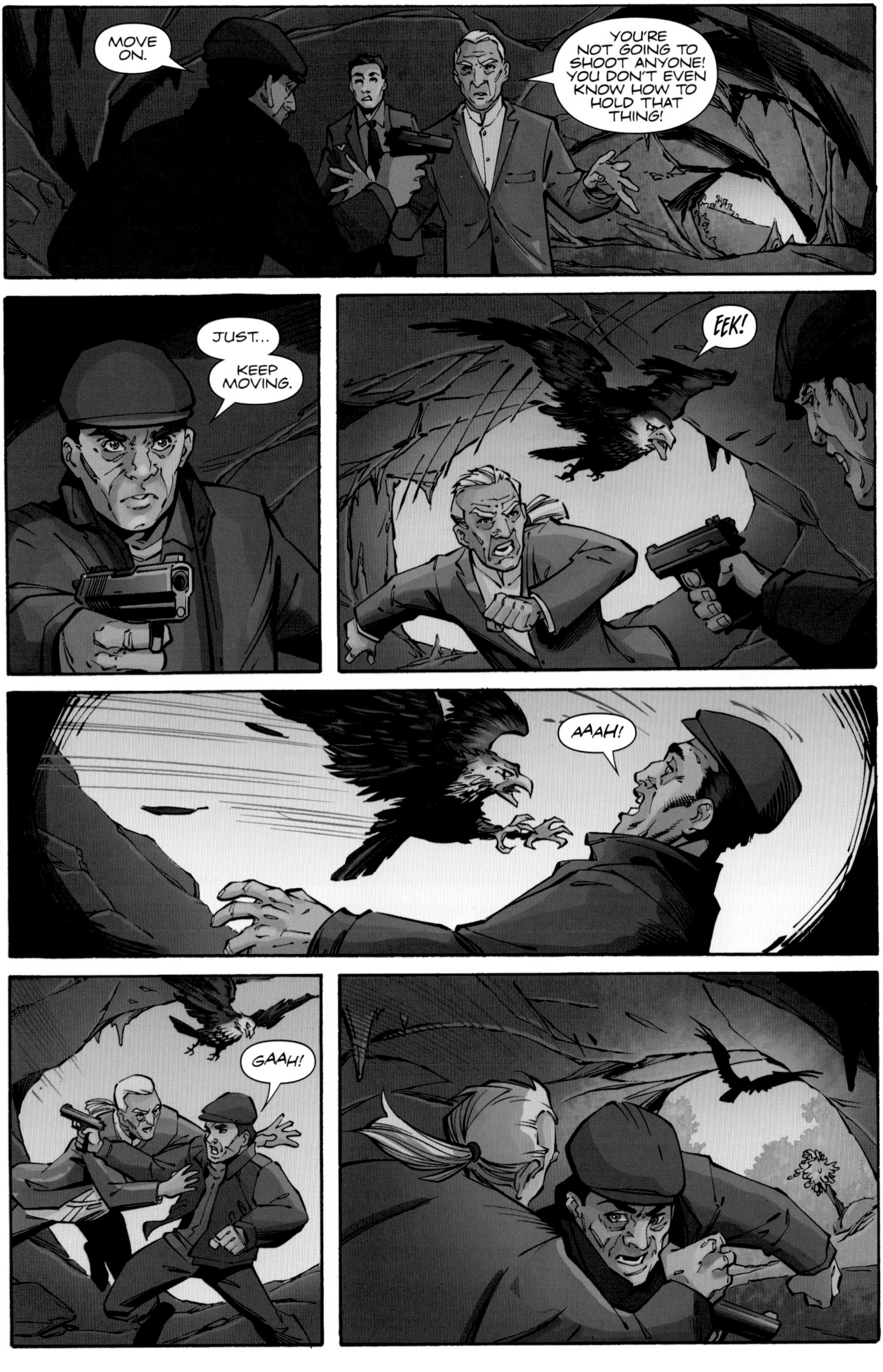
MOVE ON.
YOU'RE NOT GOING TO SHOOT ANYONE! YOU DON'T EVEN KNOW HOW TO HOLD THAT THING!
JUST...
KEEP MOVING.
EEK!
AAAH!
GAAH!

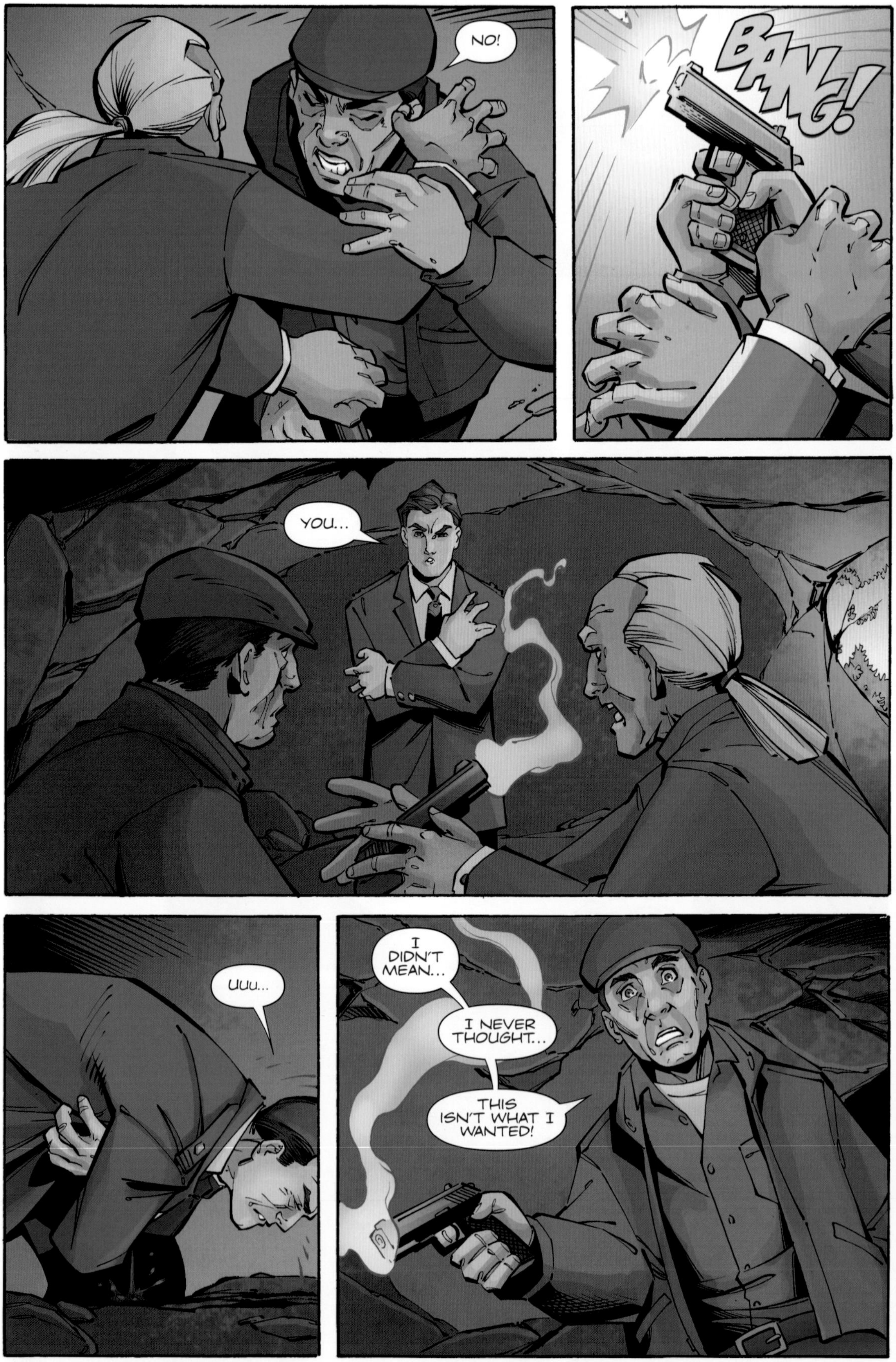
NO!
BANG!
YOU...
UUU...
I DIDN'T MEAN...
I NEVER THOUGHT...
THIS ISN'T WHAT I WANTED!

SO THIS ISN'T YOUR HOUSE?

NO! IT BELONGS TO MY EMPLOYER, MR. GREEN. WHAT IS GOING ON? IS ANY OF THIS REAL?

I'M ALMOST AFRAID TO ASK, BUT WHAT BUSINESS IS YOUR BOSS INVOLVED IN?

HE IS A POLITICIAN. WE WERE GEARING UP FOR A NATIONAL ELECTION WHEN HE...

THIS IS TOO MUCH. **PLEASE,** WHERE IS HE?

WE WERE HOPING YOU WOULD KNOW.

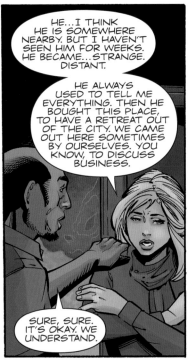

HE...I THINK HE IS SOMEWHERE NEARBY. BUT I HAVEN'T SEEN HIM FOR WEEKS. HE BECAME...STRANGE. DISTANT.

HE ALWAYS USED TO TELL ME EVERYTHING. THEN HE BOUGHT THIS PLACE, TO HAVE A RETREAT OUT OF THE CITY. WE CAME OUT HERE SOMETIMES BY OURSELVES. YOU KNOW, TO DISCUSS BUSINESS.

SURE, SURE. IT'S OKAY. WE UNDERSTAND.

THE LAST TIME ANDRO CALLED ME, HE SAID HE HAD DISCOVERED A CAVE HIDDEN BEHIND THE HOUSE. HE THOUGHT IT WAS A MAJOR FIND, SAID IT HAD ANCIENT PAINTINGS ON THE WALLS INSIDE.

HE WAS SO EXCITED. COULD NOT WAIT TO EXPLORE IT MORE. I SAID I SHOULD COME OUT AND LOOK WITH HIM... HE SAID HE WOULD CALL ME RIGHT BACK.

BUT HE NEVER DID. I CAME OUT HERE AND LOOKED AROUND, BUT HE WAS NEVER HOME. I EVEN RAN INTO HIS CREEPY DRIVER ONE TIME. DO YOU THINK HE WAS...MURDERED?

WHY DON'T WE DISCUSS THIS OUTSIDE?

WAIT, I MUST GET THE THUMB DRIVE! AND THE FILES. THERE ARE MANY THINGS HERE THAT... WELL, THAT HIS WIFE IN THE CITY WOULD NOT UNDERSTAND.

CHLOE, LISTEN TO ME. IF IT'S THE DESTRUCTION OF EVIDENCE THAT YOU'RE WORRIED ABOUT...

I THINK WE'VE GOT THAT COVERED.

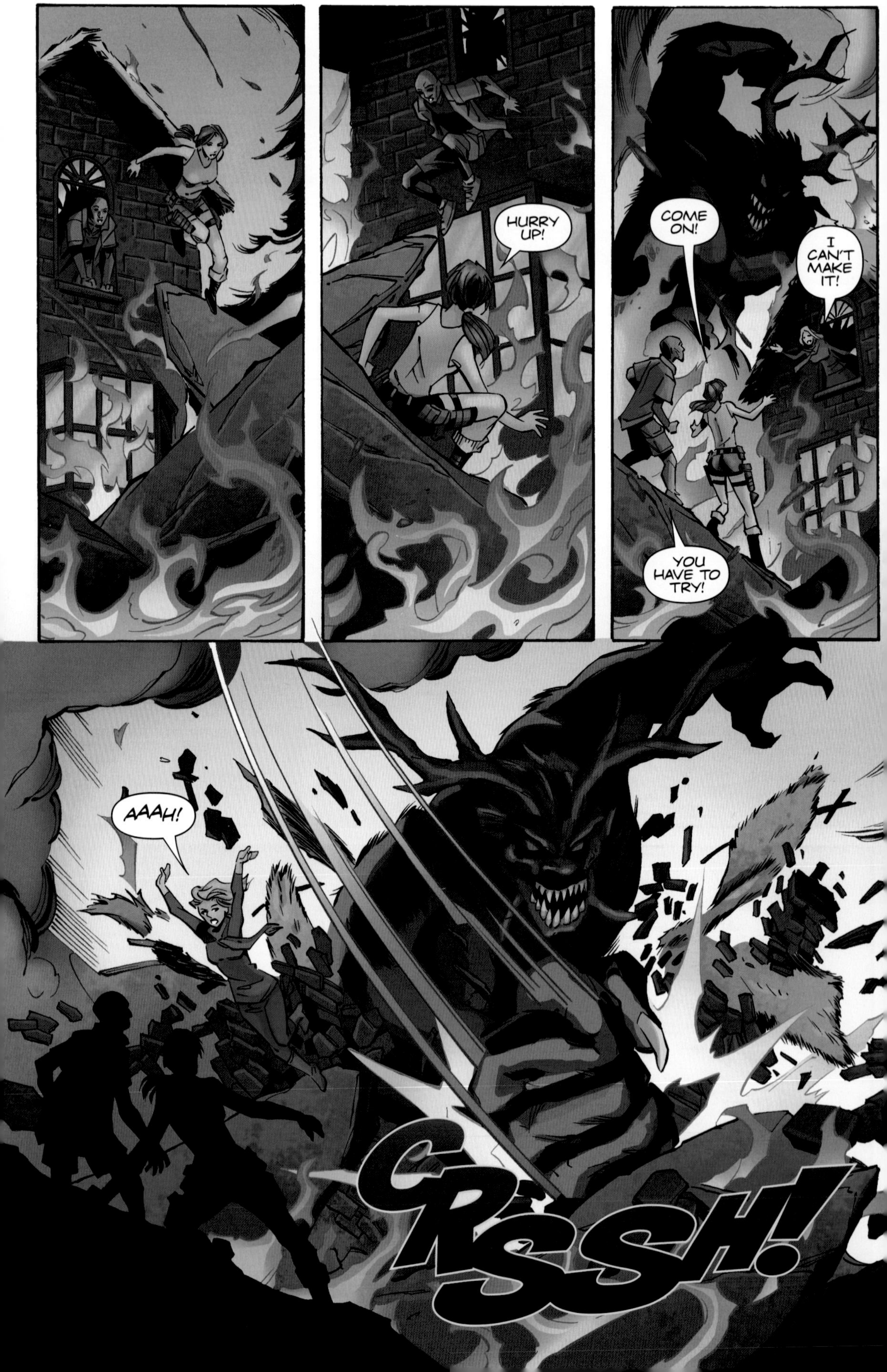
HURRY UP!
COME ON!
I CAN'T MAKE IT!
YOU HAVE TO TRY!
AAAH!
CRSSH!

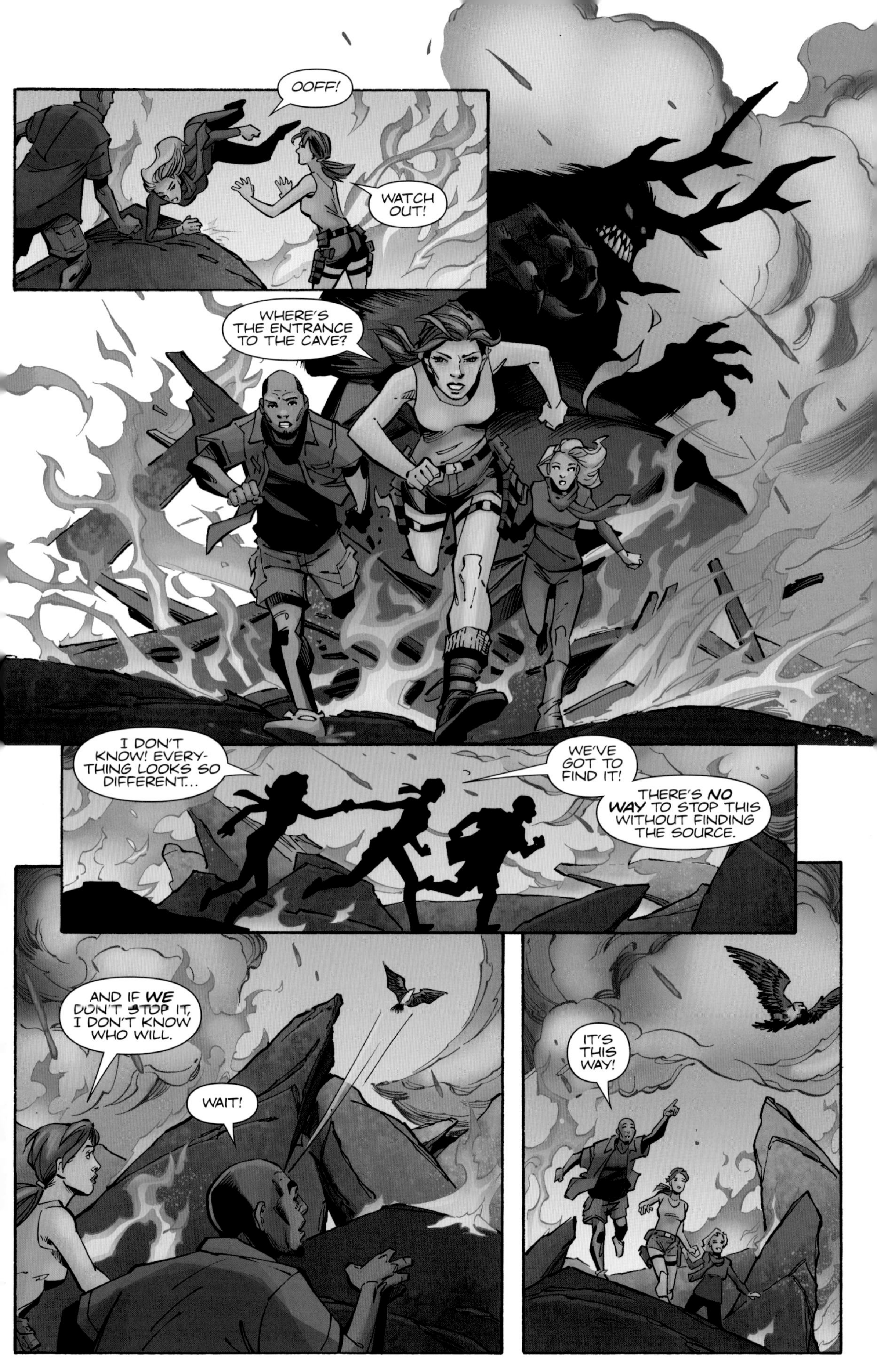
OOFF!
WATCH OUT!
WHERE'S THE ENTRANCE TO THE CAVE?
I DON'T KNOW! EVERY-THING LOOKS SO DIFFERENT...
WE'VE GOT TO FIND IT!
THERE'S **NO WAY** TO STOP THIS WITHOUT FINDING THE SOURCE.
AND IF **WE** DON'T STOP IT, I DON'T KNOW WHO WILL.
WAIT!
IT'S THIS WAY!

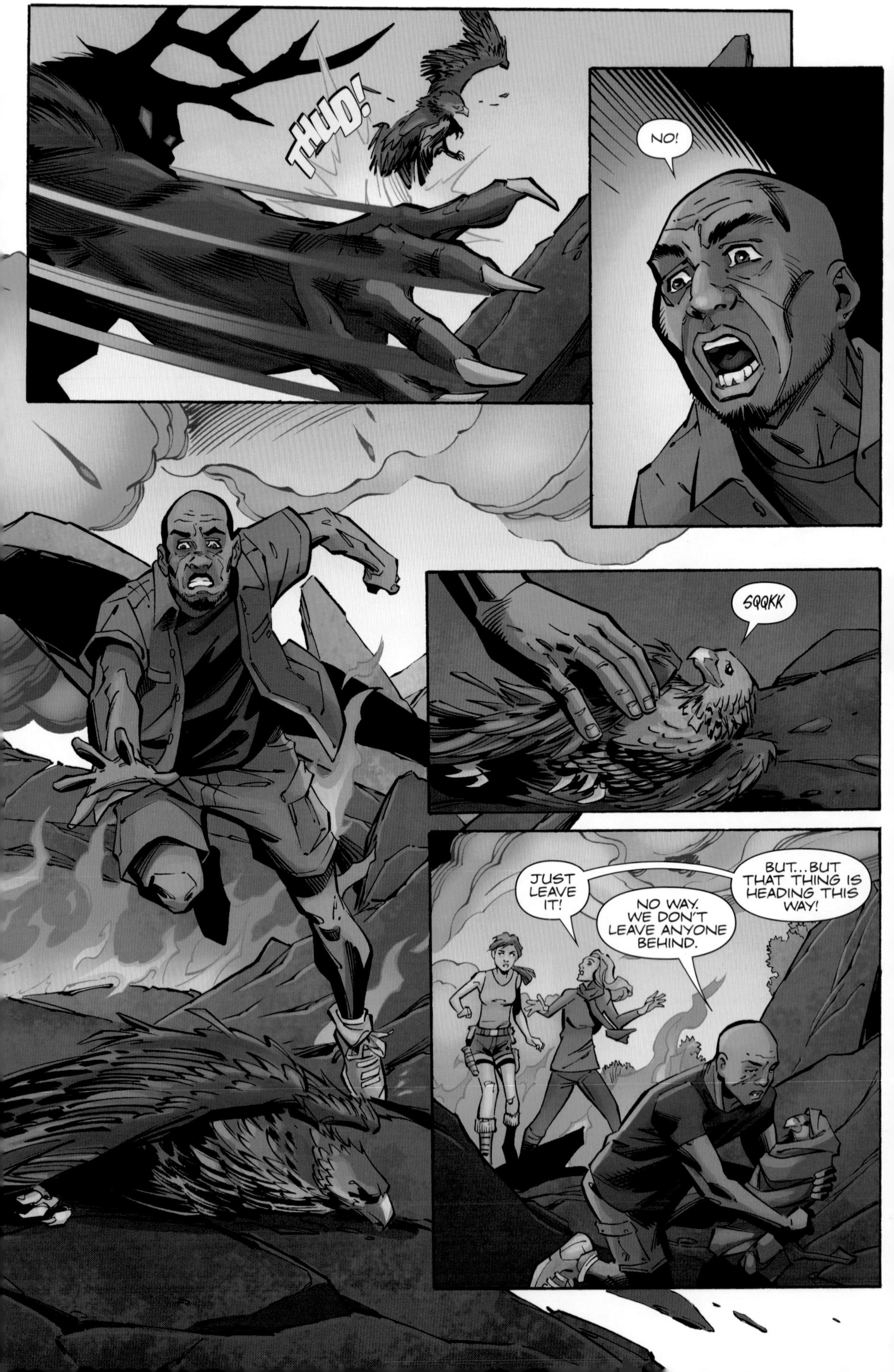
THUD!
NO!
SQQKK
JUST LEAVE IT!
BUT...BUT THAT THING IS HEADING THIS WAY!
NO WAY. WE DON'T LEAVE ANYONE BEHIND.

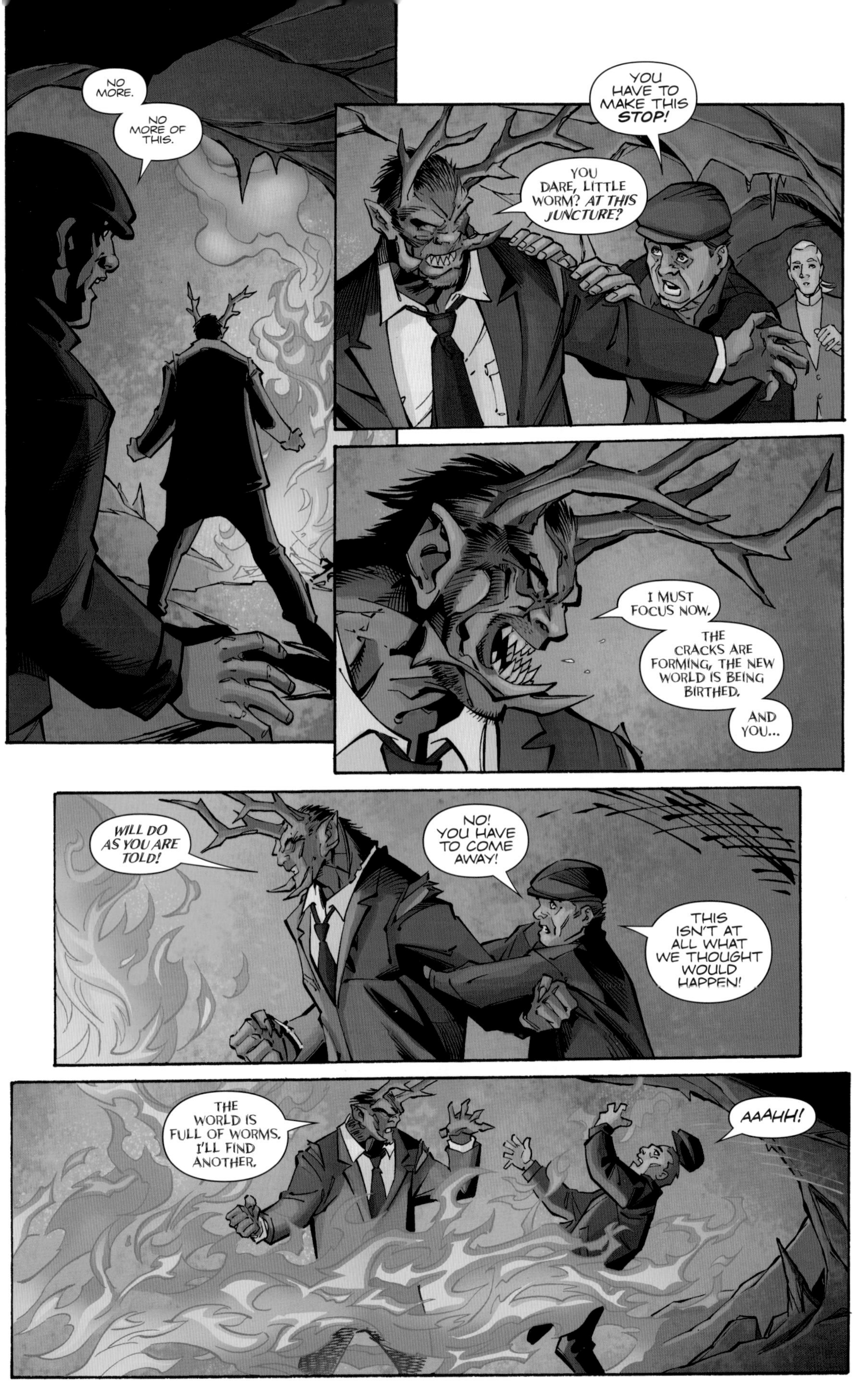
NO MORE.
NO MORE OF THIS.
YOU HAVE TO MAKE THIS STOP!
YOU DARE, LITTLE WORM? AT THIS JUNCTURE?
I MUST FOCUS NOW.
THE CRACKS ARE FORMING, THE NEW WORLD IS BEING BIRTHED.
AND YOU...
WILL DO AS YOU ARE TOLD!
NO! YOU HAVE TO COME AWAY!
THIS ISN'T AT ALL WHAT WE THOUGHT WOULD HAPPEN!
THE WORLD IS FULL OF WORMS. I'LL FIND ANOTHER.
AAAHH!

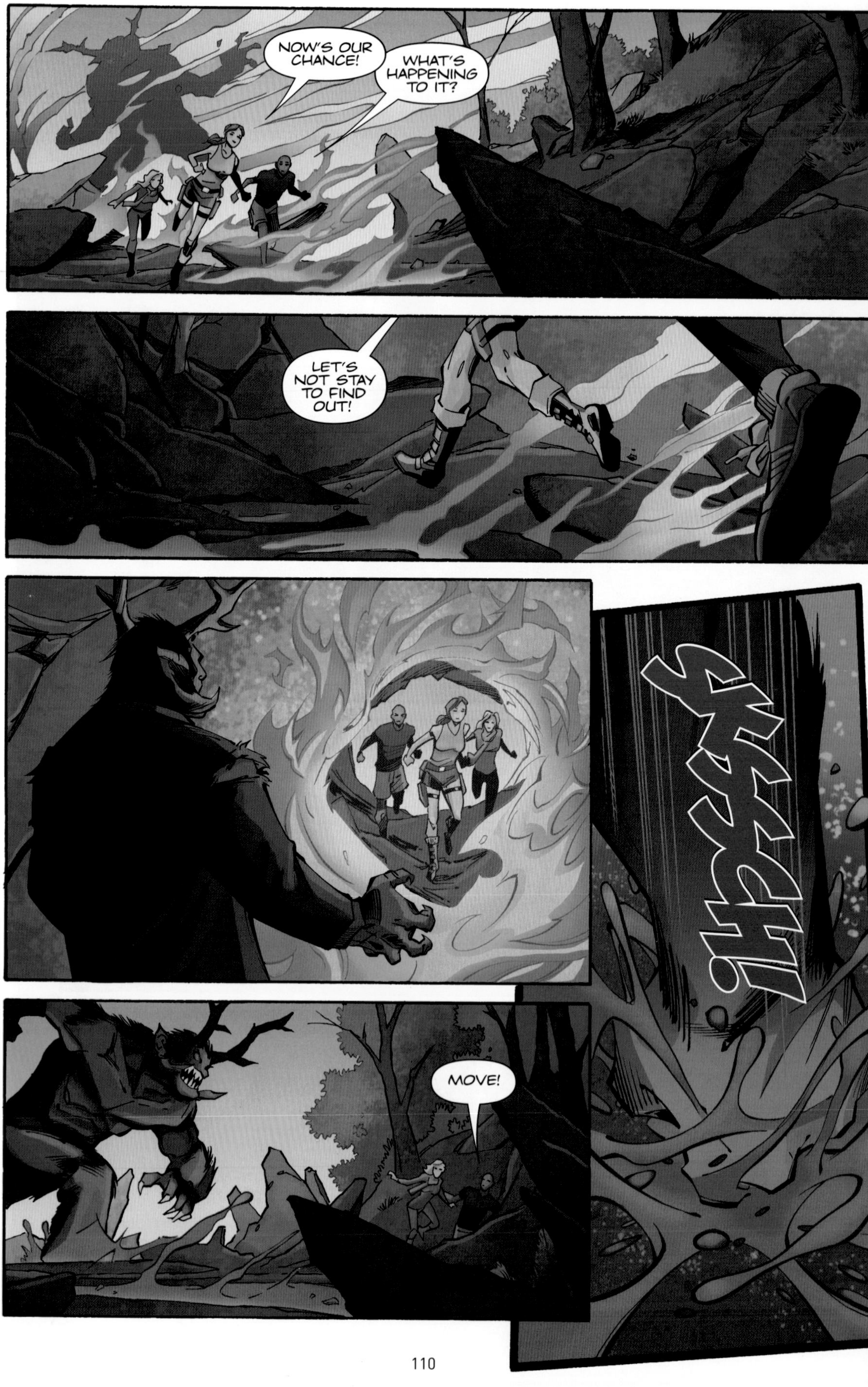
NOW'S OUR CHANCE!
WHAT'S HAPPENING TO IT?
LET'S NOT STAY TO FIND OUT!
MOVE!

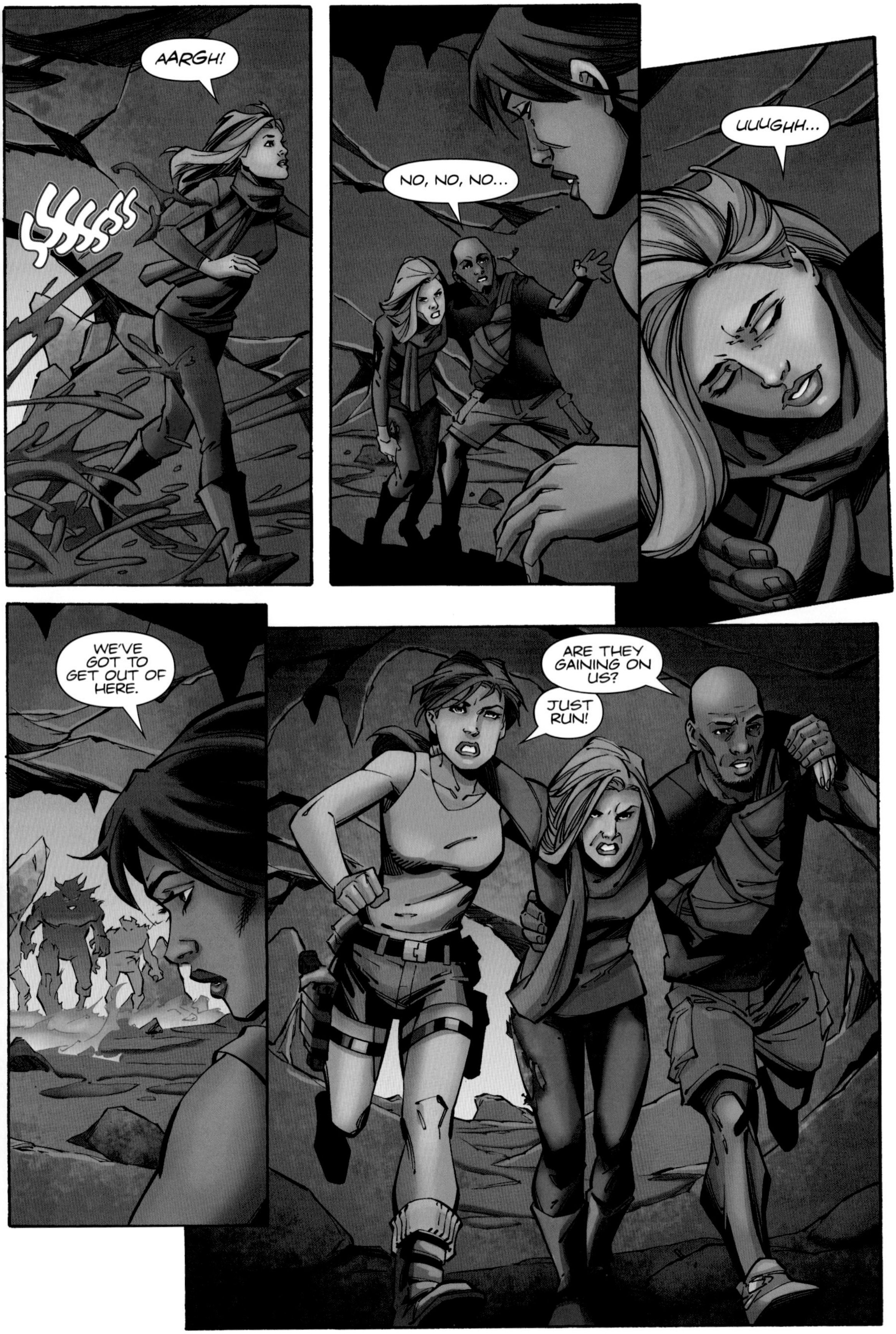
AARGH!
SSSSSS
NO, NO, NO...
UUUGHH...
WE'VE GOT TO GET OUT OF HERE.
ARE THEY GAINING ON US?
JUST RUN!

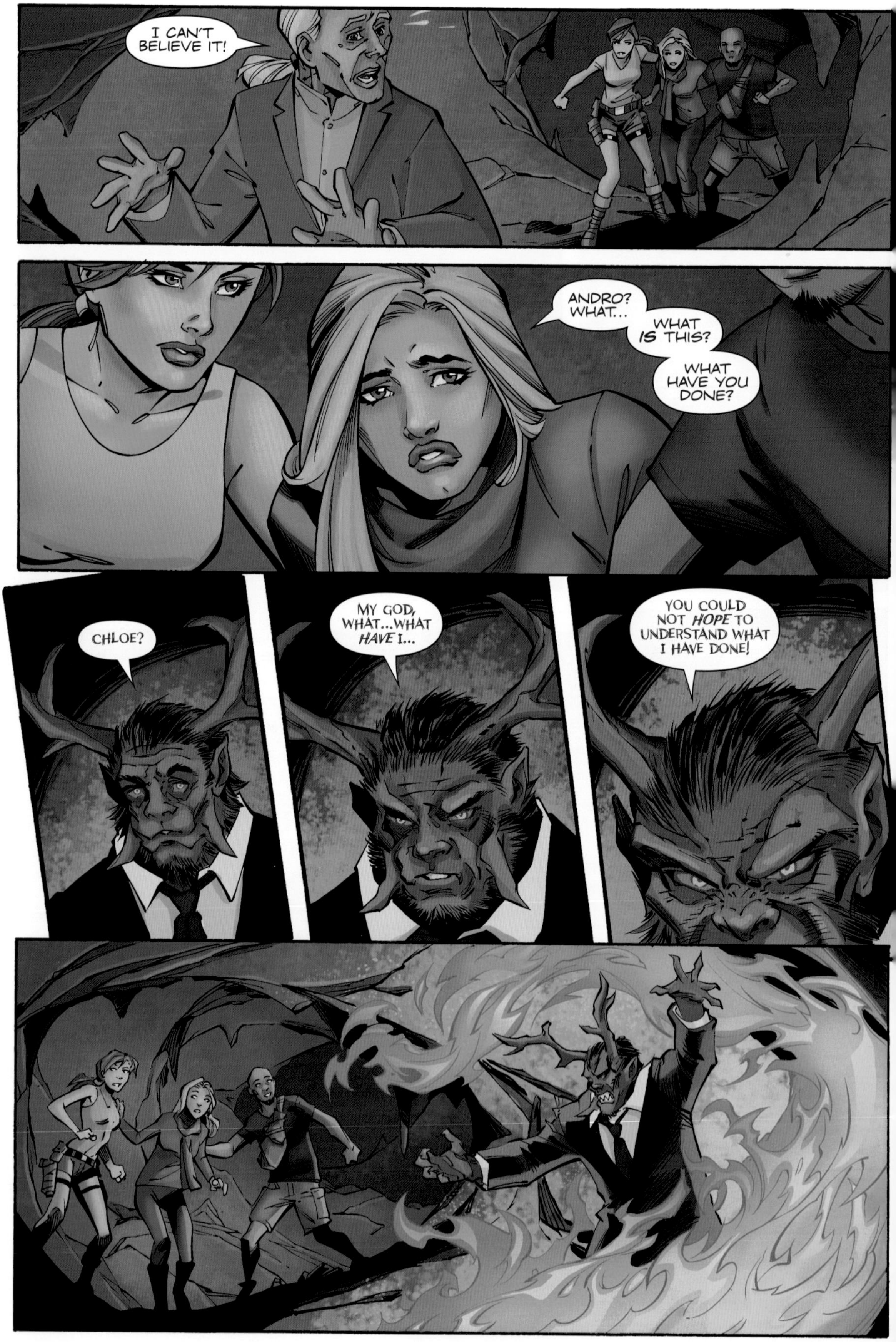
I CAN'T BELIEVE IT!
ANDRO? WHAT...
WHAT *IS* THIS?
WHAT HAVE YOU DONE?
CHLOE?
MY GOD, WHAT...WHAT *HAVE* I...
YOU COULD NOT *HOPE* TO UNDERSTAND WHAT I HAVE DONE!

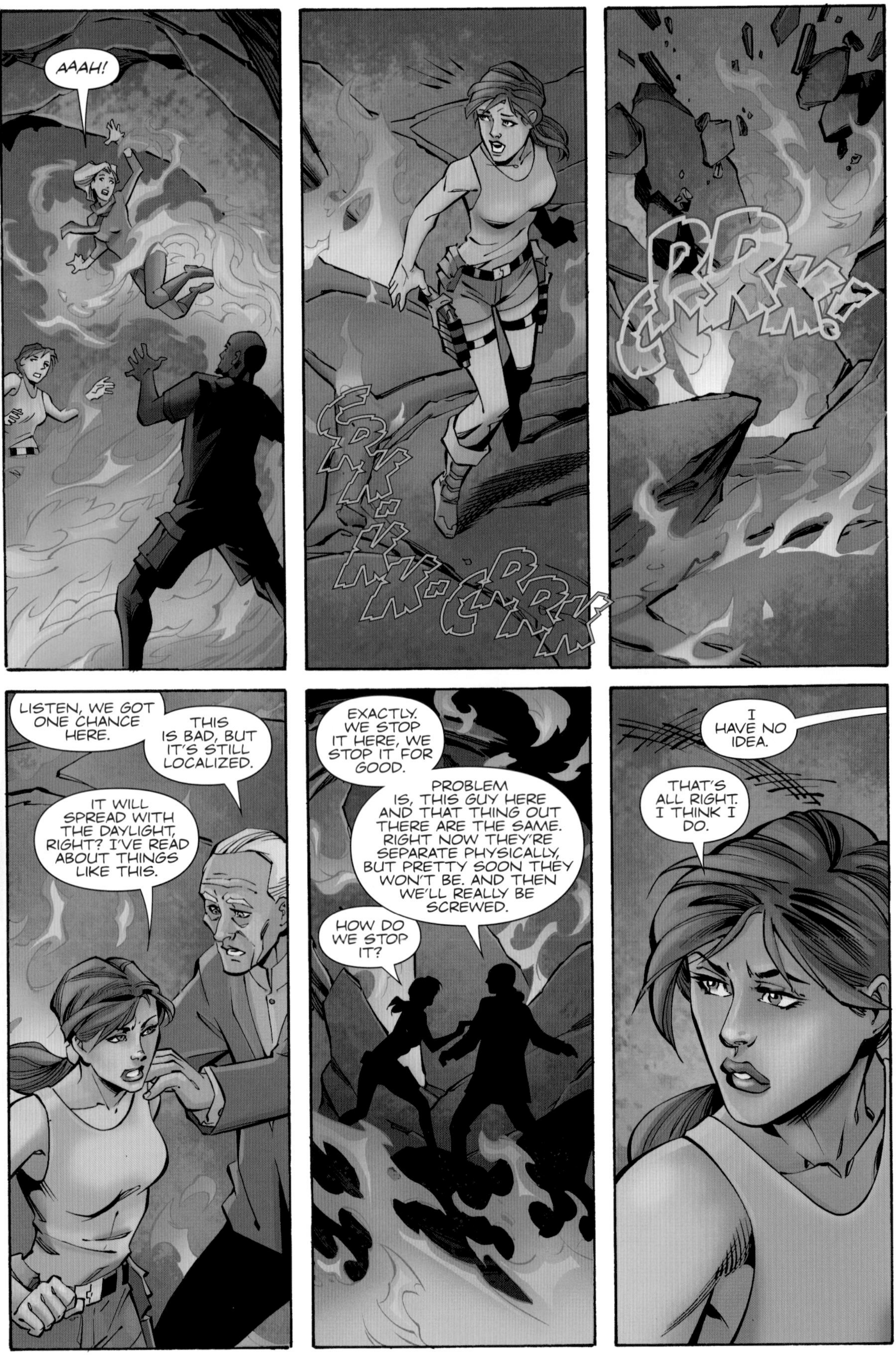
AAAH!
LISTEN, WE GOT ONE CHANCE HERE.
THIS IS BAD, BUT IT'S STILL LOCALIZED.
IT WILL SPREAD WITH THE DAYLIGHT, RIGHT? I'VE READ ABOUT THINGS LIKE THIS.
EXACTLY. WE STOP IT HERE, WE STOP IT FOR GOOD.
PROBLEM IS, THIS GUY HERE AND THAT THING OUT THERE ARE THE SAME. RIGHT NOW THEY'RE SEPARATE PHYSICALLY, BUT PRETTY SOON THEY WON'T BE. AND THEN WE'LL REALLY BE SCREWED.
HOW DO WE STOP IT?
I HAVE NO IDEA.
THAT'S ALL RIGHT. I THINK I DO.

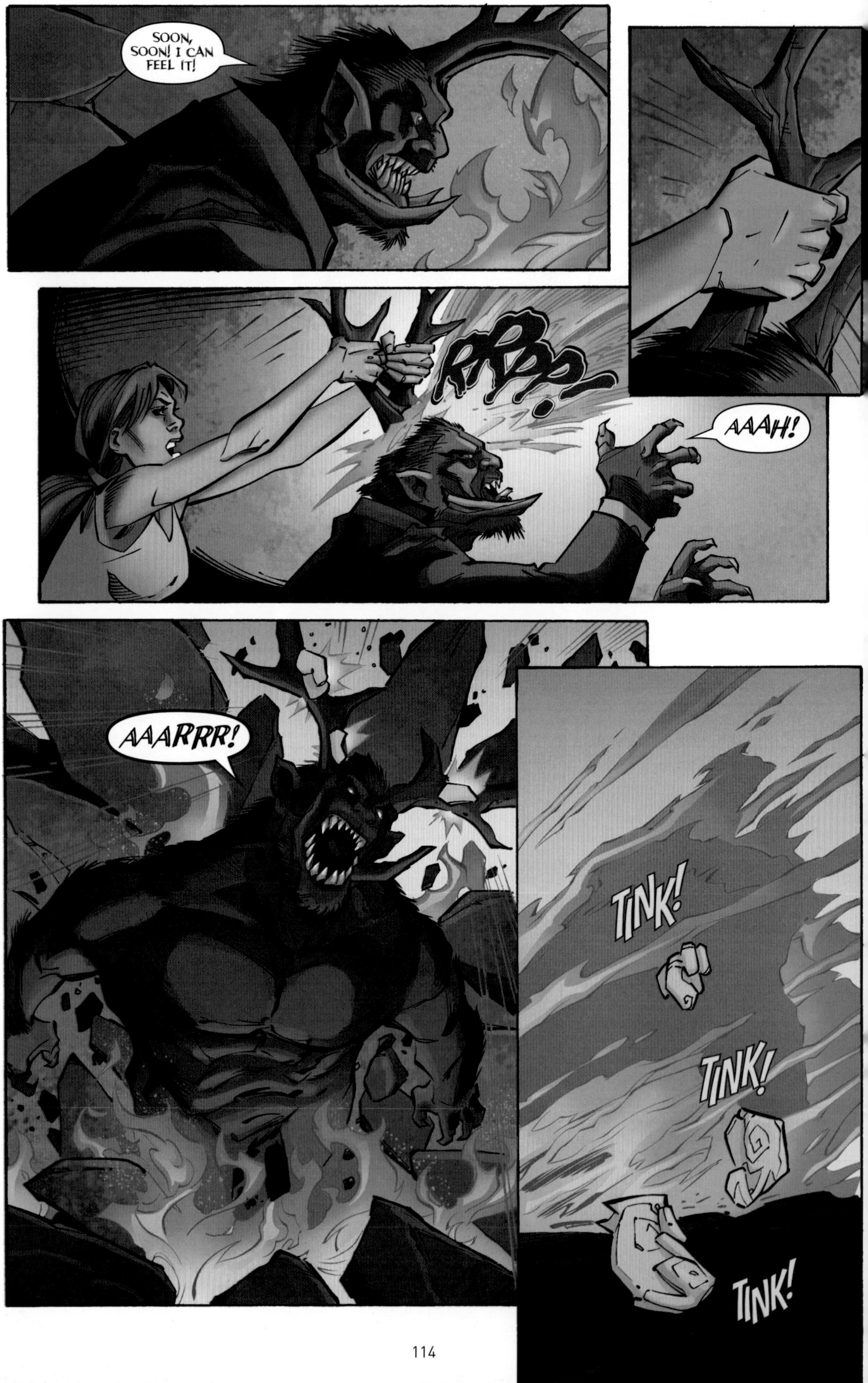
SOON, SOON! I CAN FEEL IT!
RPPP!
AAAH!
AAARRR!
TINK!
TINK!
TINK!

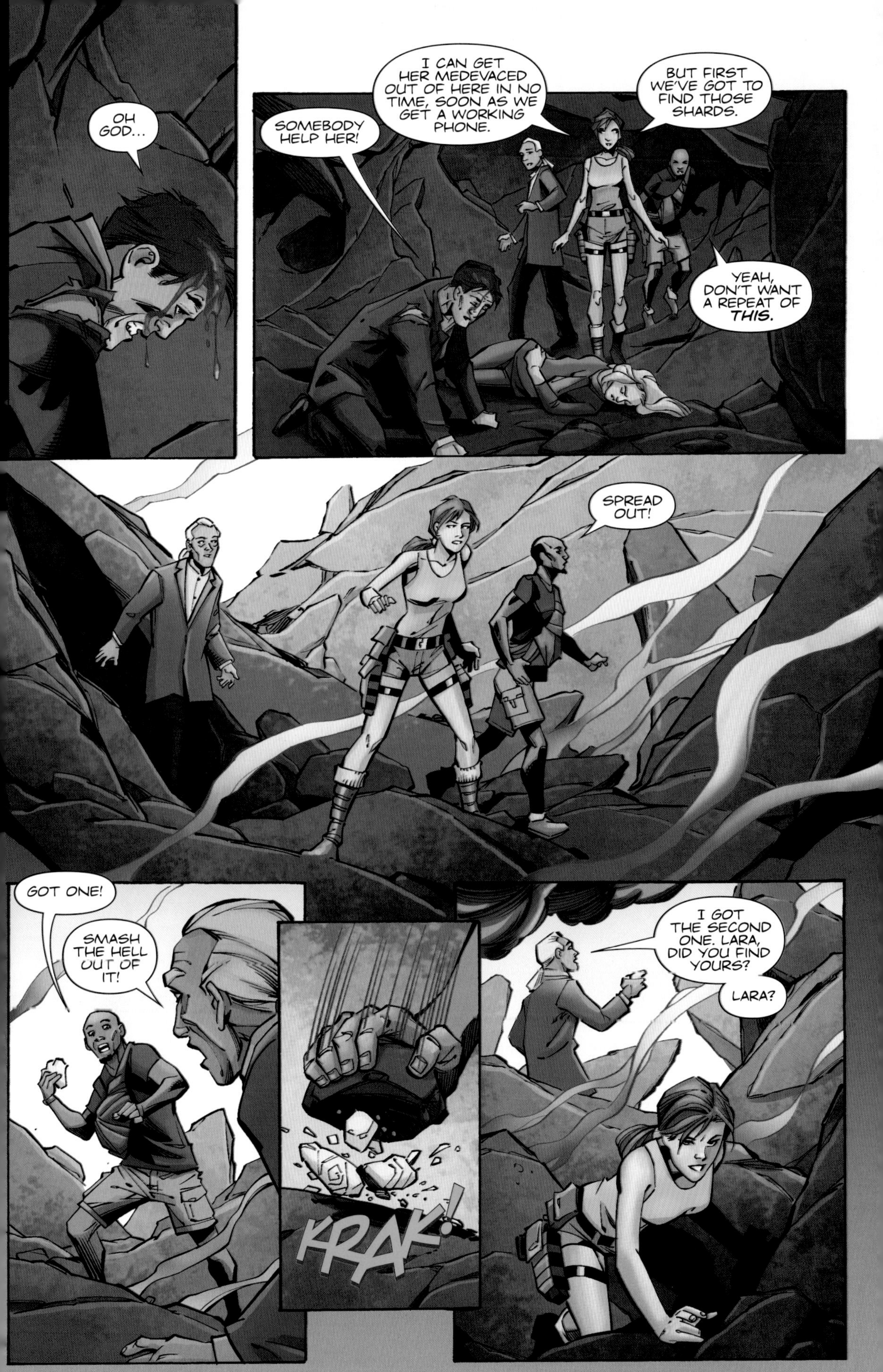
OH GOD...
SOMEBODY HELP HER!
I CAN GET HER MEDEVACED OUT OF HERE IN NO TIME, SOON AS WE GET A WORKING PHONE.
BUT FIRST WE'VE GOT TO FIND THOSE SHARDS.
YEAH, DON'T WANT A REPEAT OF THIS.
SPREAD OUT!
GOT ONE!
SMASH THE HELL OUT OF IT!
KRAK!
I GOT THE SECOND ONE. LARA, DID YOU FIND YOURS?
LARA?

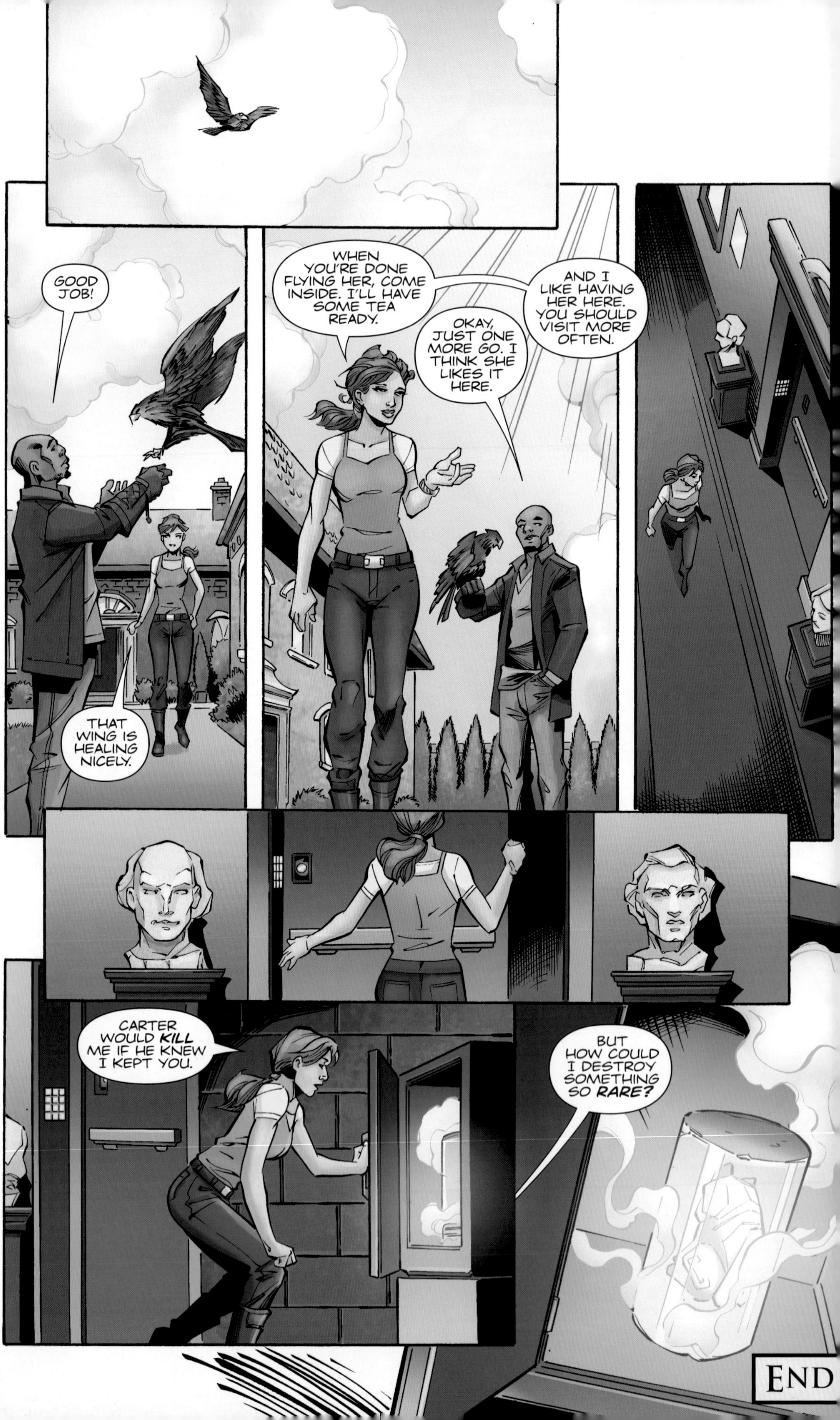
GOOD JOB!
THAT WING IS HEALING NICELY.
WHEN YOU'RE DONE FLYING HER, COME INSIDE. I'LL HAVE SOME TEA READY.
OKAY, JUST ONE MORE GO. I THINK SHE LIKES IT HERE.
AND I LIKE HAVING HER HERE. YOU SHOULD VISIT MORE OFTEN.
CARTER WOULD KILL ME IF HE KNEW I KEPT YOU.
BUT HOW COULD I DESTROY SOMETHING SO RARE?
END

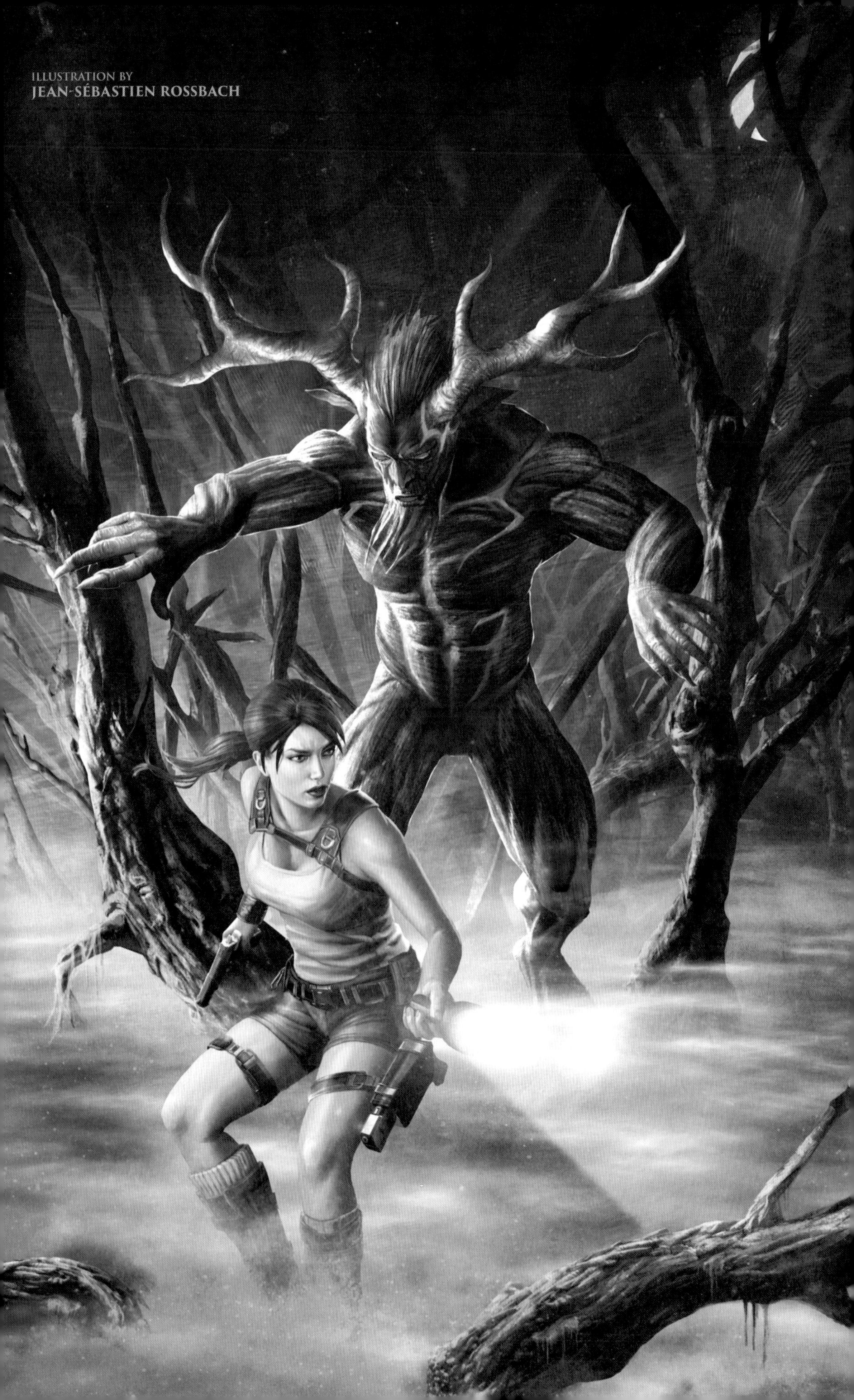

ILLUSTRATION BY
JEAN-SÉBASTIEN ROSSBACH

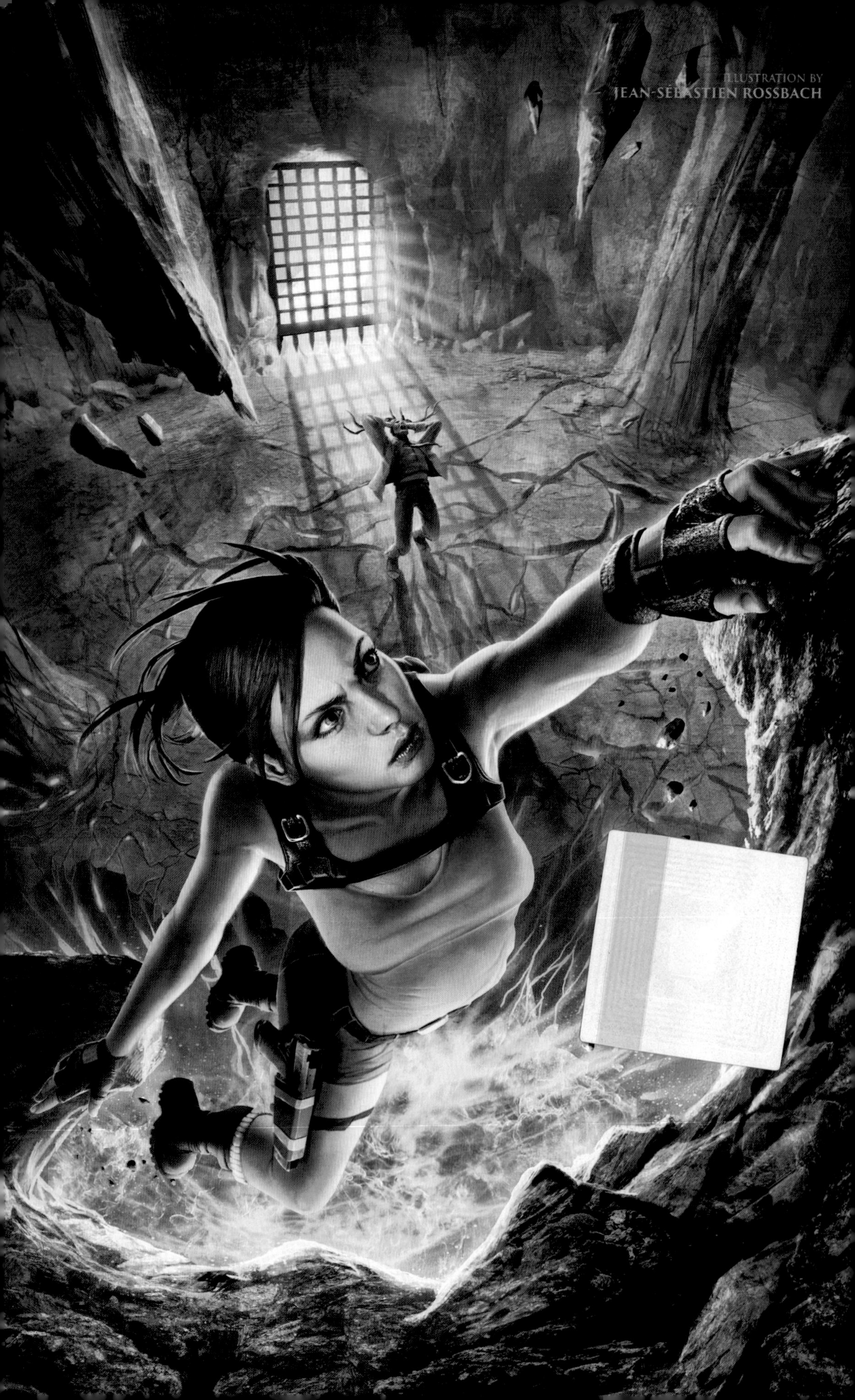
ILLUSTRATION BY
JEAN-SÉBASTIEN ROSSBACH

TOMB RAIDER

**LARA CROFT AND
THE FROZEN OMEN**

$19.99 | 978-1-61655-957-1

**TOMB RAIDER VOLUME 1:
SEASON OF THE WITCH**

$19.99 | 978-1-61655-639-6

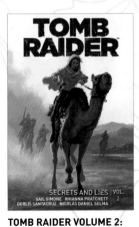

**TOMB RAIDER VOLUME 2:
SECRETS AND LIES**

$19.99 | 978-1-61655-957-1

**TOMB RAIDER VOLUME 3:
QUEEN OF SERPENTS**

$19.99 | 978-1-61655-818-5

**AVAILABLE AT YOUR LOCAL COMICS SHOP OR BOOKSTORE
TO FIND A COMICS SHOP IN YOUR AREA, CALL 1-888-266-4226**
For more information or to order direct: ·On the web: DarkHorse.com ·E-mail: mailorder@darkhorse.com
Phone: 1-800-862-0052 Mon.–Fri. 9 AM to 5 PM Pacific Time.

Tomb Raider™ © 2016 Square Enix. Developed by Crystal Dynamics. Tomb Raider, Crystal Dynamics, Square Enix and their respective
logos are trademarks and/or registered trademarks of Square Enix Holding Co., Ltd. All rights reserved. Dark Horse Books® and the
Dark Horse logo are registered trademarks of Dark Horse Comics, Inc. All rights reserved. (BL 5015)